GW01339721

a new kilo
OF KESSELSKRAMER

さらに1キロ増量！　ケッセルスクライマーの新たな1キロ

あなたがその腕に抱っこしているのは『ケッセルスクライマーの新たな1キロ』。広告代理店ケッセルスクライマーのライムグリーン色のかわいい赤ちゃん。ヘルニアを起こしそうなほど重い、私たちの創業から10年間の仕事をまとめたレンガみたいな作品集、『ケッセルスクライマーの2キロ』の後継者である。

本書の重さは2キロの半分。どんどん厳しくなる機内への手荷物制限も、これなら通過しやすくなったにちがいない。とはいえ、面白さだって負けてはいないのである。今回はケッセルスクライマーの2005年から2010年の作品を年代順に紹介。媒体がなんであれ、パワフルなメッセージを伝えようと新しい方法を模索し続ける広告代理店の奮闘の証が満載されている。

核廃棄物の色をした前表紙と後表紙のあいだには、ポスター、ビデオ、紙媒体広告、ブランド・アイデンティティ、設計ソリューション、ソーシャル・メディア、PR、展覧会、デジタル・コンテンツ、モバイル・コミュニケーション、出版、ファッション・コレクション、音楽ビデオ、TVコマーシャル、文化イベント、公共施設の環状交差点などのプロジェクトが詰めこまれている。

熱を発するこれらの作品から浮かびあがってくるのは、重要なきっかけや主要なテーマ。それらは、あとのページに続く数百ミリグラムの解説文で説明されている。

ケッセルスクライマー初心者のみなさんへ

ケッセルスクライマーの最初のアムステルダム事務所が開設されたのは1996年。ほかとは違ったことをしようという目標は、合理化された新しい作業体制から始まった。一般的な広告代理店が採用しているアカウント・ディレクター（顧客担当責任者）やトラフィック・コントローラー（作業量管理者）といった役職にはサヨナラし、戦略、コンセプト、制作面にもっと力を入れるようにしたのである。そして、戦略的ソリューション、クリエイティブな直感、非常に迅速な制作作業を基本とした、作業工程をより効率化したシンプルなモデルについて、制作担当者が依頼主と話し合うことを前提とした。ケッセルスクライマーの広告は、大規模なものや小規模なもの、地元ベースのものから国際的なものでクライアントごとにかなり多様な形態をとる。そのうえで、皮肉、ユーモア、社会的メッセージ、あるいは昔ながらのショックを与える戦術を駆使し、広告主が想定する以上に、メディアへの注目度をアップすることを目指したのである。もう幼年期は過ぎたケッセルスクライマーだが、その規模、組織、国際的スタッフの多様なバックグラウンド、そして、毎朝5杯以上は飲む濃いブラック・コーヒーのおかげで、いかなる仕事においても鋭いエッジと、嗅覚を保っている。

心と境界を広げる

一般的な意味での拡大には無関心なケッセルスクライマーは（アムステルダム事務所は約35人の規模を保っている）、事務所を拡大することよりも、精神的な成長に重きを置いている。とはいえ、地理的なこだわりはなく（世界中の仕事を手がけている）、デジタル志向のおかげで地球が狭くなっているにもかかわらず、拡大のときは訪れた。アムステルダムから223マイル離れた地に新事務所を設立したのである。新事務所KKアウトレットは2007年にその扉を開いた。活気に満ちたクリエイティブ界の中心、ロンドン、イーストエンドのホクストン・スクエアに位置するこのモダンでハイブリッドなスペースは、広告代理店にギャラリーとショップが併設されている。ここでは定期的に展覧会が開かれるかたわら、グッズや書籍が販売され、戦略が立案され、広告が制作されているのだ。本書には、KKアウトレットの初期作品も紹介されている。たとえば、モーガンズ・スパイスドの現代的冒険の探求、ブリティッシュ・フィルム・インスティテュートが開催した、ロンドン映画祭のための映画への畏敬、スノーボード用宿泊施設グループ、ルード・シャレーの、うまい具合にはずしたキャンペーンなどが特筆すべきだろう。

一番古くて最悪

ハンス・ブリンカー・バジェット・ホテルはケッセルスクライマーの一番古いクライアントだ。ケッセルスクライマーは1996年以来ずっとその広告を作り続け、ホテルの小汚いバーにもちょくちょく顔を出している。『ケッセルスクライマーの2キロ』の読者なら、このホテルが普通のマーケティング手法はまったくとらず、たくさんの欠点を馬鹿正直にさらけだしていることはご存知だろう。

広告においては一貫性を保つことや正直に事実を発表することは、なぜか忘れられがちであり、顰蹙を買う場合すら少なくない。しかしハンス・ブリンカーは、すがすがしいほどにあけすけで、10数年以上にわたり確固としてそのひどさを保っているのだ。この本のページをめくれば、その一途なメッセージにもかかわらず——あるいは、それゆえに——このホテルが前代未聞の方法ではびこっている様子を見ることができるだろう。その広告キャンペーンは、社会的メッセージ（偶然にエコ・フレンドリー・キャンペーン）、商品開発（宿泊客が自宅をちょっとハンス・ブリンカー風にできる壁紙）、あるいは、ブティック・ホテルに見せかける（ユニーク・デザイン・キャンペーン）などのアイデアを駆使して開発されてきた。ハンス・ブリンカーは、まっさらなベッド・シーツを頼んでもなかなか動いてくれないが、広告に関しては時代の流れに敏感についていくのだ。

長年にわたって考え続けてくれたことへのご褒美として、また、広告には永遠に限界がないことを証明しようと、書籍の出版も持ちかけられた。『世界最悪なホテル』というぴったりなタイトルがつけられた同書は、初めから終わりまで、高級ホテルのコーヒーテーブル・ブックにわざと逆らい、模造皮革のカバーのあいだにハンス・ブリンカーの物語と広告のすべてを収録している。ベッドのフレームがさび、配管設備に問題があり、旅行業界が危機的状況にあっても、同ホテルへの予約は急増している。そのすべてが、真実が、無限のアイデアとすばらしい結果の源になることを証明しているのである。

2.00467 kilo

It's New. It's a Kilo. It's a New Kilo of KesselsKramer
You're cradling A New Kilo of KesselsKramer, the lime-green love child of communications agency KesselsKramer. New Kilo is the heir to the hernia-inducing 2 Kilo of KesselsKramer, which collected the first ten years of the agency's work in one brick-like compilation.

A New Kilo is half as heavy as 2 Kilo – an advantage for stricter airline hand-luggage policies – but is no less involving. It chronicles the agency's output from 2005 to 2010 and bears testament to an agency that continues to find new ways to convey powerful messages through any relevant medium.

Between these nuclear-waste-coloured covers, you'll find projects in the form of poster, film and print advertising, as well as brand identities, design solutions, social media, PR, exhibitions, digital-content creation, mobile-based communications, publishing, fashion collections, music videos, TV formats, cultural events, PR and at least one public roundabout.

Emerging from this feverish outpouring are certain important moments and major themes. These are highlighted over the coming pages, in just a few hundred milligrams of words.

KesselsKramer for the uninitiated
The original Amsterdam office of the communications agency was launched in 1996. Its aim to do things a little differently started with a new, more streamlined system of working. Goodbye account directors and traffic managers, hello strategy, creative and production. The premise was that those who made the work should talk with the people who commissioned it, a simple model that created a more efficient process, one ruled by strategic solutions, creative intuition and a much quicker work yield. The communication took wildly different forms for clients both big and small, local and international, and used irreverence, irony, humour, social commentary and good old-fashioned shock tactics to engage an audience more media-aware than some brands give them credit for. KesselsKramer is no longer in its immediate infancy, yet due to its size, the structure, the varied backgrounds of an international staff and at least five strong, black coffees every morning, it manages to keep a sharp edge and keen mind on all that it does.

Expanding minds and borders
Unconcerned with expansion in the traditional sense (remaining at around 35 people in its Amsterdam base), KesselsKramer instead focused on mental growth. Yet, despite a lack of respect for geography (the agency has produced work in every continent) and this shrinking digitally-minded planet of ours, the time came to expand. The agency did so by setting up a new office just 223 miles away. KK Outlet opened its doors in 2007. Located in the thriving, creative epicentre that is Hoxton Square in London's East End, this modern, hybrid space combines a communications agency with a gallery and shop. Here, regular exhibitions take place while products and books are sold, strategies are planned and communication created. Samples from KK Outlet's early years are included here – amongst them, an exploration of modern adventure for Morgan's Spiced, the awe of cinema for the British Film Institutes' London Film Festival, and a suitably inappropriate campaign for snowboard accommodation group, Rude Chalet.

The oldest and the worst
The Hans Brinker Budget Hotel is KesselsKramer's longest-running client: the agency has been making its communication and frequenting its dishevelled bar since 1996. Readers of 2 Kilo of KesselsKramer will already know that this is a hotel that consistently eschews conventional marketing claims in favour of a brutal honesty concerning the hotel's many low points.

Consistency and honesty in communication is often mysteriously forgotten or frowned upon. The Brinker, however, has been refreshingly open and unswervingly steady about its awfulness for well over a decade. Flick forward a few grams in this book and you'll see that despite – or because of – this single-minded message, the hotel ran riot in previously unheard of ways. Campaigns have been developed using social commentary (the Accidentally Eco-Friendly campaign), product development (allowing guests to take a little bit of the Brinker home, in the form of wallpaper) or by disguising itself as a boutique hotel (the Unique Design campaign). The Brinker may not budge when you ask for fresh bed sheets but it will move with the times in its communication.
As a reward for its long-term thinking, and proof that the boundaries of communication are forever blurring, the Brinker was approached to publish a book. Appropriately titled The Worst Hotel in the World, it deliberately went jacket to jacket against luxury-hotel coffee-table books and featured the full story of the Brinker and all its communications between its mock-leather covers.
Despite the rusting bed frames, questionable plumbing and times of crisis in the travel industry, bookings continued to soar. All of which goes to show that telling the truth can be a seemingly endless source of inspiration – and high-grade results.

2.00701 kilo

ソーシャルの台頭

ケッセルスクライマーはつねに、広告において社会的交流が起きることを信じており、広告をブランドと顧客のあいだの形式ばらない、顔と顔をつきあわせた出会いの場として取り扱いたいと考えている。モバイル・ネットワーク、Ben——本書でその復活を目撃することができた——などのキャンペーンを見れば、現代の消費者に対し、広告は、リアリティを避ける必要はなく、真実を飾りたてたり、重要で、説得力があるものに見せようととりつくろう必要もないことがわかる。また、ソーシャル・メディアなどの、一対一ではなく一方通行でもない対話形式が登場したおかげで、社会（ソーシャル）という言葉は、新しくエキサイティングな局面をむかえている。ブランドが語るあらゆるストーリーが、動画や写真のシェア・サイト、インスタント・オピニオン・サイト、ブログ、動画ブログ、ソーシャル・ネットワークに翻弄される時代が突然やってきたのだ。

その結果、こうしたブランドをもつ企業は、自社に興味があったり、ファンだったりする層にも、反対に、よい印象をもたない層にも、よりオープンに情報を伝える努力をしなくてはならなくなった。公衆によって個（企業や個人など）が形成されることも、あるいは逆に、破壊されることもある新しい社会の現実は、対話をもつことと観客を参加させることをつねに信条としているケッセルスクライマーにとっては、歓迎すべきステップでもある。ゲストを発想の源とするホテルのオープニングから（こうした事例が増えているシチズンMのように）、臓器提供というデリケートな主題に取り組むウェブサイトの構築とその広告制作まで、クライアントも自身をさまざまな形で表明できるようになったのである。

「すべて」についてのすべて

全方位的、ホリスティック、インテグレート、トータルなど、広告を表現する用語は現在4,561語ある（さらに増加中である）。広告に取り組むあらゆる企業が、今後、自社独自の広告ブランドを表現する新しい方法を追求するようになるだろう。だが、これらの用語はどれも、効果的な広告を実施するための方法を説明する手段にすぎず、それだけで効果的な広告を実現するものではない。ケッセルスクライマーは、どちらかというと、複数のソリューションを、確固たる信念をもって、うまく調和させることに注力している。そして、これらのソリューションが、相互に調和するようにさまざまな媒体に植えつける。それは、世界一のパーティー用ウィスキー（J&B）を、お酒を楽しむためのインターネット・ビデオ、マイクの形をしたスポンジ、ビルの壁にぶつけられる巨大なミラーボールとともに、ウェブを通じて数千人が参加するパーティーで広告することなのかもしれない。あるいは、オランダ生まれのスノーボード・ブランドに見られるように、展示会へちょっかいをだすことから、将来のあらゆるコレクションに使えるロゴ、インターネット・ビデオ・シリーズへと消費者を導く品質表示タグにいたるまで、さまざまな広告形態を模索すること、なのかもしれない。

スタート地点からではなく、そのずっと前からスタートする

ネアンデルタール人が滅亡する直前の大昔から、広告はすでに純粋な意味での広告ではなくなっていたが、プロジェクトの早期からブランド開発を始めることが、とめようのない力を発揮するようになったのは、21世紀に入ってからのことである。商品やサービスのアイデアが、まだ企業家の脳内でのみ魅力的な神経パターンとしてスパークしている段階、まさにその瞬間こそ、効果的で一貫したブランド・イメージを構築できるのだ。そして、これを理解するクライアントも今や増えている。

このさんぜんと輝く1キロを読めば、ケッセルスクライマーが新しいブランドの誕生に立ち会っているばかりでなく、受胎の意欲的なパートナーであることもわかるだろう。おかげで、無表情できまじめな態度を追求する、お米と少々のレモンで作られた新しいタイプの夏用ビール（クラロ）が誕生したし、専門技術を親しみやすいパーソナリティで表現した新世代のコーヒー・マシーンも生まれたのだ。ビールの純度の高さを消費者に伝える、一連の紙媒体広告を打ちたいと求めたことがきっかけで始まった、最も男らしいビール・ブランドが発売するミネラル・ウォーター・ブランド（古いオランダ語のスペルでWaater）もある。長持ちする赤道上産のバラの品種ですら、ネーミング、デザイン、パッケージング、ブランド・パーソナリティという特別待遇を受けられたのだ。

また、ビジネスや観光目的の旅行者（通称シチズン・モバイル）に、贅沢なホテル・ステイを手ごろな値段で提供する急成長中のホテル・グループ、シチズンMも忘れてはならない。このケースでは、ホテルの建物の基礎が築かれるずいぶん前に、ホテル創設者が開いたミーティングからケッセルスクライマーの参加は始まった。その際に、このホテルが何を重視するかが話し合われ、情報を駆使してキャラクターが定義されたのである。ホテルの名前はすぐに決まり、それと同時に、サイン、デジタル広告、キー・カード、入室禁止プレート、メニュー、オープニング・イベント、PRプロジェクト、フレグランス入り石鹸、元気なゲスト向けの目立たないコンドーム・パッケージが開発された。そして最後に、スタッフと彼らのゲストへの接し方という、最も重要な事柄のための全工程が吟味されたのである。

2.00935 kilo

The rise of social
KesselsKramer has always believed in social interaction in communication, preferring to treat advertising as an informal, face-to-face meeting between brand and audience. Campaigns for the likes of mobile network, Ben – the resurrection of which can be witnessed in this book – realized that communication doesn't have to avoid reality, or gloss over the truth to be attractive, meaningful or persuasive to a modern audience. So with the advent of social media – and a dialogue that is rarely conducted one to one, or one way – the term social is given new and evermore exciting dimensions. Every story told by brands is suddenly at the mercy of video and photo-sharing sites, instant opinion sites, blogs, vlogs and social networks.

As a consequence, these companies have to work harder and more openly to reach an audience who is willing to investigate them, celebrate them or hang them out to dry. The new social reality, where the public shapes or breaks you, is seen as a welcome step from an agency that has always believed in dialogue and audience involvement. For clients, this has manifested itself in a variety of ways – from the launch of a hotel that lets the guests be its inspiration (as with citizenM, more on this coming up), to the creation of a site and associated communication that tackles the delicate subject of organ donation.

It's all about the all
There are currently 4,561 (and counting) terms to describe communication that promises it all. 360 degrees, holistic, integrated, total – any company involved in communication will seek new ways to describe their own brand of communication. Since all these terms are simply ways to describe a means to deliver effective communication rather than ends in themselves, KesselsKramer prefers to focus on single-minded harmonious solutions. These solutions are then planted in different media in such a way that they work in harmony with each other. It might be communicating the world's number-one party whisky (J&B) via a party that could be attended by thousands of guests via the web, connected to a responsible drinking online film, connected to a sponge in the shape of a microphone, connected to a giant mirror ball slammed into the side of a building. It might be announcements on behalf of a snowboarding brand born in The Netherlands, where multiple terrains of communication have been explored from trade-show interventions to a new logo for all future collections to hang tags that connect you to a series of online films.

Don't start at the start, start long before that
Shortly before the fall of Neanderthal man, advertising stopped being purely about advertising. However it took until the 21st century before early-initiated brand development became an unstoppable force. There is now a growing band of entrepreneurs who understand that a consistent and effective personality could be built at a time when the product or service is nothing more than an attractive neural pattern firing in their brains.

Presented within this single glowing kilo, you will see that KesselsKramer has been not only at the birth of new brands, but also a willing partner in their conception. This has resulted in a new kind of summer beer called Claro, made with rice and a chaser of no-nonsense, deadpan attitude. It has helped produce a new generation of coffee machines that replaces technicalities with personality. Or a brand of table water (named Waater, the old Dutch spelling) introduced by the most manly beer brand in the Netherlands and initiated when the client called for a series of press advertisements telling the public about the purity of its beer. Even a long-lasting rose bred on the equator got the full treatment – naming, design, packaging and brand personality.

Then there's citizenM, a rapidly expanding group of hotels offering affordable luxury to a new breed of business and leisure traveller (dubbed 'citizen mobile'). In this case, KesselsKramer's involvement began with meeting those involved in the hotel's inception, talking about what it stood for, and using the information to define its character, long before the foundation of the first building was ever placed. Soon, the hotel was christened and along with the naming came the development of signage, digital communication, key cards, do not disturb hangers, menus, launch events, PR stunts, even soap fragrances and discreet condom packaging for frisky guests, eventually filtering all the way through to the most important part – the staff and the way they interact with guests.

2.01168 kilo

徹底的に学ぶ

自社プロジェクトは、ケッセルスクライマーの活動の中心となっている。それは、コーヒーが入るのを待つ間のひまつぶしになるからではない。こうしたプロジェクトは、未来のプロジェクトのための小さな大学のようなものだからだ。これらのおかげで、新しいアイデアを実行することができ、めちゃくちゃにしたり、再評価したりして、満足の行く形で完成することができるのである。そして結局は、広告における新しい領域の理解にもつながる。過去には、こうした活力源は世界最下位の2つのサッカー・チームについてのドキュメンタリー映画（ジ・アザー・ファイナル：ケッセルスクライマーの2キロに収録）や、子ども向けの短編TV番組シリーズ（Kijkers）だった。最近では、ケッセルスクライマーは、出版、イベント、展覧会、商品開発、ブランディングを以前にもまして深く探求している。多数の写真集の出版（『in almost every picture』シリーズなど）は、J&Bの輝ける歴史に関する書籍や『ザ・ワースト・ホテル・イン・ザ・ワールド』の制作に役立っている。無数のアート・プロジェクトや、ケッセルスクライマーが手がけた作品の展覧会は、ベネチア・ビエンナーレのためのドローグ・デザインとのコラボレーションや、オランダのブレダに設立された世界初のグラフィック・デザイン美術館のオープニング展覧会と、その宣伝につながっている。そして、ケッセルスクライマー自身のブランド（do）。1996年に誕生して以来、消費者に参加を求めるこのブランドの実験は、進んだ考えをもつクライアントのブランド広告制作に役立ってきたのである。このように、自社プロジェクトは、なんらかの形をともなって、未来と現在の両方のブランドがその可能性を探るために、キラキラ輝く新しい道筋をつくってくれるだろう。それは、これまで軽視されてきた、一見したところつまらない写真に着目する雑誌『ユースフル・フォトグラフィ』であろうが、プログレッシブ・エレクトロ・バンド（LeLe）であろうが、どんなものであれ、そして、どんな形であれ変わらない。

　ケッセルスクライマーの物語においては、それらすべてが、とてもまばゆい次のストーリーへの序章となっているのだ。ジムに定期的かつ頻繁に通っているような熱心な読者なら、『ケッセルスクライマーの新たな1キロ』と『ケッセルスクライマーの2キロ』を一緒に楽しみたくなることだろう。それ以外の読者は、お好みの椅子を引っ張りだし、好きな飲み物を嗜りながら、面白そう、と思えるキャンペーンのページをめくっていただきたい。

　（注）：著者はみずからを「communication agency」と位置づけ、文中でもその役割については「communication」という言葉を使用しておりますが、日本語では、読みやすさを考慮した上で、便宜上、「広告」と翻訳しております。

www.kesselskramer.com
www.kkoutlet.com
www.kesselskramerpublishing.com

2.01402 kilo

Learning from the inside out

Self-initiated projects are at the heart of what KesselsKramer does. Not because they fill in time while waiting for the coffee to brew. Instead, they are like mini-universities for future projects. This is where new ideas can be initiated, messed up, reappraised and then worked out to satisfactory completion.

Eventually, such projects help gain understanding in new areas of communication. In the past, this lifeblood has meant the creation of a documentary about the two lowest-ranking football teams in the world (The Other Final, as found in 2 Kilo of KesselsKramer) or a series of TV shorts for children (Kijkers).

More recently it has seen the agency delve further into the fields of publishing, events and exhibitions, product development and branding.

The publishing of numerous photography books (such as the 'in almost every picture' series) has helped feed the creation of books about the illustrious history of J&B or The Worst Hotel in the World. Numerous art projects and exhibitions for work of its own devising has led KesselsKramer to collaborate with Droog Design for the Venice Biennale, as well as provide the opening exhibition and associated communication for the world's first graphic design museum in Breda, Holland. Experimentation with its own brand 'do', a brand that has been inviting audience participation since its inception in 1996, has helped with the advancement of brands for forward-thinking clients.

So whether it is a magazine promoting a series of previously disregarded and seemingly innocuous images (Useful Photography) or a music video for a progressive electro outfit (LeLe), these are projects which can soon, in one form or another, provide glittering new avenues for future and current brands to explore for themselves.

All of which concludes the prologue to this, the extremely luminescent next instalment in the saga of KesselsKramer. The avid reader – one who regularly frequents the gym – may wish to enjoy a New Kilo of KesselsKramer along with 2 Kilo of KesselsKramer. For the rest of you, pull up a seating device of your preference, sip a beverage of your choice and flip to a campaign that finds your favour.

www.kesselskramer.com
www.kkoutlet.com
www.kesselskramerpublishing.com

2.01636 kilo

www.piebooks.com

fresh delivery:
a new kilo
of kesselskramer

a new kilo of KesselsKramer, poster
Poster communicating the fresh arrival of a new kilo of KesselsKramer, a book chronicling the work of communications agency KesselsKramer between 2005 and 2010.
a new kilo of KesselsKramer／ポスター：広告代理店ケッセルスクライマーによる2005〜2010年の作品を年代別に紹介した作品集『a new kilo of KesselsKramer』。その発刊告知ポスターは、生まれたてのみずみずしい感覚を伝えている。

2.02103 kilo

VitraHaus – welcome home.

Vitra, poster, print and in-store
Renowned designer and manufacturer of contemporary furnishings, Vitra, created a multi-purpose building on their campus near Basel, Switzerland. Called VitraHaus, each of its floors contains all the inspiration needed to make houses into homes. This poster celebrates its opening under the line 'The VitraHaus- Welcome Home'.

Vitra／ポスター、紙媒体、店内ツール：コンテンポラリー家具の有名デザイナーであり、製造業者でもあるヴィトラはスイスの都市バーゼル近郊に多目的ビルを建設。この「ヴィトラ・ハウス」と呼ばれる建物では、各階で、家をただの建物から暖かい家庭に変えるために必要な、あらゆるアイデアを紹介。本ポスターは「The VitraHaus- Welcome Home＝ヴィトラ・ハウスへお帰りなさい」というキャッチ・フレーズのもと、ビルのオープニングを祝したもの。

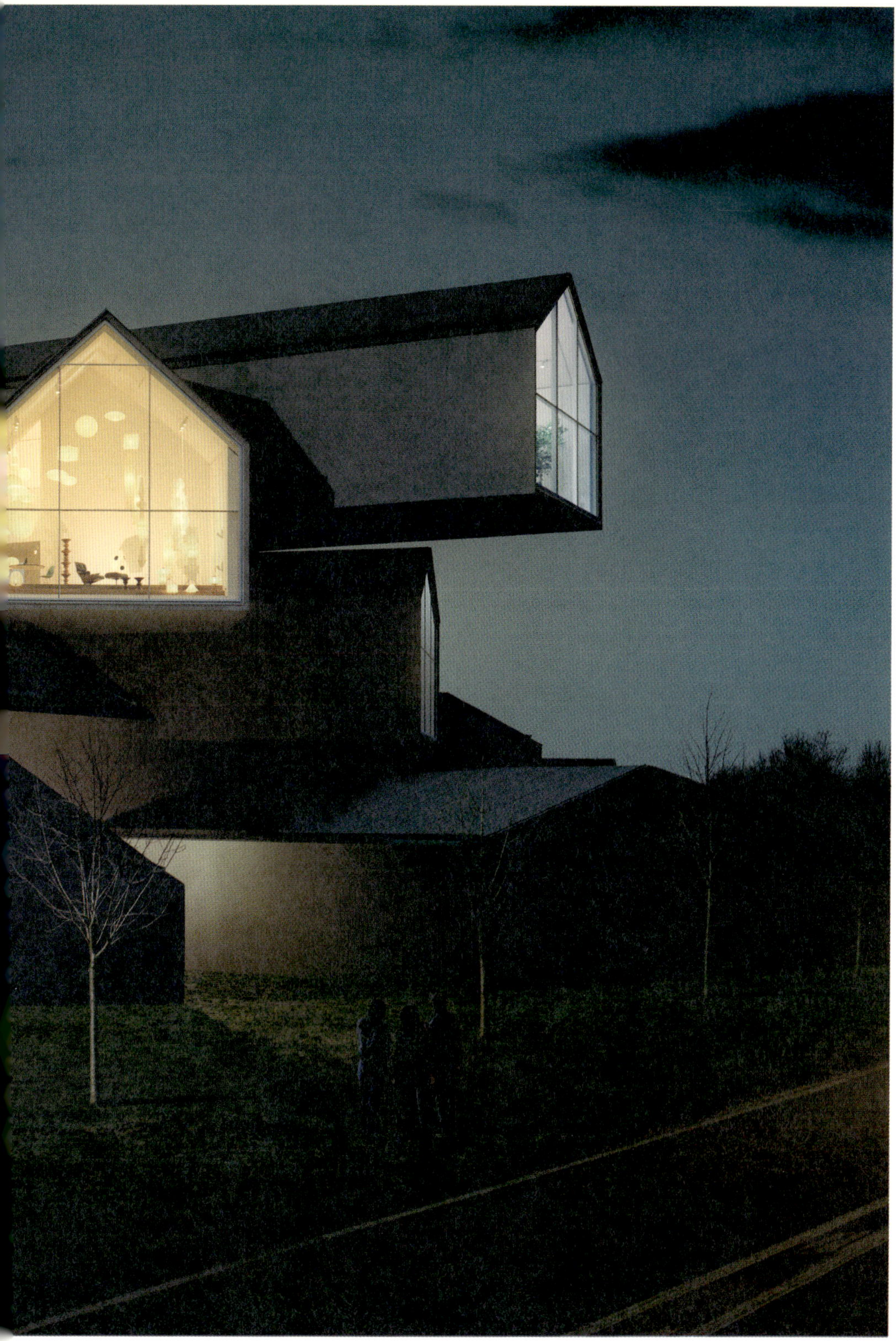

28 CUPS OF BAD COFFEE TO GET TO THE SLOPES

PROTEST
TO GET THERE

JONAS HAGSTROM & MIIKKA HAST — PROTEST.EU

2.02804 kilo

Protest, poster, print and online

Protest's winter work was based around the theme 'countdown to get there.' Just how many cups of bad coffee, laundry days and uninspiring dates do you have to experience until it's time to fulfil your life's true purpose: snowboarding? Press and posters focused on the little things we must endure before it's time to go boarding while web-based films dealt with the journey to the slopes.

Protest／ポスター、紙媒体、インターネット：プロテストによるウィンター・コレクションのテーマは「countdown to get there ＝あちらに行くまでのカウントダウン」。人生の真の目的、スノーボードをする日まで、何杯まずいコーヒーを飲み、何回洗濯をし、何日たいくつな日々をすごすのだろう？ 出版物やポスターでは、スノーボードに行く日までに耐え続けなければならない日常の些事にフォーカスする一方、インターネット・ビデオでは、ゲレンデへの旅を題材にしている。

Protest, poster, film and event
Snowboard brand Protest also makes surf gear. The brand's strategy rallied their audience to let no obstacle get in the way of boarding and to demonstrate this, an island was built that allowed truly dedicated surfers to eat, sleep, check their email and use the toilet without leaving the water. Posters and online featured the island. It was also recreated for the world surfing championships, allowing surf fans to use it for real.

Protest／ポスター、ビデオ、イベント：スノーボード・ブランドのプロテストは、サーフィン関連商品も製造している。同ブランドの戦略は、ユーザーが障害なく波乗りを楽しめるようにすること。その一環として、熱心なサーファーたちが海から上がらずに食事をしたり、睡眠をとったり、eメールをチェックしたり、トイレに行ったりできるような島が建造された。この島はポスターとインターネット広告に掲載されたのち、サーフィン・ファンたちが実際に使えるよう、世界サーフィン・チャンピオンシップに合わせて再建された。

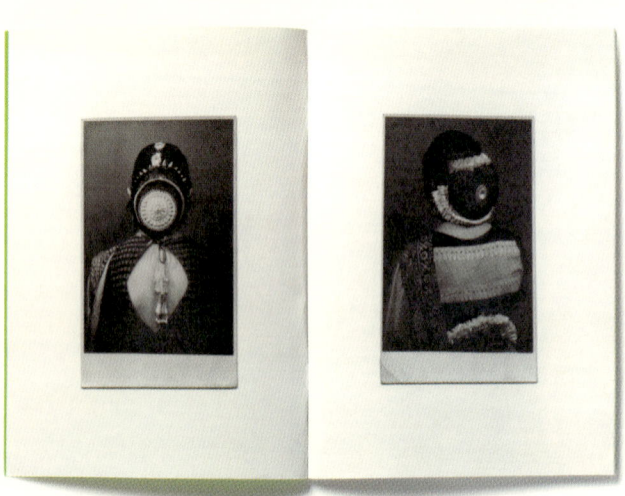

Bombay Beauties, book
A found photography book that compiles images discovered in Mumbai. This series creates a snapshot of everyday life in the metropolis formerly known as Bombay: hairdressers, Bollywood stars, even wedding photos hint at its millions of untold stories.
Bombay Beauties／書籍：ムンバイで見つけた写真をまとめたファウンド・フォト（日常生活で偶然見つけた写真）集。美容師やボリウッド・スターから結婚写真まで、語られることのない無数の物語をほのめかす写真を集めた本書は、かつてはボンベイと呼ばれていた巨大都市における日常生活のスナップショットである。

2.03271 kilo

do sin, product
Part of KesselsKramer's ever-evolving brand do, a brand which asks for user intervention, this soap helps people purify themselves in both mind and body. Select the sin of which you're most guilty, break it off, jump in the shower and scrub until you're cleansed.
do sin／商品：常に進化し続ける、ケッセルスクライマーのブランド、do。ユーザーの参加により成立するこのブランドの石鹸do sin (sinは罪の意) は、人の心と体の両方をきれいにするためのもの。自分が犯した最大の罪を選んでポキッと折り、シャワー室に飛び込んで、清められるまでごしごし洗おう。

2.03505 kilo

Bushmills, online films
Bushmills Irish whiskey celebrates authentic male bonding. 'Bushmills Brothers' shows different aspects of boys-together behaviour and highlights the moment when friendship became more fraternal.
Bushmills／インターネット・ビデオ：ブッシュミルズのアイリッシュ・ウィスキーは、真の男同士の絆を支持。そのキャンペーン「ブッシュミルズ・ブラザーズ」では、さまざまな形の男同士のつきあいを紹介し、友情が兄弟愛のように深まる瞬間に焦点をあてている。

in almost every picture #8, book
This edition of the long-running found photography series tells the tale of Oolong, a rabbit with an unusually flat head. This very small mantelpiece was used to display all kinds of household objects over a period of many years until his unfortunate demise. During his lifetime, Oolong became the star of a website during blogging's first wave and has been revived, in spirit at least, for this book.

in almost every picture #8／書籍：長年にわたり刊行されているファウンド・フォト・シリーズ『in almost every picture＝ほとんどどの写真にも』の第8集では頭が平らなうさぎ、ウーロンの物語が取りあげられた。ウーロンの頭は、家の中のあらゆるものをディスプレイするために使われる、とても小さな台座。惜しまれつつ亡くなるまで、長年にわたって台座の役を務めたウーロンは、ブログ・ブームの第一波とともに、生涯を通じて、ウェブ界のスターとして評判を呼んだ。そして本書により、少なくとも読者の心の中に生き返ったといえよう。

2.03972 kilo

Mavi, poster campaign
Mavi is a premium Turkish jeans brand that prides itself on doing things differently. This desire to be unconventional lead to The Mavi Way. The above campaign appeared in Berlin during the Bread and Butter fashion trade fair and helped outline a new way of living, one that twists logic on its head.

Mavi／ポスター・キャンペーン：マヴィは、ユニークに行動することにプライドをもつトルコの高級ジーンズ・ブランド。この、型にはまりたくない、という想いが「The Mavi Way＝マヴィ的な方法」の誕生につながった。「ブレッド＆バター・ファッション展示会」の間、ベルリンでは上図のキャンペーンが展開され、頭上に掲げられた不条理なメッセージが、新しい生き方を提示した。

MAIL & FEMALE
LINGERIE
SEX TOYS
DVDS
MASSAGE OILS

WWW.MAILFEMALE.COM
NIEUWE VIJZELSTRAAT 2 (HOEK WETERINGCIRCUIT), AMSTERDAM
PIN-UP BY QIU YANG.

Mail & Female, print
Amsterdam's oldest sex shop for women wanted to celebrate classic pin-ups. This image showed an updated version of this tradition, by taking the term 'pin-up' literally.
Mail & Female／紙媒体：アムステルダムで最も老舗の女性向けセックス・ショップが、クラシックなピンナップをテーマに取りあげることを希望。写真は、「pin-up＝（ピンで）留める」という言葉を文字通り表現し、この手法の新しい形を提示している。

2.04439 kilo

2.04673 kilo

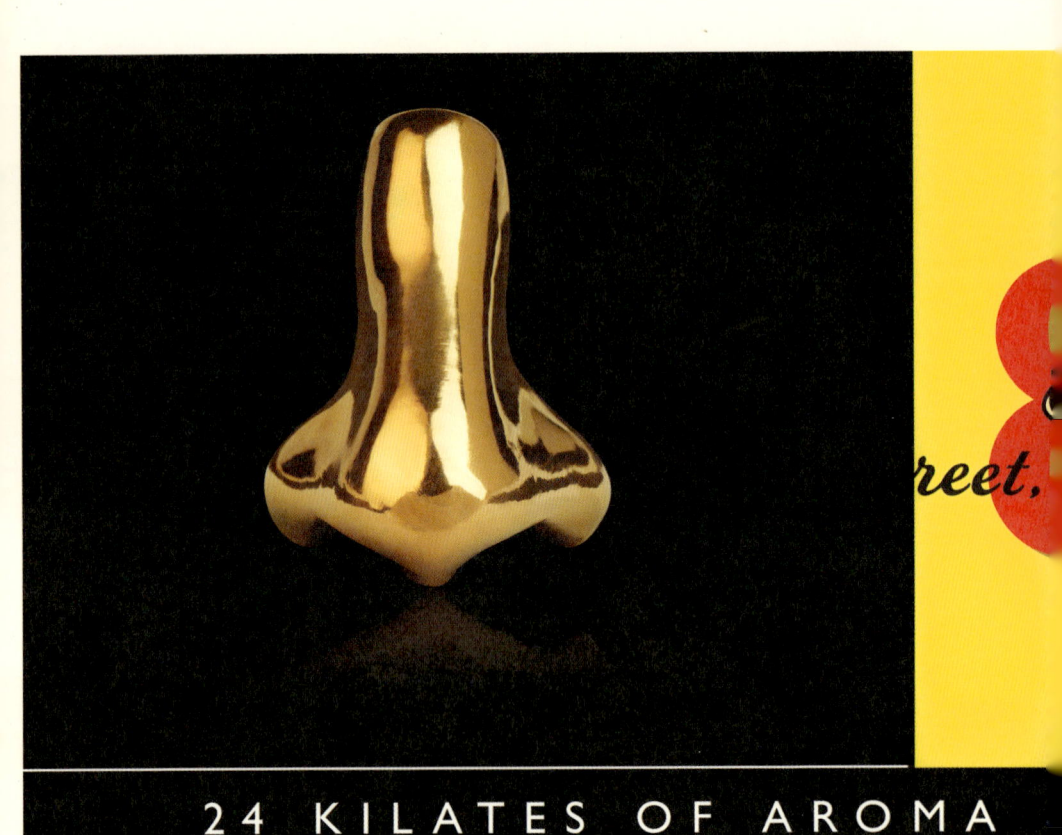

24 KILATES OF AROMA

J&B, poster and online
A campaign that asked Spanish consumers to hunt down the golden nose and mouth of J&B, the ultimate symbols of the brand's ability to stimulate the senses of any whisky fan. Print and posters drove customers to a website where they searched for these symbols of aroma and taste through a complex and involving series of clues, games and competitions. Two lucky winners received the actual golden nose and mouth. Each statuette weighed one kilo and represented roughly 25,000 euros.

J&B／ポスター、インターネット：スペインの消費者たちに、J&Bの金の鼻と唇を捕まえるよう呼びかけるキャンペーン。金の鼻と唇は、同ブランドが、ウィスキー愛好家たちの感覚をいかに刺激するかを表す究極のシンボル。印刷物とポスターが、ウェブサイトへと顧客をいざない、そこを訪れた者は、手がかりやゲームやコンテストが盛りだくさんの楽しいコンテンツの中で、この芳香と味覚のシンボルを探し回った。二人の幸運な勝利者が、本物の金でできた鼻と唇を獲得。これらの小像は、それぞれ1キロの重さがあり、価値は約25,000ユーロに達した。

TASTE AT JBONLINE.ES

J&B, online film
A web-based announcement of J&B's online treasure hunt which asked people to find the golden nose and mouth. The film featured the nose and mouth as characters on a journey around an abstract version of London.
J&B／インターネット・ビデオ：金の鼻と唇を探すよう求めるJ&Bのオンライン宝探しに関するウェブベースの告知。動画のストーリーは、抽象化されたロンドンを鼻と唇が旅するという設定。

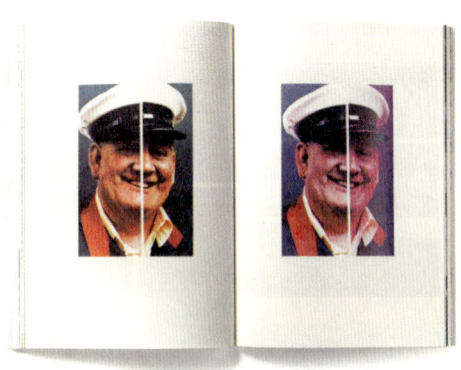

Useful Photography #009, magazine
Useful Photography is a magazine celebrating uncelebrated photography: the images that are used purely for practical purposes. This edition collects oddities from the world of photography manuals, showing readers how to take better pictures and identify potentially disastrous errors.
Useful Photography #009／雑誌：『ユースフル・フォトグラフィ』は、実用的な目的のために撮影された名もなき写真にスポットをあてる雑誌。本号では、写真の手引書から少し風変わりな作品が集められ、読者にどうやったらよい写真が撮れるか、そして、どんなときにひどい写真になってしまうかを手ほどきしている。

2.05374 kilo

J&B, poster, online and event

J&B regularly hosts epic, unconventional parties all over the planet. Its Transylvania event took place in Dracula's castle and included a programme heaving with unusual acts under the theme 'energize the night', as well as digital back-up for those who couldn't make it to the party.

J&B／ポスター、インターネット、イベント：J&Bは世界中で定期的に盛大でユニークなパーティを開催している。トランシルヴァニアでのイベント会場は、ドラキュラ伯爵の城。「夜に力を！」をテーマにした独特な出し物が場を盛りあげた。イベントの模様は、パーティに出席できなかった人たちも楽しめるようデジタル・データで記録された。

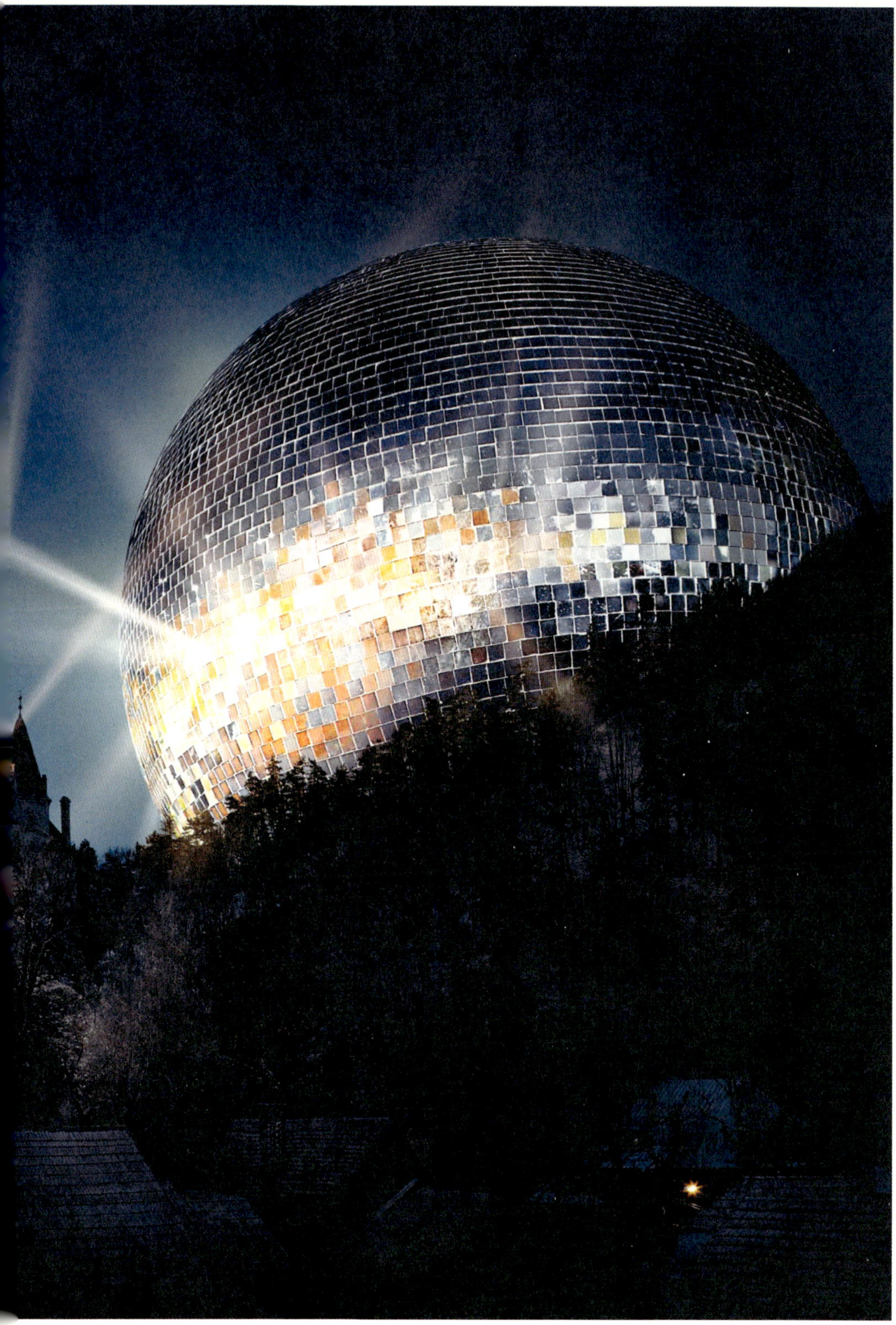

Het Goud Van Lopik, art installation
The Dutch town of Lopik had a roundabout that it wanted to make more meaningful by commissioning a sculpture. The solution involved casting a series of golden statuettes based on local people's designs. This gold was then buried under the roundabout beneath the sign Het Goud Van Lopik ('The Gold of Lopik'). A book accompanied the project.
Het Goud Van Lopik／アート・インスタレーション：オランダの街ロービックが、環状交差点をもっと有意義にしようと彫刻の設置を求めた。その結果、地元住民のデザインをベースに金の小像がいくつか作られ、環状交差点の「Het Goud Van Lopik＝ロービックの金」と記された標識の下に埋められた。同プロジェクトについては書籍も出版されている。

2.06075 kilo

Het Goud Van Lopik, book
The book of the artwork shows pieces subsequently buried beneath the roundabout of Lopik. As the art itself was now entombed, this was the only way for people to view the creative endeavours of the good citizens of Lopik. Made in collaboration with Hans Aarsman.
Het Goud Van Lopik／書籍：ロービックの環状交差点に埋められた作品を紹介する書籍。作品が埋葬されてしまった今、同書はロービックの素晴らしい市民たちの制作努力を目にできる唯一の機会となっている。ハンス アースマンとの共同制作。

2.06308 kilo

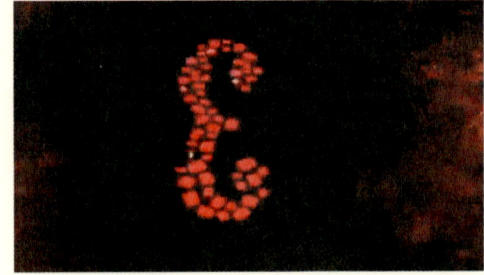

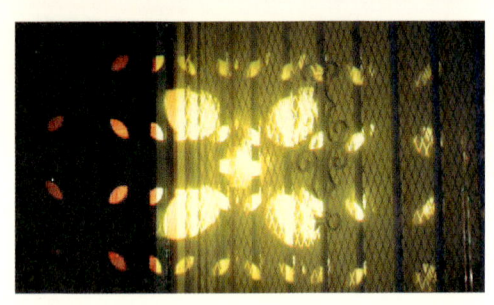

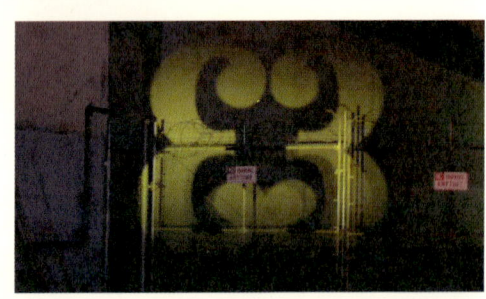

J&B, films
A group of international artists, designers and film-makers reinterpreted J&B whisky's ampersand logo. The resulting series of six films, each displaying a markedly different style, were shown on big screens in nightclubs and bars.
J&B／ビデオ：国際的なアーティスト、デザイナー、ビデオ制作者たちのグループがJ&Bウィスキーのロゴの「&」を再解釈した。その結果、6本の映画シリーズが制作され、それぞれにまったく異なるスタイルが提示された。これらのビデオはナイトクラブやバーの大型スクリーンで上映された。

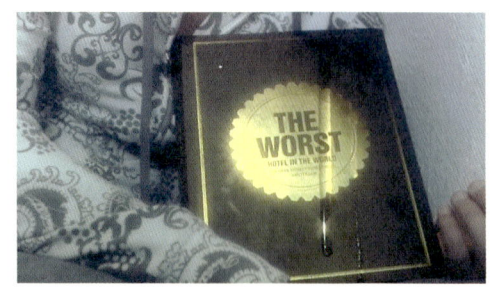

Hans Brinker Budget Hotel, online films
Two films made to celebrate the launch of The Worst Hotel in the World (a book telling the story of the Hans Brinker Budget Hotel). One film presents the book between the buttocks of a comatose backpacker. The other reveals the book on the lap of a drunken, dribbling guest.
Hans Brinker Budget Hotel／インターネット・ビデオ：《ワースト・ホテル・イン・ザ・ワールド＝世界最悪なホテル》（ハンス・ブリンカー・バジェット・ホテルの物語を伝える本）の出版を祝し、2本のビデオが制作された。その1本では、本は、無気力そうなバックパッカーのお尻のあいだにはさまれ、もう1本では酔っ払ってよだれをたらしている宿泊客の膝のうえにのせられている。

Hans Brinker Budget Hotel, book
The full sordid story of the notorious Hans Brinker Budget Hotel. The Worst Hotel in the World collects the hostel's history and campaigns for the very first time. The book also includes interviews with the staff, a report on the Brinker's economy versus the world's economy, and various others behind the scenes insights. Thoughtfully, a DVD of all commercials of the Brinker is not included.
Hans Brinker Budget Hotel／書籍：悪名高きハンス・ブリンカー・バジェット・ホテルのむさくるしい物語の全貌をまとめた『ワースト・ホテル・イン・ザ・ワールド』は、同ホテルの歴史とキャンペーンを紹介した初めての本。スタッフへのインタビュー、ブリンカーの経済状態と世界の景気を対比したレポート、さまざまな裏話なども掲載されている。ブリンカーの全コマーシャルを収録したDVDを付けなかったのは、賢明な判断だったといえよう。

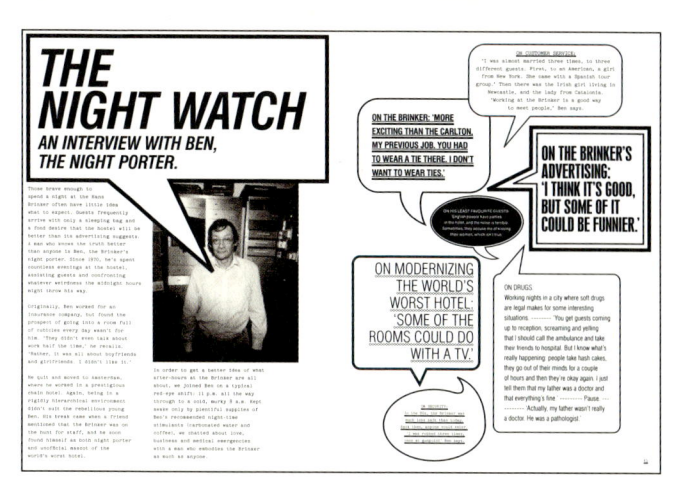

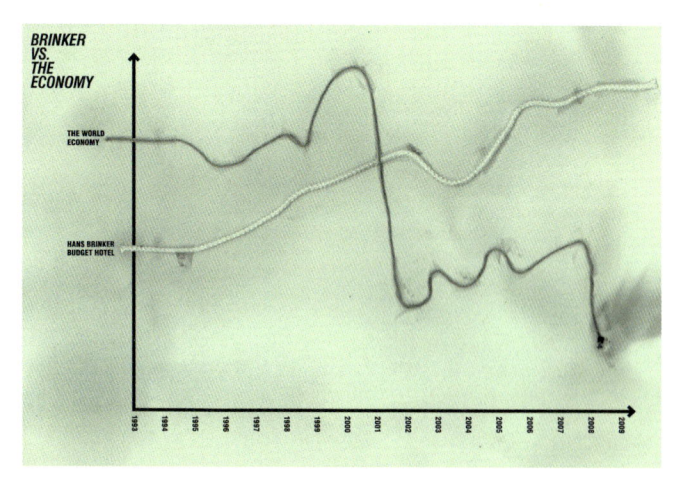

THE NIGHT WATCH
AN INTERVIEW WITH BEN, THE NIGHT PORTER.

Those brave enough to spend a night at the Hans Brinker often have little idea what to expect. Guests frequently arrive with only a sleeping bag and a food desire that the hostel will be better than its advertising suggests. A man who knows the truth better than anyone is Ben, the Brinker's night porter. Since 1970, he's spent countless evenings at the hostel, assisting guests and confronting whatever weirdness the midnight hours might throw his way.

Originally, Ben worked for an insurance company, but found the prospect of going into a room full of cubicles every day wasn't for him. "They didn't even talk about work half the time," he recalls. "Rather, it was all about boyfriends and girlfriends. I didn't like it."

He quit and moved to Amsterdam, where he worked in a prestigious chain hotel. Again, being in a slightly hierarchical environment didn't suit the rebellious young Ben. His break came when a friend mentioned that the Brinker was on the hunt for staff, and he soon found himself as both night porter and unofficial mascot of the world's worst hotel.

In order to get a better idea of what after-hours at the Brinker are all about, we joined Ben on a typical red-eye shift; 11 p.m. all the way through to 8 a.m. Kept awake only by plentiful supplies of Ben's recommended night-time stimulants (carbonated water and coffee), we chatted about love, business and medical emergencies with a man who embodies the Brinker as much as anyone.

ON THE BRINKER: 'MORE EXCITING THAN THE CARLTON, MY PREVIOUS JOB. YOU HAD TO WEAR A TIE THERE. I DON'T WANT TO WEAR TIES.'

ON CUSTOMER SERVICE: 'I was almost married three times, in three different guests. First, to an American, a girl from New York. She came with a Spanish tour group.' Then there was the Irish girl living in Newcastle, and the lady from Catalonia. "Working at the Brinker is a good way to meet people," Ben says.

ON THE BRINKER'S ADVERTISING: 'I THINK IT'S GOOD, BUT SOME OF IT COULD BE FUNNIER.'

ON MODERNIZING THE WORLD'S WORST HOTEL: 'SOME OF THE ROOMS COULD DO WITH A T.V.'

ON DRUGS
Working nights in a city where soft drugs are legal makes for some interesting situations. ——— You get guests coming up to reception, screaming and yelling that I should call the ambulance and take their friends to hospital. But I know what's really happening people take hash cakes, they go out of their minds for a couple of hours and then they're okay again. I just tell them that my father was a doctor and that everything's fine ——— Pause. ——— 'Actually, my father wasn't really a doctor. He was a pathologist.'

BRINKER DUST BALL HALL OF FAME

UNDER BED, ROOM 401

LOBBY | CORNER, ROOM 314
LOCKER, ROOM 317 | UNDER MATTRESS, ROOM 212
SHOWER DRAIN, ROOM 108 | BEHIND TOILET, ROOM 108

BRINKER VS. THE ECONOMY

THE WORLD ECONOMY

HANS BRINKER BUDGET HOTEL

9

2.07243 kilo

Hans Brinker Budget Hotel, poster campaign
The Worst Hotel in the World is a book dedicated to the Hans Brinker Budget Hotel, KesselsKramer's oldest client. The poster campaign shows the book being put to good use in the hotel.
Hans Brinker Budget Hotel／ポスター・キャンペーン:『ワースト・ホテル・イン・ザ・ワールド』は、ケッセルスクライマーの最もつきあいが古いクライアント、ハンス・ブリンカー・バジェット・ホテルに捧げられた本。そのポスター・キャンペーンでは、同書がホテル内でうまく活用されている様子が紹介されている。

Libelle Anniversary Edition, editorial
Dutch women's magazine Libelle commissioned a photo story from KesselsKramer for their anniversary edition. The result is a strange tale describing how papier mâché bunnies could undo the damage magazines do to our environment.
Libelle 記念号／エディトリアル：オランダの女性誌『Libelle』が、ケッセルスクライマーに記念号用のフォト・ストーリーを制作するよう依頼。その結果、雑誌が環境に与えるダメージを張子のウサギがいかに解消できるかを語る風変わりな物語ができあがった。

2.07710 kilo

2.07944 kilo

Libelle Anniversary Edition, editorial
In Libelle magazine's story of how to make the world a better place, a tribe of papier mâché bunnies are created to return thousands of magazine pages to the woods from where they came. Created with photographer Amira Fritz.
Libelle 記念号／エディトリアル：どのようにしたら世界をよくできるかに関する『Libelle』誌の特集のために、張子ウサギの一群が制作された。これは数千ページにおよぶ雑誌の紙を、その故郷である森に帰す試み。撮影は、写真家のアミラ・フリッツ。

2.08178 kilo

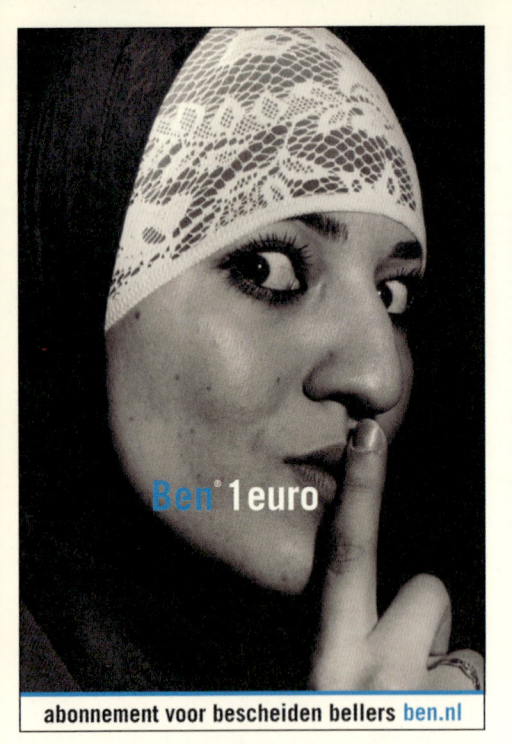

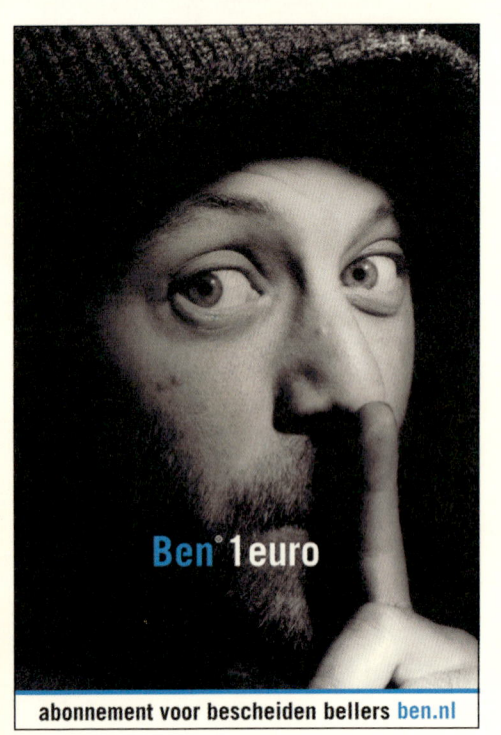

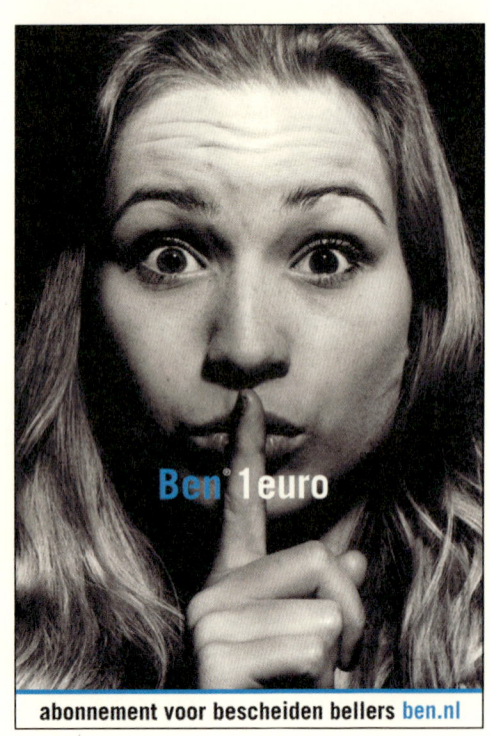

Ben, poster campaign
Dutch mobile phone network Ben is based around a more personal, social service (the brand is a person's name but is also the verb 'to be.') Here, it launched a new subscription for 'modest callers.' We see portraits of reserved phone users – because even those who don't talk a lot have something to say. The headline reads: Ben 1 euro ('I am one euro').
Ben／ポスター・キャンペーン：オランダの携帯電話ネットワーク、Benは、より個人的で社会的なサービスを基本としている（同ブランドは人名であると同時に「になる」という動詞でもある）。同社は「控えめな通話者」という新サービスを開始。話すことは少なくても何かを伝えたい人がいることから、広告には遠慮がちな電話ユーザーの顔写真が使われている。キャッチ・フレーズは「Ben 1 euro＝私は1ユーロ」

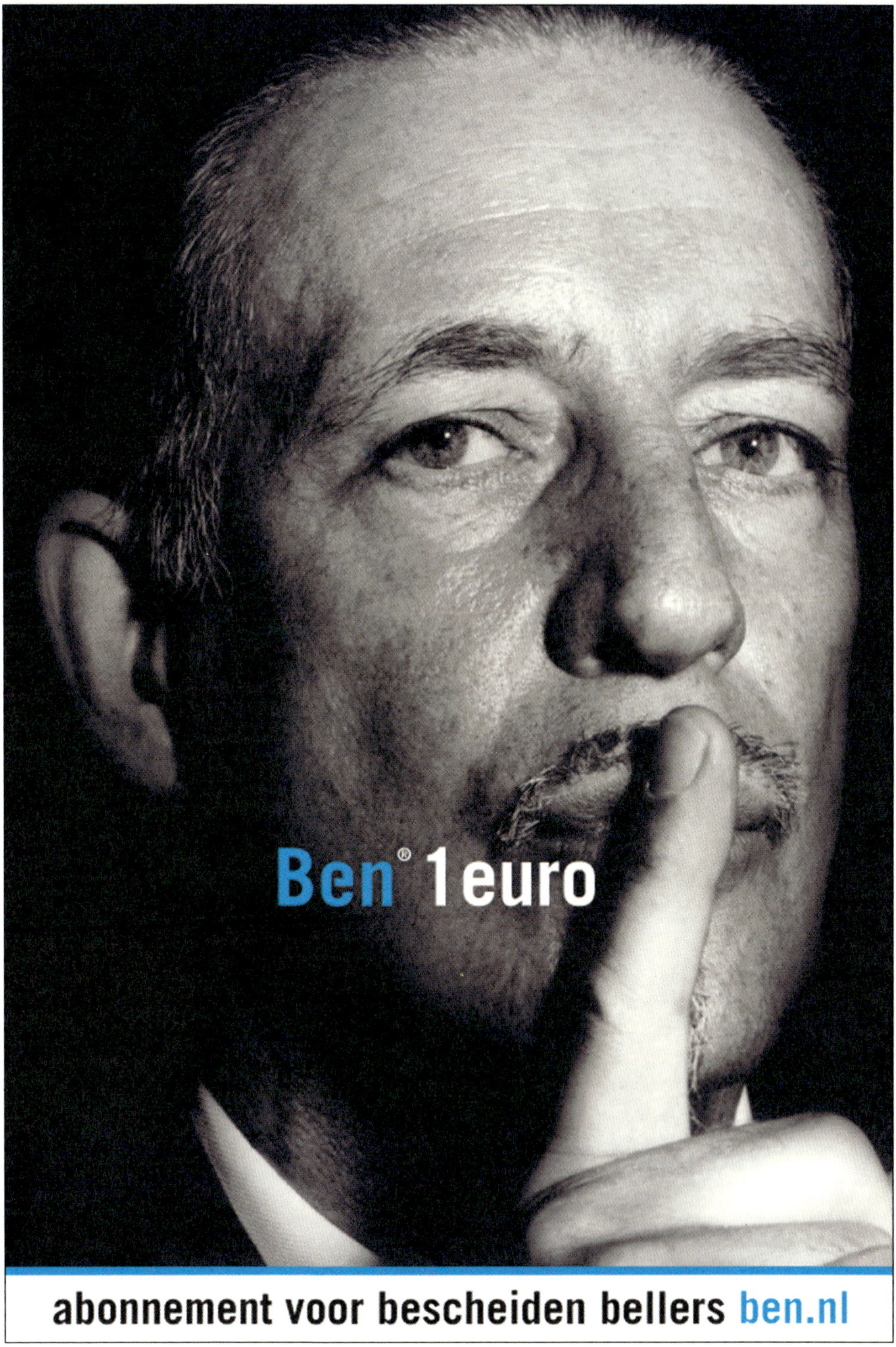
Ben® 1euro
abonnement voor bescheiden bellers ben.nl

Ben®aan

Ben vrij om te komen en vrij om te gaan. Ben.nl

Ben®aan

Ben vrij om te komen en vrij om te gaan. Ben.nl

Ben, poster campaign
Ben's flexible subscription means you can have an on/off relationship with this mobile phone provider. Posters demonstrated this by showing a couple who were, themselves, on and off again. The headlines read: 'Ben On (I am on)' and 'Ben Off (I am off)'.
Ben/ポスター・キャンペーン：Benの「フレキシブルな加入」とは、この携帯電話会社と常時契約し続ける必要はないことを意味している。ポスターでは、くっついたり、別れたりしているカップルを使ってこれを表現。キャッチ・フレーズは、「Ben On=つきあいましょう」と「Ben Off=さようなら」

2.08879 kilo

Ben® uit

Ben vrij om te komen en vrij om te gaan. Ben.nl

Ben® uit

Ben vrij om te komen en vrij om te gaan. Ben.nl

Ben, poster campaign
This campaign for Ben continues to highlight the flexibility of the mobile-phone provider. The poster on the left reads 'I am still here,' and on the right 'I am welcome'. In this way, the company shows that it appeals to all kinds of customers.

Ben／ポスター・キャンペーン：Benのフレキシブルさに焦点があてられた、ほかのキャンペーン例。左側のポスターの見出しは「私はまだここにいます」。そして、右側は「ようこそ」。同社があらゆるタイプの顧客を対象としていることを示している。

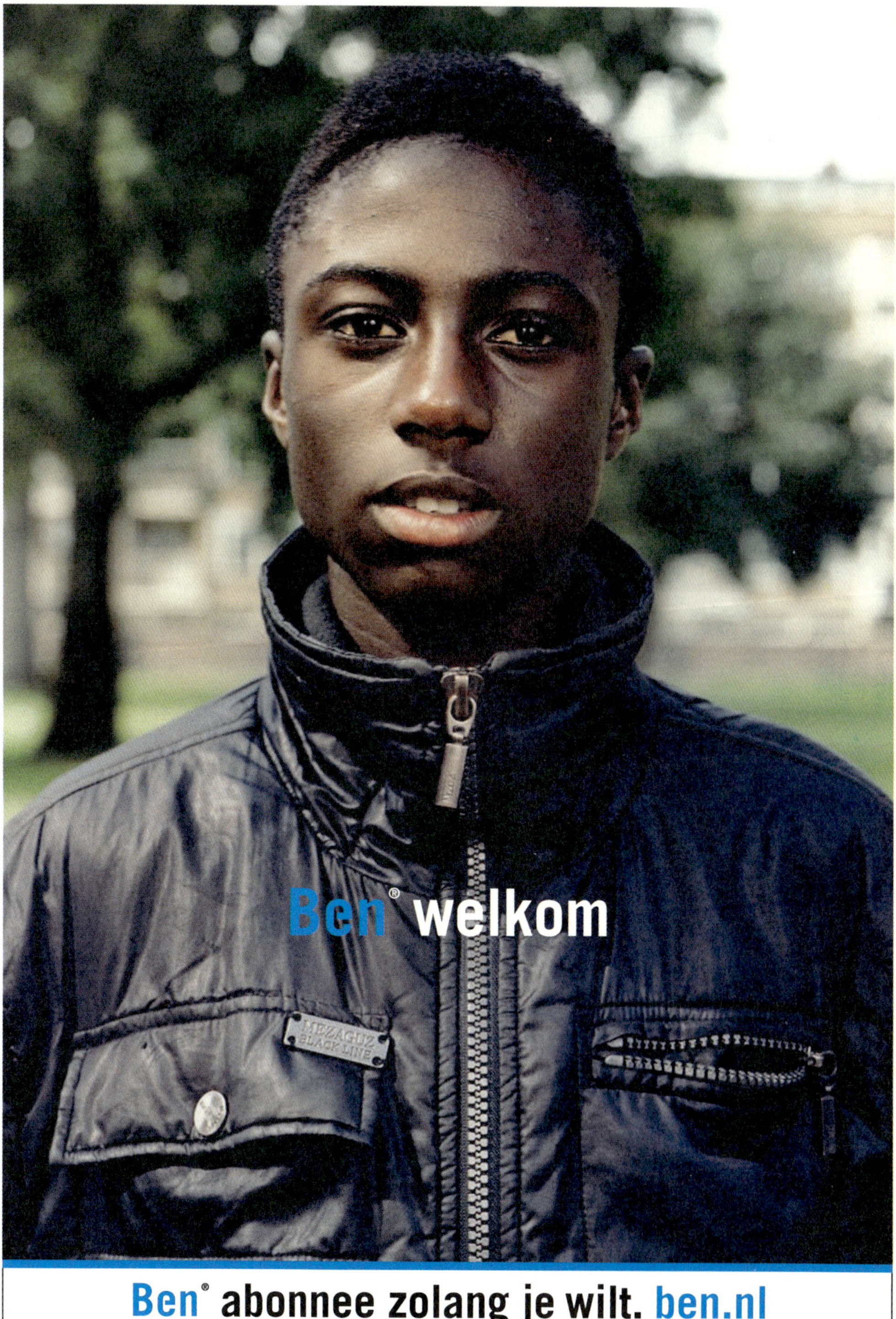

Ben® welkom
Ben® abonnee zolang je wilt. ben.nl

Ben, poster campaign
Further examples of the Ben campaign focusing on flexibility of service. The text reads, anti-clockwise from top left: 'I am happy with what I've got', 'I am new,' 'I am inseparable.' and 'I am free to go'.
Ben／ポスター・キャンペーン：Benがサービスのフレキシブルさに力を入れていることを示す、さらに別のキャンペーン。キャッチ・フレーズは、左上から時計と反対回りに「私は手に入れたものに満足しいてる」「私は新しい」「私は離れられない」「私は好きなところへ行く」

KK Exports, exhibition
This showcase of KesselsKramer work was initiated by Australian communications agency The Surgery, who exported a huge assortment of KesselsKramer posters, as well as associated films, commercials and books, to unusual gallery spaces in Melbourne and Sydney.
KK Exports／展覧会：オーストラリアの広告代理店ザ・サージェリーが開催したケッセルスクライマーの作品展。ケッセルスによる膨大なポスターが、関連ビデオ、コマーシャル、書籍とともにメルボルンとシドニーの個性的なギャラリー・スペースに展示された。

Protest, print campaign
'Do whatever you can to get there' announced this Dutch boarding brand. This seasonal campaign continued the theme by showing snowboarders leaving behind a trail of the boring objects and distractions that were getting in the way of true happiness on the slopes.
Protest／紙媒体キャンペーン：「あそこに行くために、できる限りなんでもしよう」は、オランダのスノーボード・ブランド、プロテストのキャッチ・フレーズ。このテーマにのっとり、スロープの上で味わえる幸福の前に立ちはだかる、たいくつなものや、気休めのたぐいを置き去りにしていくスノーボーダーたちを、季節のキャンペーンで表現した。

2.10514 kilo

Protest, hang-tag films
A collection of short films featuring Protest riders overcoming anything and everything that stands between them and the slopes. The series was created with a number of upcoming international filmmakers with the goal of reminding boarders to conquer every obstacle, constantly seek fresh powder and, above all else, enjoy the ride.
Protest／インターネット・ビデオ（商品タグにURLを掲載して告知）：プロテストの短編ビデオ集は、みずからとスロープのあいだに立ちはだかる、あらゆる障害を克服していくスノーボーダーたちを描いている。新進気鋭の世界的映像作家たち多数によって制作された、本シリーズが目指すのは、すべての困難を乗りこえ、つねに新鮮なパウダー・スノーを求め、そして、なによりボーディングそのものを楽しむことを、スノーボーダーたちに忘れないでいてもらうことだ。

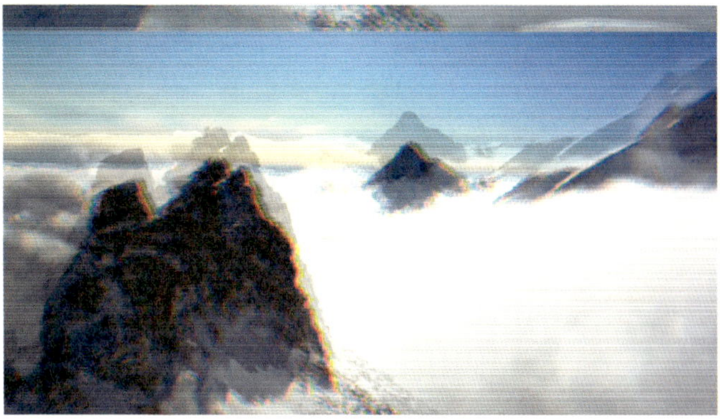

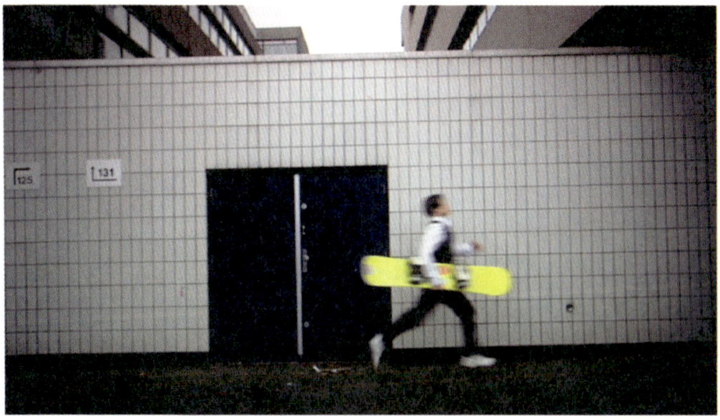
125
131

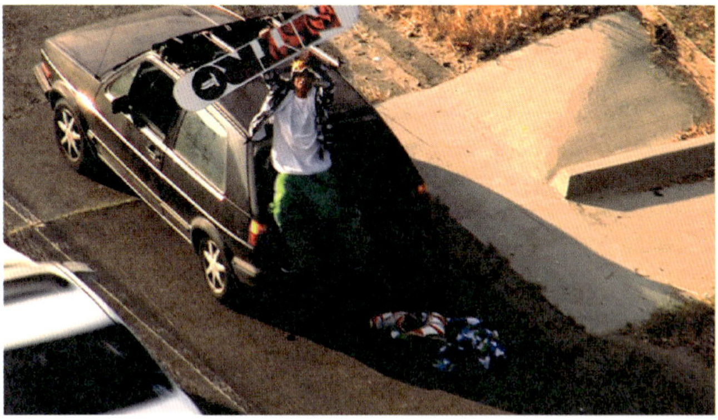

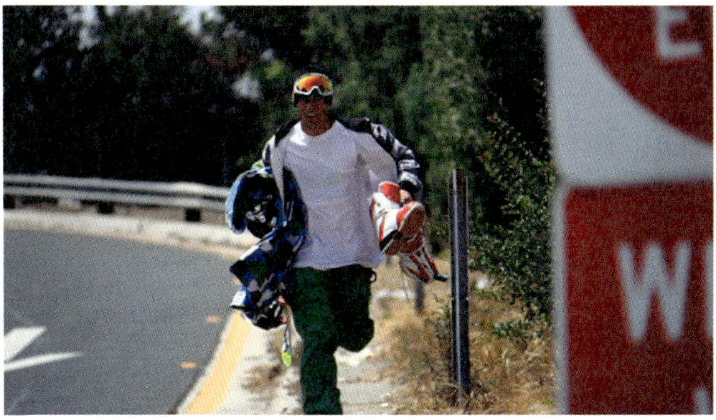

Dutch Ministry of Health, poster, print and web
When it comes down to it, organ donation is a simple decision: would you like to save a life or not? This organ donator registration campaign makes an issue normally shrouded in moral implications feel more practical, by leaving the question open and directing the audience to the website JaofNee.nl (YesorNo.nl). A sample headline from above reads, 'If you can save someone's life, would you do it?'

オランダ厚生省／ポスター、紙媒体、ウェブ：臓器提供に直面した者にとって、提供の意思を左右するのは、シンプルに「命を救いたいか否か？」である。ウェブサイト「JaofNee.nl＝イエスorノー.nl」の閲覧者に、オープンで直接的な質問を投げかけ、通常はモラルでがんじがらめになってしまうこの問題を、もっと現実的に感じられるよう目指すのが、本臓器提供者登録キャンペーンだ。上図のキャッチ・フレーズの例をひとつあげると、「だれかの命を救うことができるとしたら、あなたは救いますか？」

Dutch Ministry of Health, TV commercial
The words 'Ja' or 'Nee' are sung out by different individuals to the strains of Dutch birthday song, Lang zal je leven (Long may you live).
オランダ厚生省／テレビ・コマーシャル：さまざまな人たちが歌う「Ja＝イエス」あるいは「Nee＝ノー」の言葉は、オランダの誕生歌「Lang zal je leven＝あなたが長生きしますように」の旋律に乗せて発せられたもの。

Dutch Ministry of Health, extra materials
Further material for the Organ donation campaign for different occasions and communication sites, including brand book, flyers, stickers, badges and other handouts.
オランダ厚生省／そのほかのツール：ブランド・ブック、フライヤー、ステッカー、バッジなど、臓器提供キャンペーンのさまざまな機会や、宣伝の場で使われる多様なツール。

2.11682 kilo

Ja
Nee
Ja
ik ben orgaandonor
Nederland zegt
Ja
Nee
Ben jij al donor? JaofNee.nl
Nederland zegt
Ja
Nee
Ben jij al donor? JaofNee.nl
Ja
Nee
Ben jij al donor? JaofNee.nl

Benthem Crouwel, poster campaign
KesselsKramer helped create a book celebrating 30 years of Dutch architects, Benthem Crouwel. These posters appeared on the sides of buildings featured in the book. Copy reads: 'This is page 102'.
Benthem Crouwel／ポスター・キャンペーン：ケッセルスクライマーは、オランダの建築家ベンテム・クラウェルの30周年を祝した書籍の制作を手伝った。そのポスターは、同書に掲載されたビルの側面に掲示された。コピーは「これはP.102に掲載」とうたっている。

30 years of architecture by Benthem Crouwel

now in the shops or via www.010.nl

Benthem Crouwel, poster campaign
A second wave of posters for Benthem Crouwel featured buildings constructed from copies of the book. The title BCAD refers to Benthem Crouwel's past and present (A.D. as in '2009 A.D.'). The book was designed by Studio Lauke.

Benthem Crouwel／ポスター・キャンペーン：ベンテム・クラウェルのためのポスター第2弾は、作品集で建てたビルを取りあげた。タイトルの『BCAD』は、ベンテム・クラウェル（BC）の過去と現在（AD＝紀元後の意。通常、2009.A.D.など、西暦の年号の前後に付けられる）をさしている。ブック・デザインはスタジオ・ラウケが担当。

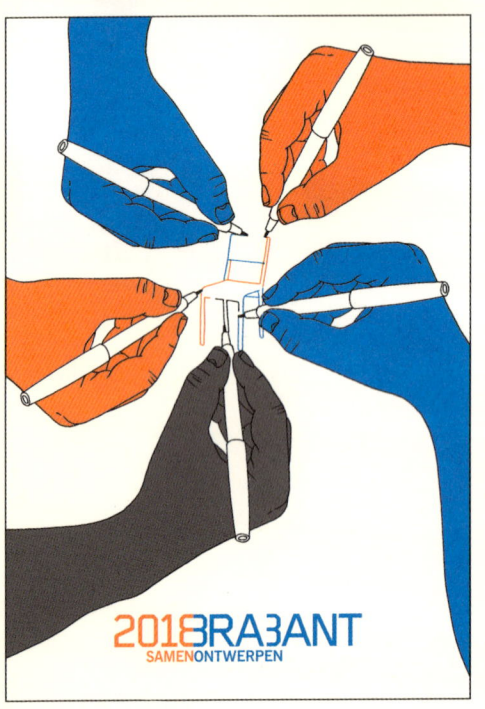

Brabant Cultural Capital, poster campaign
The Dutch town of Brabant was selected as the country's cultural capital. These materials helped lobby for this great honour and were produced with the backing of five cities in the area.
Brabant Cultural Capital／ポスター・キャンペーン：オランダの街ブラバントが、国の文化首都に選ばれた。この大いなる栄誉に向けたロビー活動を支援したポスターは、同地区の5都市の後援により制作された。

citizenM, packaging
Each item produced by hotel chain citizenM (which stands for 'citizen mobile') contains an element of the brand's playful, guest-orientated character. This water packaging tells the story of its contents, from clouds to rivers and rain right up to its current state as a source of refreshment.
citizenM／パッケージング：ホテル・チェーン、シチズンM (citizen mobileの略語) が制作した各アイテムには、同ブランドの顧客第一主義を感じさせる楽しい工夫が取りいれられている。飲料水用パッケージは、雨が雲から川へと移動して現在の状態になるまでを説明し、その内容物が清涼飲料水になるまでのストーリーを語っている。

2.12850 kilo

**A chair grown for living.
The new Vegetal is here.**

Vegetal is a new chair planted by Ronan and Erwan Bouroullec and grown by Vitra. A chair that comes in 6 colours. A chair that will blossom naturally in any living space indoors and out. No watering required.

vitra.

Only at authorised Vitra retailers: Tueraessed tis augueril nonsent lortio ea alit adignis corem nit iusto ad ea ad magna con exero ea core tem euis augiam, conullamet nit velismo doluptat ad tissi te dunt lutpatie veliquis num quis am nulla commy nibh exeril irit ulla feugueraesse velent utatem volorti scipsum doluptat praessi. Iquis dolor sit la facillaorper sum digna core totie dolorerit landre dolobor peraessis nit illaorem adit iriusto commolo rtismol oborem duisl dignibh ex ea alis nulluptat, con utat la faccumm olobore Non vercip et dionumsan ut outpatue facincipsum veniam volobortie molobore corperatet luptat. Ut aute core facinis duis niatum zzrilit lore min vel dolobore modolent vel irit lore. www.vitra.com

Vitra, print and poster
This campaign drew attention to the organic, fluid shapes of Vitra's Vegetal chair designed by Ronan and Erwan Bouroullec. By showing it literally sprout from the ground, the image underlined its natural, plant-like form.
Vitra／印刷物、ポスター：ロナン＆エルワン・ブルレックが設計したヴィトラの「ベジタル・チェア＝植物のように成長する椅子」の有機的で流動的な形に注目を集めるためのキャンペーン。椅子がまさに地面から芽生えているように見せることで、その植物のようなナチュラルな形状を強調している。

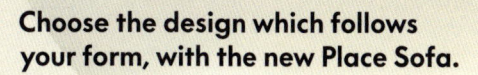

Vitra, print and poster
This poster points out that Vitra's Place Sofa is moulded to perfectly fit the human form.
Vitra／紙媒体、ポスター：ヴィトラの「プレイス・ソファ」が人間の形に完璧にフィットするよう成形されていることを表すポスター。

**Introducing perfect balance
for the modern office.**

The new AC 4 by Antonio Citterio. It takes
the most advanced ergonomic features and
balances them beautifully with the lightest
of forms. Meaning that, while you see
elegance, you feel comfort and support.
Learn more at www.vitra.com/ac4

vitra.

Dionum zrit ute vullam iusta conumsa ndiam, sequatue dolor siscidusim vero dolor iuscidusis ex eui tie magna feu feu fac cum iure tat lor ip etol duis

---

Vitra, print and poster
The AC 4 is an office chair that seeks to do what no office chair has done before: balance
ergonomics and design. In this campaign, the AC 4 was seen perched on top of a carefully
arranged display of office equipment.
Vitra／紙媒体、ポスター：「AC4」は、人間工学とデザインをうまく釣り合わせ
るというこれまでのオフィス・チェアが成しえなかった領域を追求する商品。本
キャンペーンでは、AC4は、精巧に配置されたオフィス機器の上にとまっている
ように演出された。

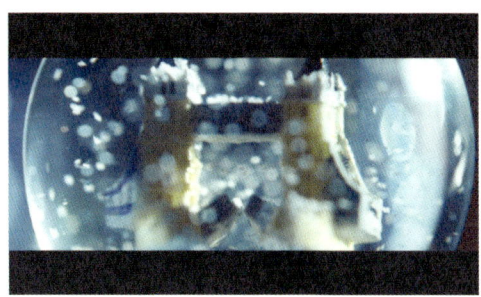

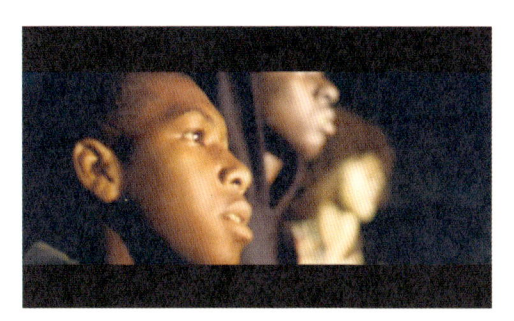

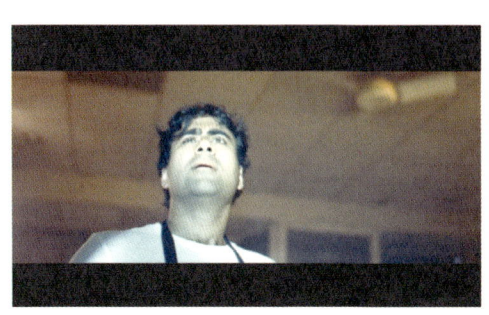

BFI London Film Festival, poster campaign and cinema commercial
The power of cinema to affect people's everyday lives is shown using a simple visual metaphor: faces lit up by a projector in ordinary situations. This work was produced at London's KK Outlet.
BFI London Film Festival／ポスター・キャンペーン、映画コマーシャル：映画が人の日常生活に与える力が、シンプルな視覚的メタファを使って表現された。そのメタファとは、映写機でライトアップされた日常の人々の顔。本作品はロンドンのケッセルスクライマーのスタジオ、KKアウトレットで制作された。

Hans Brinker Budget Hotel, poster and films
The Hans Brinker has been the patron of a celebrated art prize for ten years. This anniversary poster featured a mysterious group worshipping the prize's trophy: a toilet-brush. In supporting films, the ceremony was brought to life, and the dubious origin of the toilet-brush trophy explored.
Hans Brinker Budget Hotel／ポスター、ビデオ：ハンス・ブリンカーは10年にわたり有名な芸術賞を後援している。その10周年を記念するポスターの題材は、賞のトロフィとしてトイレブラシをあがめるあやしげな一団。この儀式をリアルに紹介し、トイレブラシ・トロフィのうさんくさい起源まで探求するビデオも制作された。

Tree Paintings, book
A photobook that took trees marked for destruction as its theme. Each photo featured a different swirl of spray paint applied to the tree by a woodsman. The result is a record of a strange series of accidental artworks.
Tree Paintings／書籍：切り倒すための印がつけられた木をテーマにした写真集。各写真には、木こりがさっとつけたさまざまなスプレー・ペイントが写っている。その結果、一連の奇妙な偶発的アート作品の記録ができあがった。

Ben® vrij om te komen

Ben® vaak
500 min/sms + 100 gratis sms van €19,99 voor **€15,99** p. mnd.
Ben® regelmatig
250 min/sms + 100 gratis sms van €9,99 voor **€6,99** p. mnd.
Ben® soms
100 min/sms van €5,99 voor **€4,99** p. mnd.
Ben® zuinig
50 min/sms van €3,99 voor **€2,99** p. mnd.
Bestel direct op Ben.nl - of bel 079-7504222 - zie actievoorwaarden op **Ben®.nl**

Ben, print campaign
Ben's print campaign continues the mobile company's communication strategy of championing flexible rates. The copy reads 'Free to come' (left-hand side) and 'Free to go' (right-hand side). The ads appeared on consecutive pages.
Ben／紙媒体キャンペーン：紙媒体キャンペーンでも、フレキシブルな料金に挑戦する、携帯電話会社 Ben の宣伝戦略が展開された。キャッチ・フレーズは「来るのも自由」（左）、「去るのも自由」（右）。これらの広告は連続したページに掲載された。

Ben® vrij om te gaan

Slechts 1 maand opzegtermijn. Ben®.nl

Ik zal altijd mijn best voor je doen. Dat beloof ik. Maar het zou natuurlijk kunnen dat jij ooit, zomaar ineens, op mij bent uitgekeken. Ik hoop ook van niet, natuurlijk. Maar als je ooit weg wilt, kan dat altijd. Ook al ben je pas 1 maand abonnee. Even goede vrienden.

De groeten van Ben®

2.14720 kilo

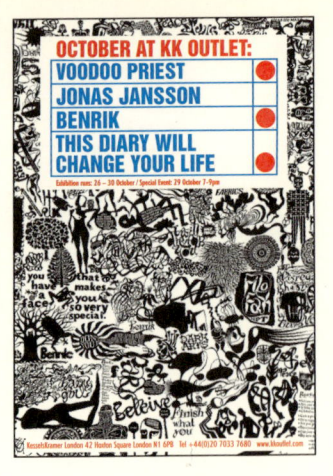

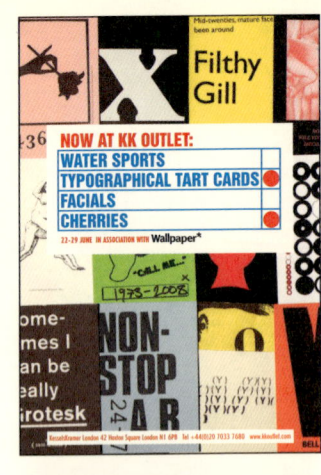

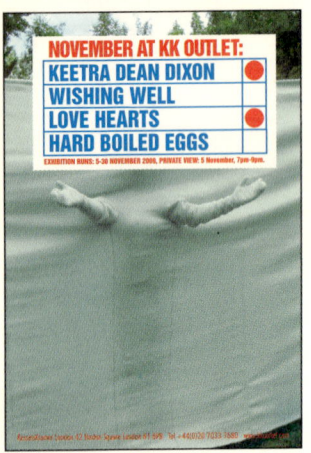

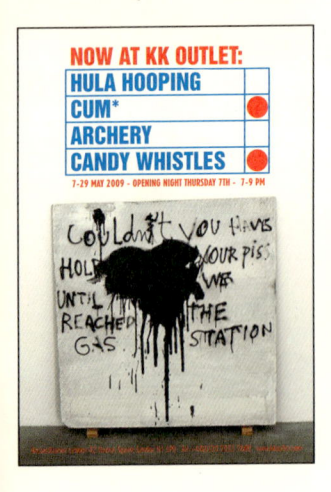

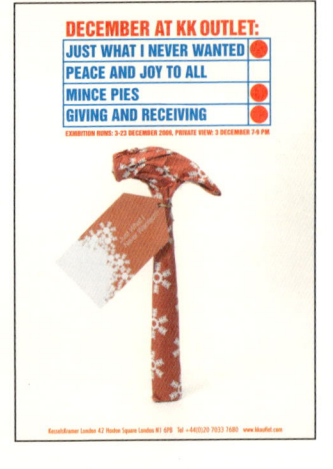

KK Outlet, posters and exhibition space

KK Outlet stages regular exhibitions showcasing the work of interesting and unusual artists. Above are a selection of posters advertising these events. On the right-hand side: KK Outlet's exhibition space.

KK Outlet／ポスター、展示スペース：KKアウトレットは定期的に、個性的で興味深いアーティストの作品を紹介する展覧会を開催している。上図はこれらのイベントを宣伝するためのポスターの一部。右ページはKKアウトレットの展示スペース。

9
2.15187 kilo

jacht-op-jan-modaal.nl

Jan Modaal heeft 8.6 verschillende seksuele partners.

NORMAAL

Image by Olaf Breuning

Niet Normaal, print, poster and online campaign
Work for Niet Normaal, an art exhibition that asked visitors to consider what society judges as normal. The campaign was based on 'the hunt for Average Joe', with posters, press and online visualizing unlikely facts about the behaviour of the supposed 'average' person (for example: 'Average Joe has 8.6 sexual partners'). In a second phase (see right), posters advertised some of the work seen at the exhibition.

Niet Normaal／紙媒体、ポスター、インターネット・キャンペーン：社会がなにを正常と判断すると思うかを訪問者にたずねる芸術展「Niet Normaal＝正常ではない」のための作品。そのキャンペーンでは「標準的なジョー探し」をベースに、ポスター、出版物、インターネットで想像上の「標準的な」人の行動にありえなさそうな事実が視覚化された（たとえば「標準的なジョーは8.6人のセックス・フレンドをもつ」など）。第二段階では（右図参照）、ポスターで展示作品の一部が宣伝された。

2.15421 kilo

16 december 2009 - 7 maart 2010 - nietnormaal.nl

Tentoonstelling Niet Normaal

Beurs van Berlage, Amsterdam

Marc Quinn - Stuart Penn, 2000

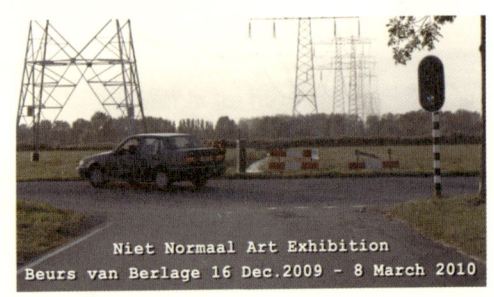

Niet Normaal, online films
Two short clips for a digital audience to support the Niet Normaal exhibition. In one, a man jumps into a swimming pool full of saliva to illustrate that 'Average Joe produces two swimming pools full of saliva in his lifetime'. In the second execution, a man is stuck at a traffic light for what seems like an eternity. Copy reads 'Average Joe spends two weeks of his life waiting at traffic lights'.
Niet Normaal／インターネット・ビデオ：展覧会Niet Normaalのプロモーション用に制作された、デジタル・ユーザー向けの2本の短編ビデオ。ひとつは唾液でいっぱいのプールに飛び込む男の話で、「標準的なジョーは唾液でいっぱいになったスイミング・プールを生涯に2つ作る」を説明するためのもの。もうひとつは、永遠に続きそうな赤信号に立ち往生している男を描いたもの。その見出しは「標準的なジョーは人生のうちで二週間を信号機が変わるのを待って過ごす」

Niet Normaal, extra materials
Extra material for the Niet Normaal campaign, showing its simple house style of red on white.
Niet Normaal／そのほかのツール：「Niet Normaal」のキャンペーンのための
そのほかのプロモーション・ツール。白地に赤のシンプルな自社ツールが使われ
ている。

2.16121 kilo

Dutch Funeral Museum, poster
A poster for an exhibition at the gallery section of Tot Zover, the Dutch Funeral Museum. The exhibition was curated by KesselsKramer and comprised a photo story detailing a man's relationship with his wife: from their first meeting, to childbirth, to her mental illness and eventual suicide.
Dutch Funeral Museum／ポスター：オランダ葬儀博物館「Tot Zover」のギャラリー部門で開催された展覧会のためのポスター。ケッセルスクライマーがキュレーションした同展は、ある男とその妻との関係を、ふたりの最初の出会いから、子どもの誕生、妻の精神障害、その果ての自殺まで克明に物語るフォト・ストーリーで構成された。

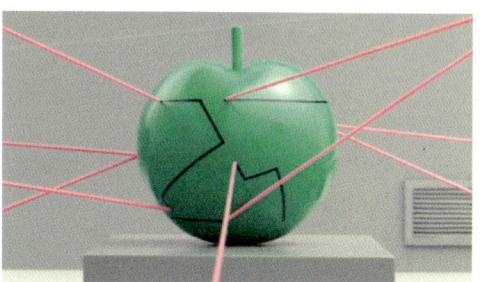

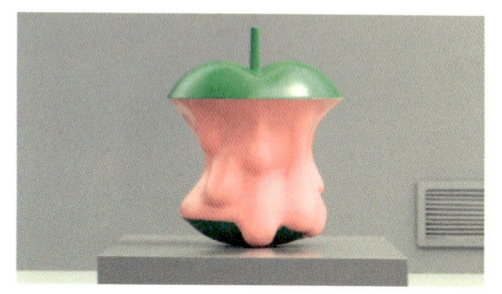

Het Klokhuis, brand identity and films
One of the longest, running Dutch children's television shows needed a new identity. The show's focus is educational, with installments dedicated to broadening kids' knowledge base. Given this theme, an idea based on curiosity seemed fitting. Here, the trademark Het Klokhuis apple is experimented upon and revealed to contain all kinds of scientific marvels.
Het Klokhuis／ブランド・アイデンティティ、映像：オランダで最も長く放送されている子ども番組に、新しいアイデンティティが必要になった。この番組は、子どもたちの知識を広げるためのツールを使った教育に焦点をおいている。このテーマなら、好奇心にまつわるコンセプトが最適だろう。そこで、トレードマークであるHet Klok-huisリンゴが実験に使われ、番組がさまざまな科学的驚きを内包している様子が表現された。

2.16589 kilo

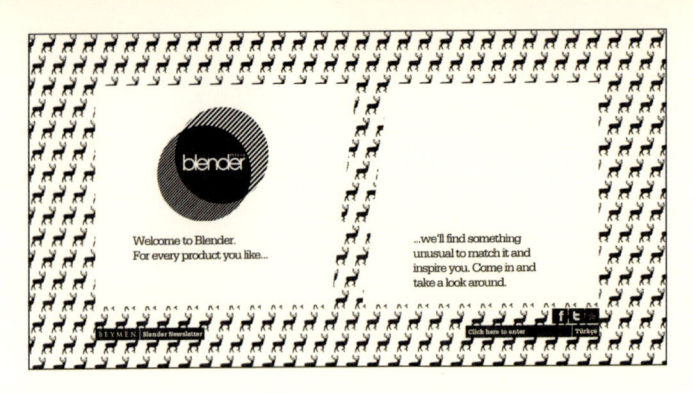

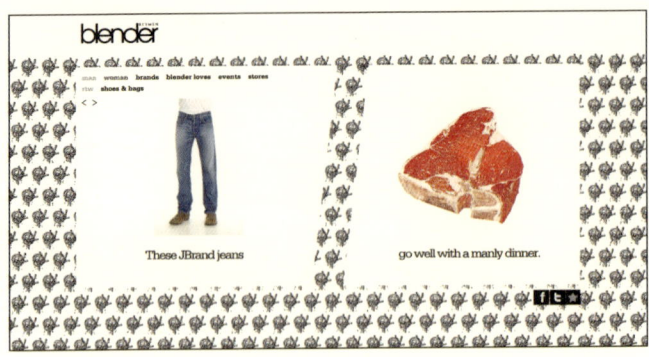

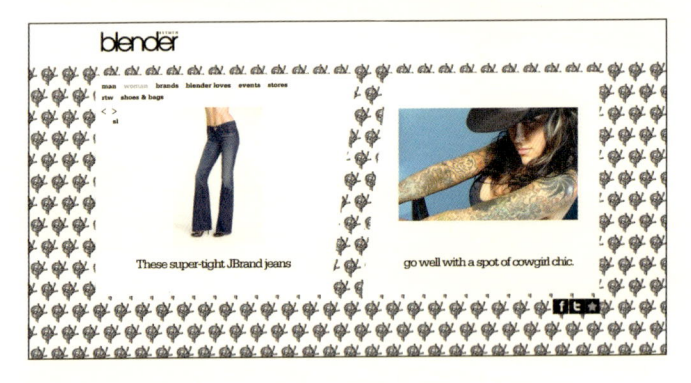

Blender, website
Istanbul's most prestigious department store asked for a new website. The result is based on the shop's name, Blender, recommending whatever situation or product blends best with the user's initial choice of apparel.
Blender／ウェブサイト：イスタンブールで最も高級な百貨店が新しいウェブサイトの制作を求めた。その結果、店名のブレンダー（blend=調和する）をベースにしたウェブサイトができあがり、ユーザーが最初に選んだ洋服に最もブレンドする状況や商品をすすめた。

Rude Chalet, posters, booklet, online, events
Rude Chalets are snow chalets aimed at the snowboarding in-crowd, a group known for their distrust of marketing ploys. To bypass this hard-wired cynicism, a fictional but almost real town was created in posters, press and online. Called Rudeville and populated by weird and wonderful snowboarders, it addressed the target as friends not consumers.

Rude Chalet／ポスター、小冊子、インターネット、イベント：ルード・シャレーは、スノーボーダー向けの山小屋で、そのターゲットとは、マーケティングの策略に不信感を抱くことで有名な、排他的だが究極のスノーボードを求めるグループ。彼らのゆるぎない不信感を取り去るため、実在しないが非常にリアルな町が、ポスター、出版物、インターネット上につくられた。ターゲットを消費者ではなく、友人として扱う、ルードビルというこの町には、ユニークですばらしいスノーボーダーたちが訪れた。

Morgan's Spiced, print and poster campaign
Morgan's Spiced is made with exotic ingredients from all over the world. These origins are linked to its target consumer: young men with a taste for adventure. The lifestyle of these 'modern adventurers' are described in posters, television and press.
Morgan' s Spiced／紙媒体、ポスター・キャンペーン：モーガンズ・スパイスドは世界中のエキゾチックな原料でできている。その原産地が、ターゲット消費者である「味の冒険をいとわない若者」に結びつけられた。この「現代の冒険家たち」のライフスタイルはポスター、テレビ、出版物で紹介された。

Morgan's Spiced, TV commercial
The lives and attitudes of Morgan's Spiced modern adventurers are shown in this clip. Fearlessly exploring every aspect of everyday life, they hike intrepidly across parks and urban streets on a quest for the holy grail of contemporary man: the pub.
Morgan's Spiced／テレビ・コマーシャル：モーガンズ・スパイスドの、現代の冒険家たちの生活と生き方が示された映像。日常生活のあらゆる局面を、恐れも知らずに冒険する彼らは、現代人の聖杯、つまりは究極の目的であるパブを求めて、公園や街中を勇敢に歩き回るのだった。

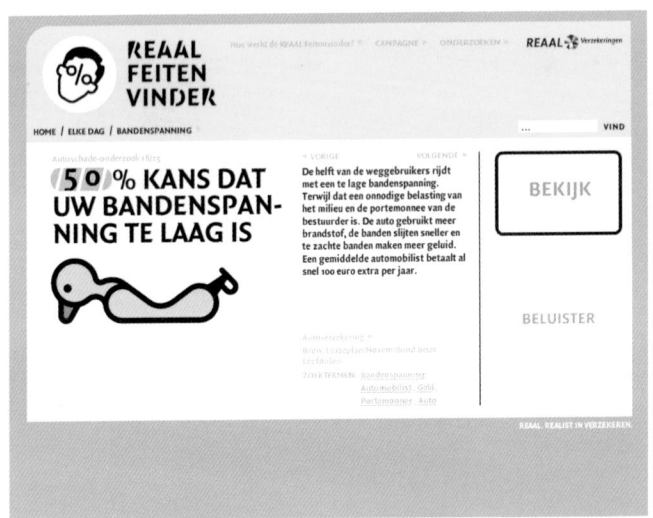

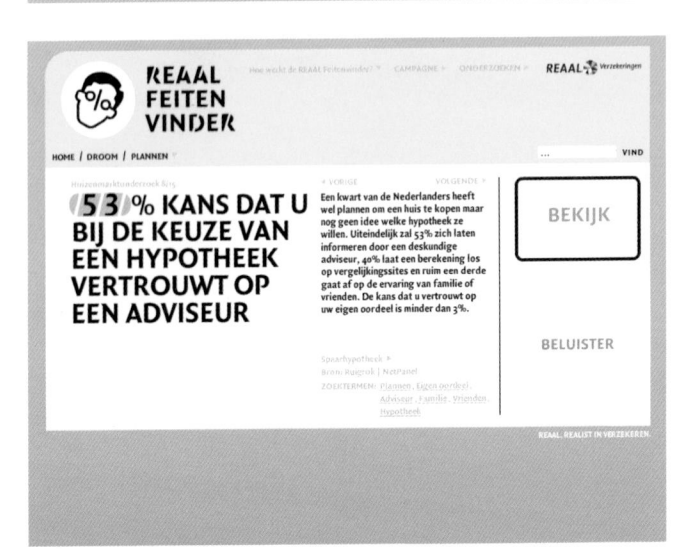

REAAL Insurance, website
The online version of the insurance company's long-running campaign based on unlikely-sounding (but true) statistics. All the facts from many years of communications are collected here and made accessible via keywords. The original research reports from which the facts are drawn can also be accessed.
REAAL Insurance／ウェブサイト：ありえなさそう（だけど本当の）統計に基づいた保険会社のロングラン・キャンペーンのインターネット版。長年の宣伝活動から得られたあらゆる事実が一手に集められ、キーワードで探せるようになっている。事実の情報源であるオリジナルの報告書にもアクセスできる。

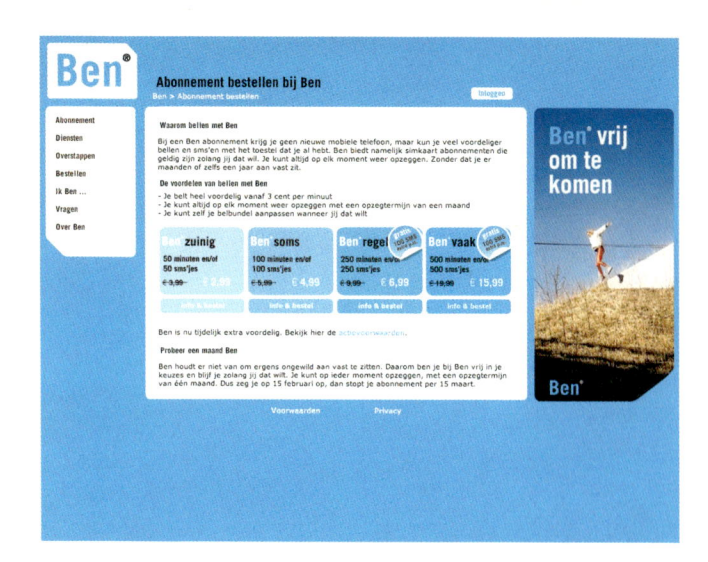

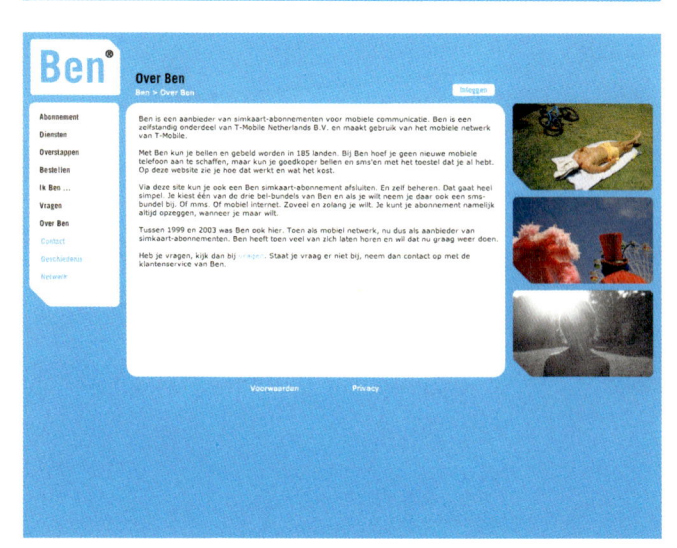

Ben, website
The mobile phone network Ben has a very sales-driven website, with subscriptions shown up front. Next to them, space for banners allows the company to either communicate other services or display messages based on the mobile provider's philosophy.
Ben／ウェブサイト：携帯電話ネットワーク、Benのウェブサイトは、非常にセールス面を重視し、加入者数をトップに掲載している。ほかのサービスについての宣伝や、携帯電話会社としての哲学に基づいたメッセージなどを、そのとなりのバナー用スペースに掲示している。

Ursus, TV and poster campaign
Ursus is a flavoured vodka which once enjoyed huge success in Greece. KesselsKramer's London office, KK Outlet, was invited to rediscover this glory. This particular incarnation saw Ursus promote itself as a new kind of cocktail mix. In TV and posters, peculiar visual mixes highlighted the drink's suitability as an ingredient in a variation on the classic cosmopolitan cocktail.

Ursus／テレビ、ポスター・キャンペーン：アーサスは、かつてギリシャで大成功を収めたフレーバーつきウォッカ。ケッセルスクライマーのロンドン・オフィス、KKアウトレットが、この栄光を再発見するよう依頼された。特別な再生プロジェクトの結果、アーサスは、新しいタイプのカクテル・ベースとして宣伝された。テレビとポスターでは、風変わりなビジュアルをミックスさせ、この飲料が、クラシックなコスモポリタン・カクテルの材料に適していることを強調している。

Ursus Red Cosmopolitan
A Mix Less Ordinary

To Nights Less Ordinary

2.18692 kilo

ター画像。今回のテーマはアーサス・レッド・モヒートとカイピリーニャ。

Ursus Red Mojito
A Mix Less Ordinary

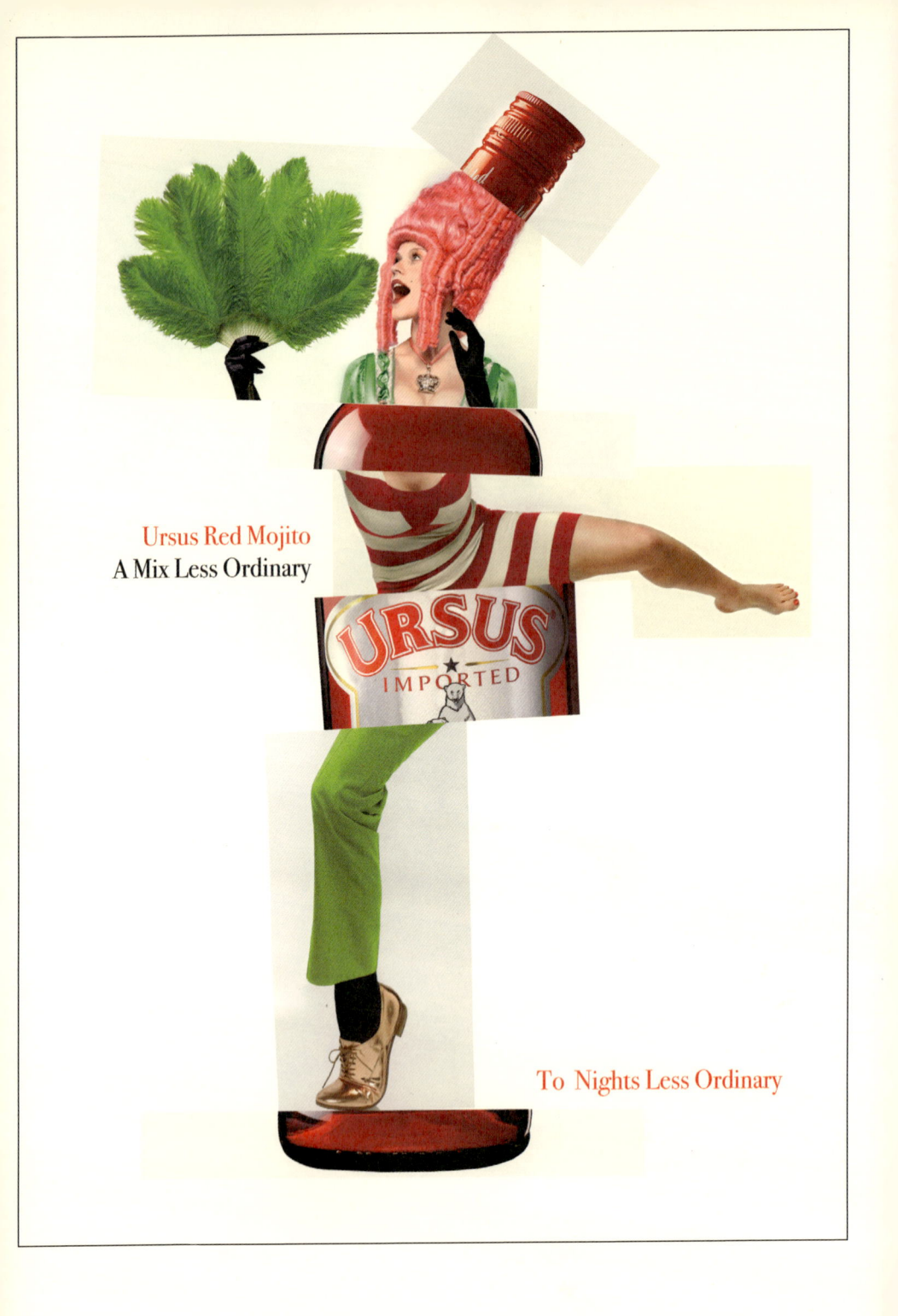

To Nights Less Ordinary

Ursus, poster campaign
More poster images featuring unusual mixes, this time for the Ursus Red Mojito and Caipirinha.
Ursus／ポスター・キャンペーン：個性的なミックスを表現した、そのほかのポスター画像。今回のテーマはアーサス・レッド・モヒートとカイピリーニャ。

Ursus Red Caipirinha
A Mix Less Ordinary

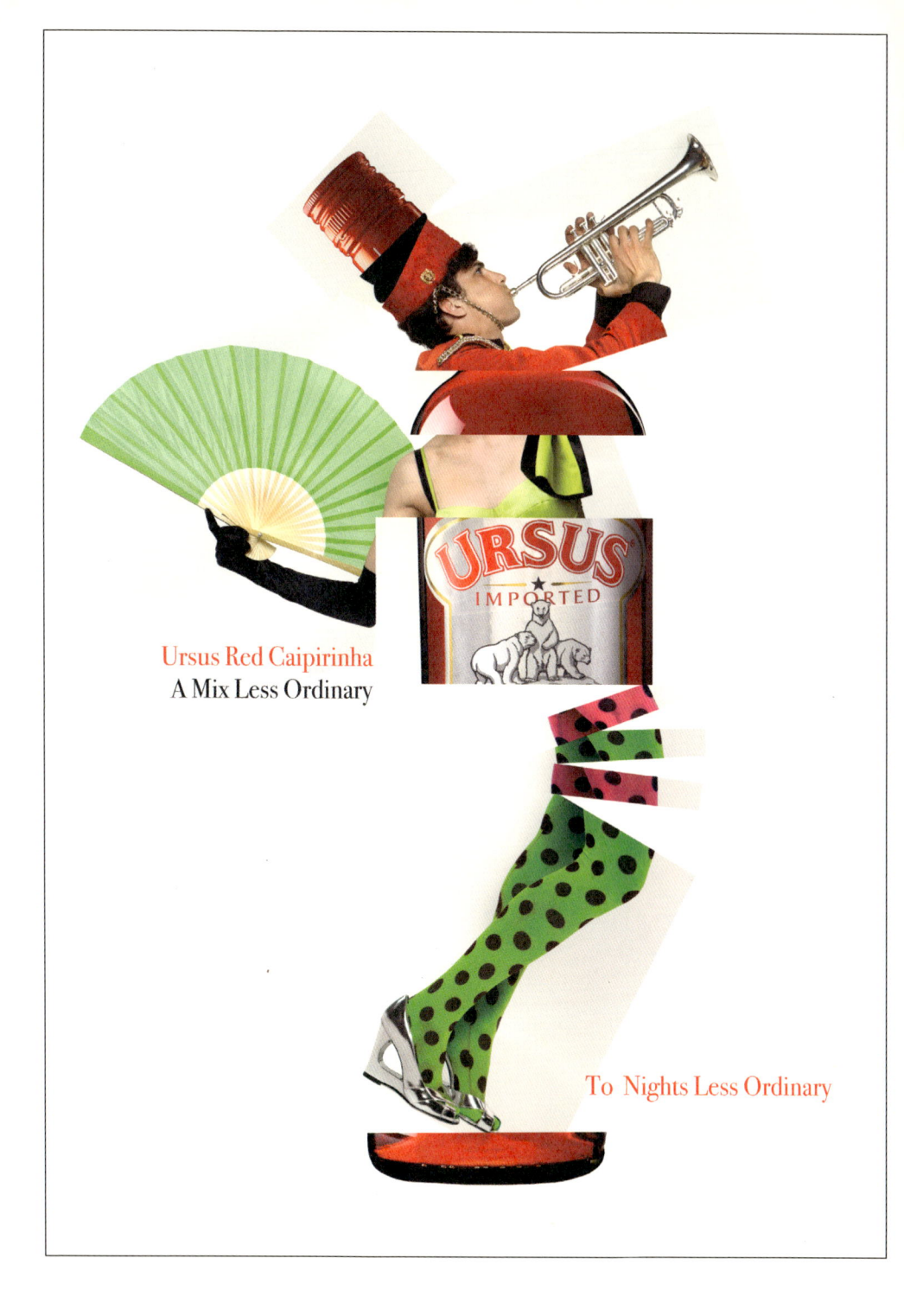

To Nights Less Ordinary

Ben, poster campaign
When the Dutch mobile provider Ben, whose name and personality were initiated by Kessels-Kramer, returned to the market, it called for a large-scale launch. As well as an epic TV ad, mysterious posters appeared all over Amsterdam. Each image showed a person covering their face. A short time later, these images were replaced with a second version: the same person making a peek-a-boo face. The headline utilizes the double meaning of Ben as a proper name and the verb 'to be' by saying: Ben is back/I am back.

Ben／ポスター・キャンペーン：ケッセルスクライマーが、名称とパーソナリティを考案したオランダの携帯電話会社、Benが市場に復活する際に、同社は大々的なキャンペーンの開催を強く求めた。そこで、壮大なテレビ・コマーシャルに加えて、ミステリアスなポスターがアムステルダムじゅうに展開された。各ポスターには、顔を手で覆った人が掲載され、しばらくすると、その画像は次のバージョン「同じ人物が、いないいないばあ、をしている写真」に切り替わる。見出しには、Benがもつ、ひとの名前と動詞「になる」の二重の意味を活かした「Benが戻ってきた、私は戻ってきた」が採用された。

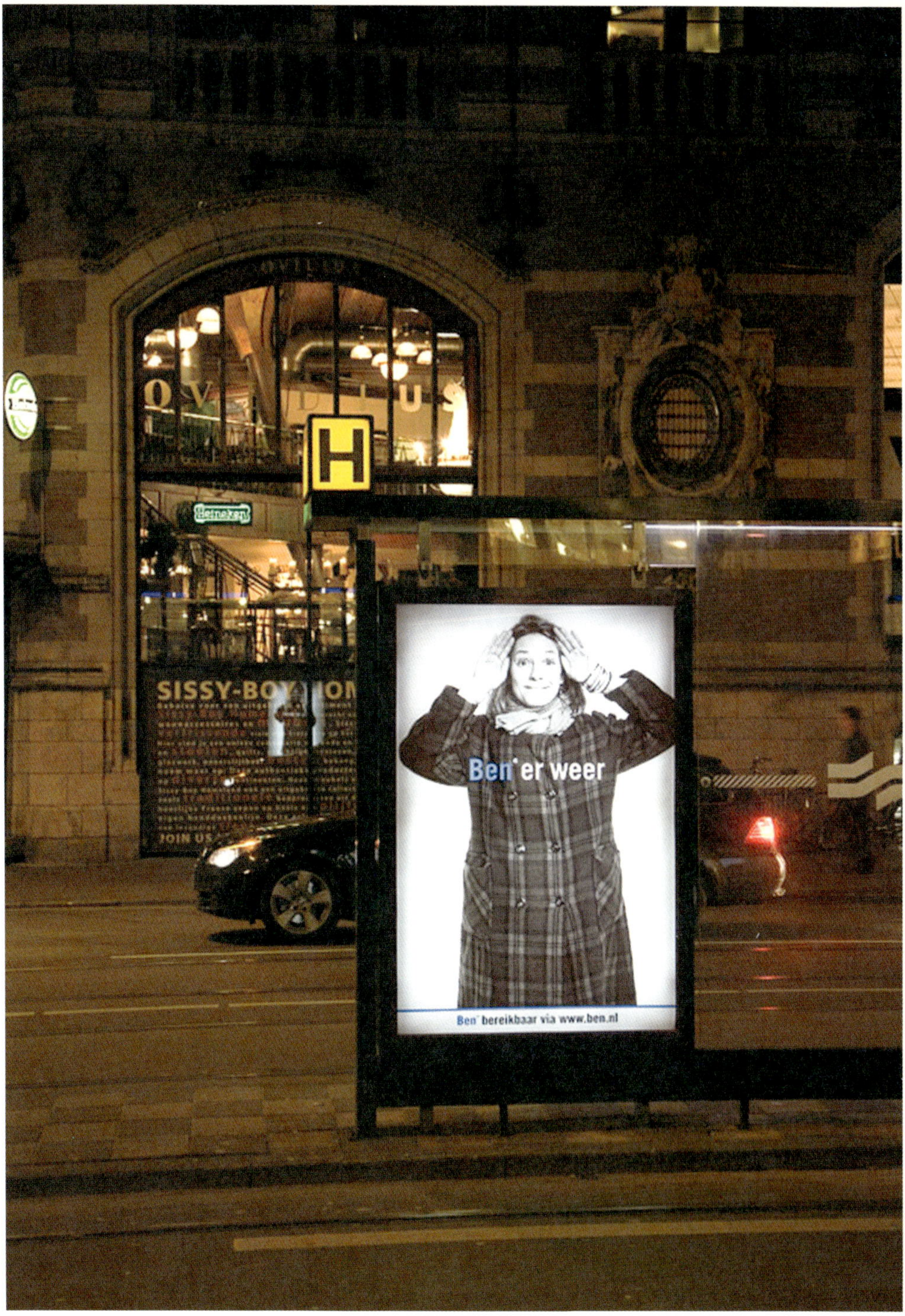
H
Heineken
Ben' er weer
Ben' bereikbaar via www.ben.nl
JOIN US

Ben, poster campaign
Further executions in the Ben relaunch campaign featuring a wide cultural cross section of the Dutch community.
Ben／ポスター・キャンペーン：Benの再生キャンペーンのそのほかの例。オランダの地域社会が、幅広い民族構成で成り立っていることをテーマにしている。

2.19860 kilo

Ben, TV commercial
Mobile provider Ben returned to The Netherlands with two epic three-minute films shown simultaneously on two channels. On one channel, viewers were asked if they already knew Ben from its iconic past in this market. If so, they were invited to keep watching. Otherwise, they could switch and get acquainted with this friendliest of phone companies.

Ben／テレビ・コマーシャル：2チャンネルで同時放送される2本の壮大な3分間映像を引っさげて、携帯電話会社Benがオランダに帰ってきた。視聴者は、片方のチャンネルで、かつて市場において象徴的な存在だった時代からBenを知っているか？とたずねられた。イエスの場合は、そのまま放送を見続けるよう促され、ノーの場合はチャンネルを切り替えれば、とても親しみやすい電話会社Benについての紹介が受けられた。

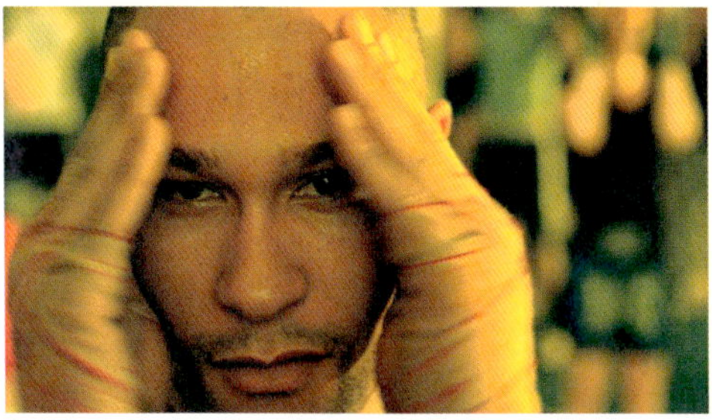
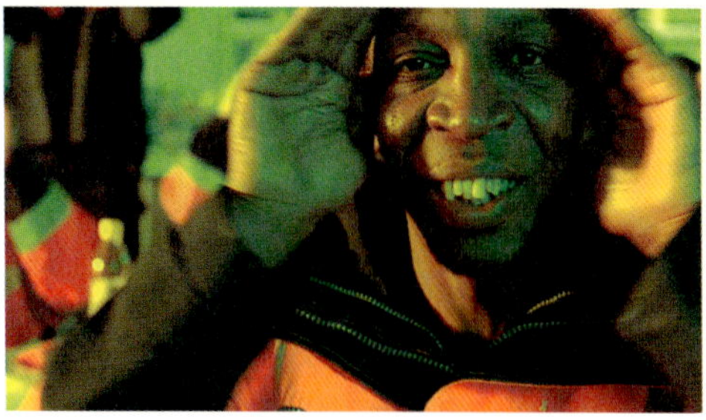
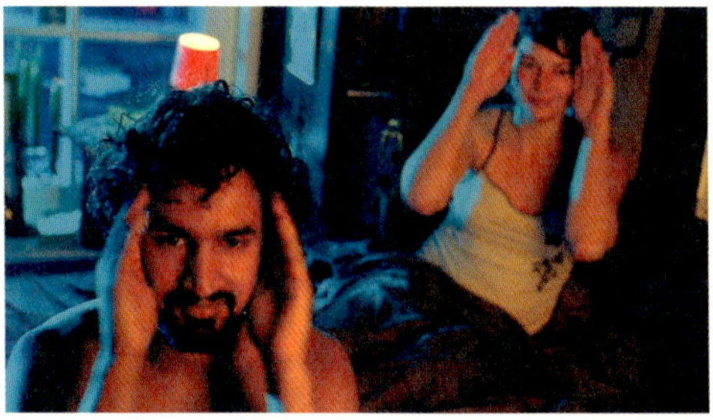
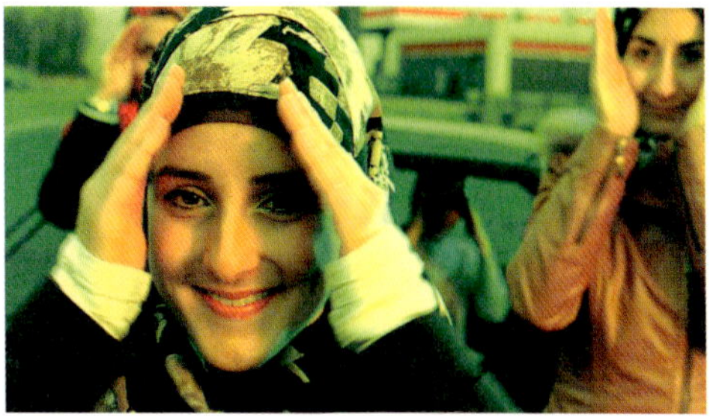
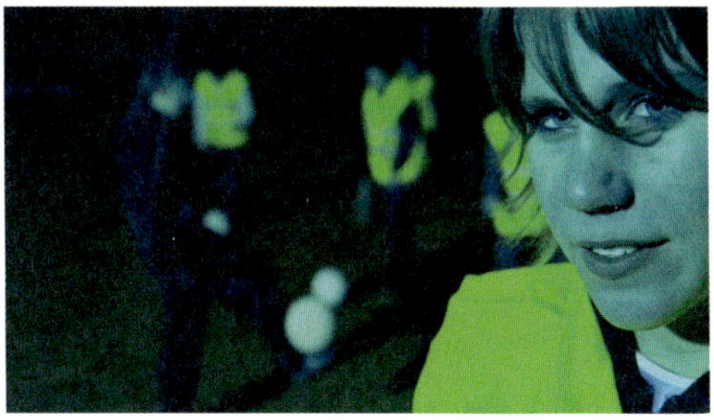
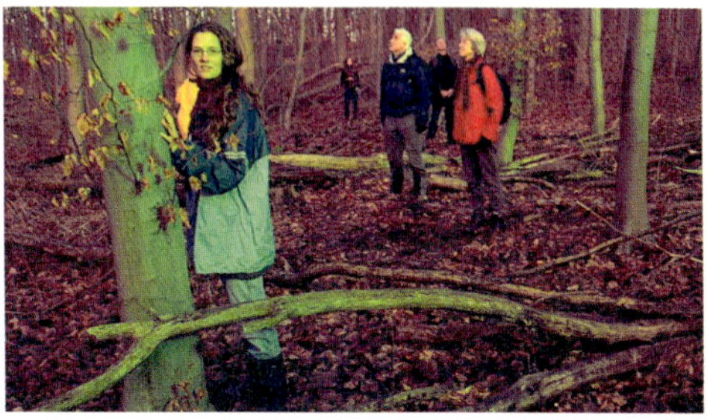
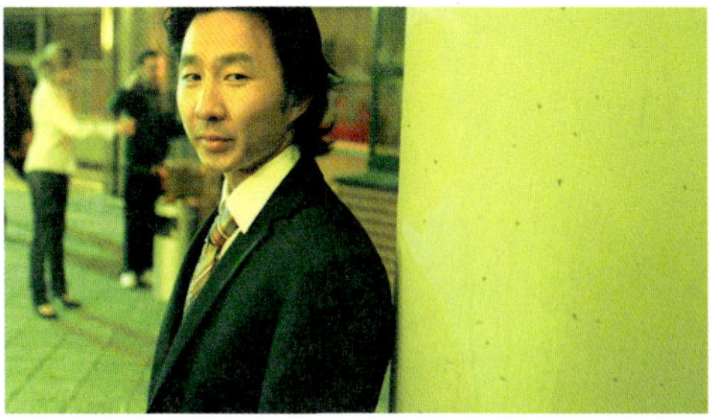
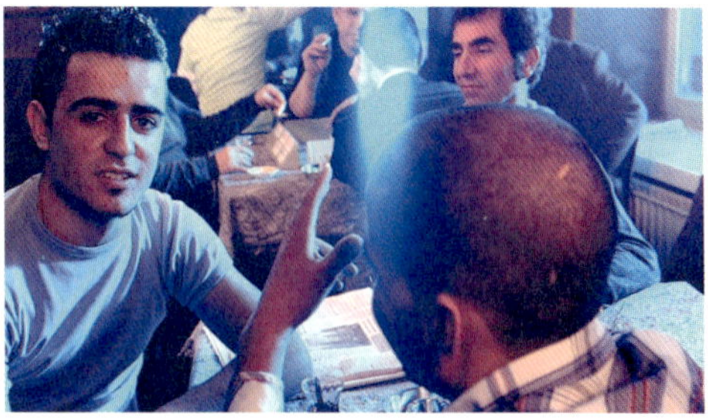

Ben, print campaign
Simple print ads which stated 'Greetings from Ben', intended to welcome and surprise new customers.
Ben／紙媒体キャンペーン：シンプルな紙媒体広告。そのメッセージ「Benから、こんにちは！」は、新規顧客を歓迎し、驚かせることを意図したもの。

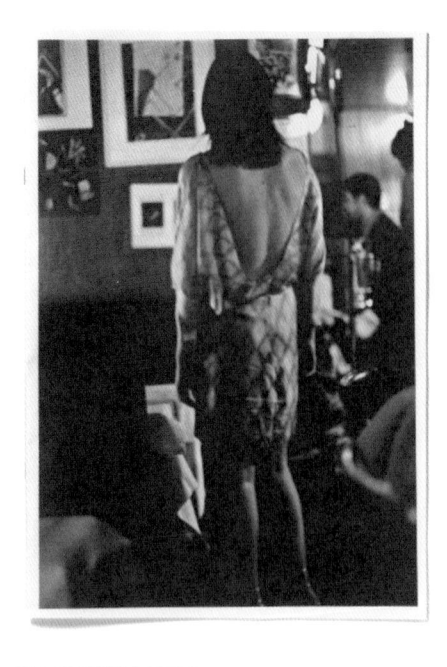

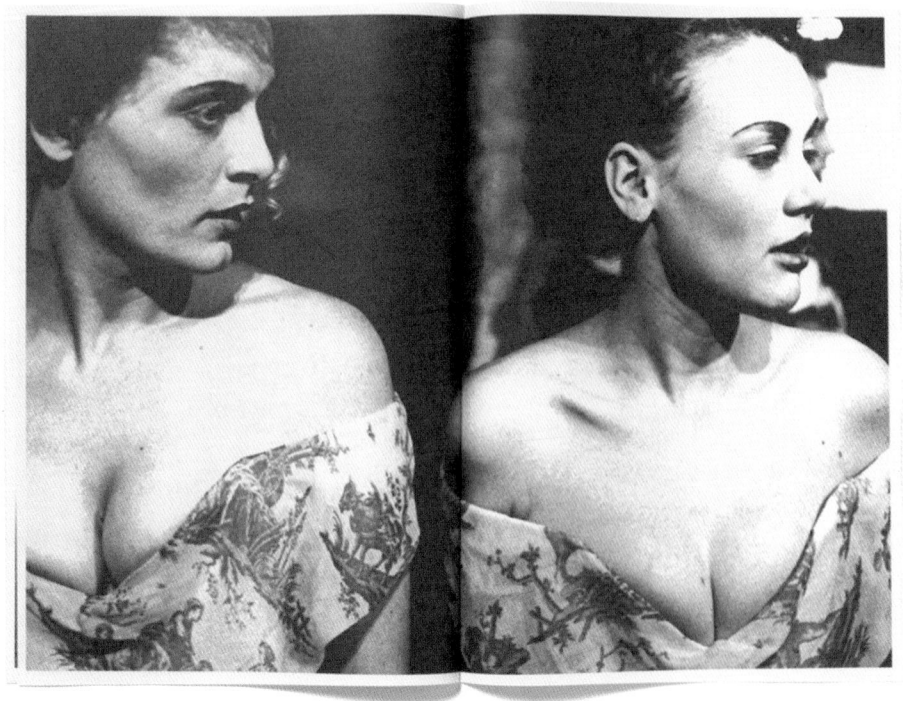

Bart Julius Peters, newspaper
Self-promotion for this Dutch photographer's images. The newspaper format supports his strong black-and-white style.
Bart Julius Peters／新聞：オランダの写真家のセルフ・プロモーション用写真。新聞のフォーマットが、そのモノクロ・スタイルの強い印象をさらに高めている。

UitMarkt, poster campaign
The cultural season in The Netherlands is announced by the Uitmarkt, the biggest festival of its type in the country. In these images, we see folks from all over Holland preparing to attend.
UitMarkt／ポスター・キャンペーン：国内最大級の文化フェスティバル、アウトマルクトからオランダの文化シーズン到来が告知された。これらの写真は、参加を待つオランダじゅうの人々を紹介したもの。

UIT
AMSTERDAMS UIT BURO
MARKT'08:
LEEUWARDEN GAAT OOK
29/30/31 AUG.
OOSTELIJK
HAVENGEBIED
AMSTERDAM

WHO CARES ABOUT SOUP OF THE DAY?

WHEN THE WAVES ARE EPIC, YOU HAVE TO BE QUICK
PROTEST PRESENTS: THE DROP-IT-ALL SESSIONS
SPONTANEOUS EVENTS AT EUROPE'S BEST SURF SPOTS
SIGN UP FOR TEXT AND EMAIL ALERTS AT PROTEST.EU
SEE YOU OUT THERE!

Protest, print, poster and mobile campaign
For millions of boarders, their 9 to 5 is spent dreaming of the freedom they feel riding the perfect wave. In this campaign for Protest, that freedom was brought closer by the 'Drop it all Sessions'- spontaneous happenings which sprung up on beaches when conditions were perfect. SMS messages encouraged consumers to 'drop it all' and join Protest partying and surfing.

Protest／紙媒体、ポスター、モバイル・キャンペーン：大勢のサーファーたちにとって、仕事をしている9時から5時までは、完璧な波に乗っているときに味わえる、自由を夢見るための時間。プロテストのキャンペーンでは、この自由は「仕事は全部おしまい！」という呼びかけを合図に、波のコンディションさえ完璧なら、ビーチで自然に体験できた。携帯のショートメールが、消費者に「仕事は全部おしまい」にして、プロテストのパーティーとサーフィンに参加するよう呼びかけた。

THE DROP-IT-ALL
SESSIONS BY

PROTEST

Protest, print, poster and mobile campaign
Further executions for the 'Drop-it-all' Sessions in which surfers escape the humdrum to live the dream.
Protest／紙媒体、ポスター、モバイル・キャンペーン：「仕事はおしまい」キャンペーンのそのほかの例。サーファーたちが退屈さから逃げ出し、夢に生きるさまが描かれている。

THE DROP-IT-ALL
SESSIONS BY
PROTEST

THE DROP-IT-ALL
SESSIONS BY
PROTEST

2.22196 kilo

Protest, brand manual
An introduction to the Protest character for designers and other third parties. The book contains a fold-out map highlighting various aspects of the Protest world, packaged with a series of stickers so boarders can mark the places they've been and the places they want to go.
Protest／ブランド・マニュアル：プロテストの特徴をデザイナーなどのサードパーティに伝えるためのツール。本マニュアルには、プロテストの世界のさまざまな局面に焦点をあてた折込地図が同封されている。ボーダーたちが、今までに行ったことがある場所や、行ってみたい場所に印がつけられるよう地図にはシール・セットがついている。

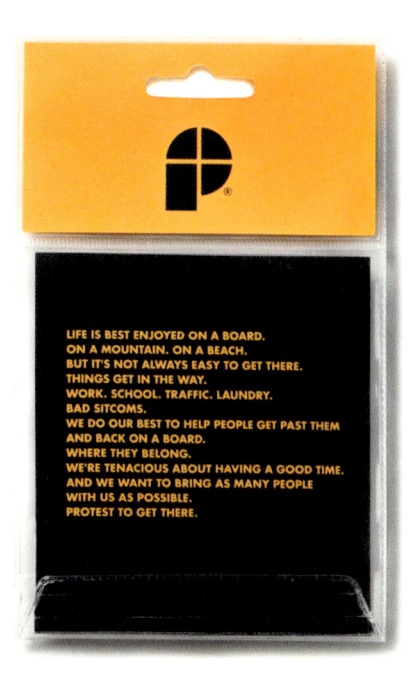

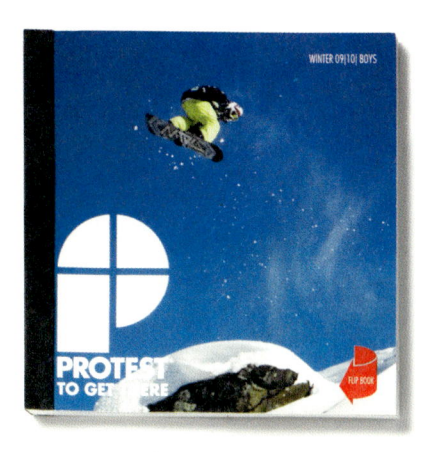

Protest, extra materials

Communication for trade shows formed a large component of the brand's marketing mix. However, such events are the antithesis of boarding. Protest offered the lucky few a chance to escape the humdrum of the show, jump into a helicopter, and fly at high speed to the nearest snow. A flip book showing the Protest collection in all its lo-fi animated glory was also handed out at trade events.

Protest／そのほかのツール：展示会の宣伝のため、同ブランドは、大規模なマーケティング・ミックスを行った。かしこまったこの種のイベントは、そもそもボーディングとは正反対の存在。そこでプロテストは、少数のラッキーな客が、退屈な展示会から逃げ出して、ヘリコプターに飛び乗り、最も近くのスロープまで高速で到着できるチャンスを提供。展示会では、同ブランドのコレクションを、クールでチープなクオリティで見せる、ばらばら漫画も配布された。

Protest, extra materials

A big pile of extra Protest gear, showing the campaign in all its 360-degree glory including stickers, posters, tape, T-shirts and even hang tags. KesselsKramer also worked with Protest to develop their new logo, which would subsequently appear on all new collections.

Protest／そのほかのツール：豊富に用意された、プロテストのそのほかの宣伝ツール。ステッカー、ポスター、テープ、Tシャツから品質表示タグまで、キャンペーンを全方位から紹介している。ケッセルスクライマーは、プロテストの新しいロゴも制作。その後、ロゴはすべての新しいコレクションに使用された。

8 2.23131 kilo

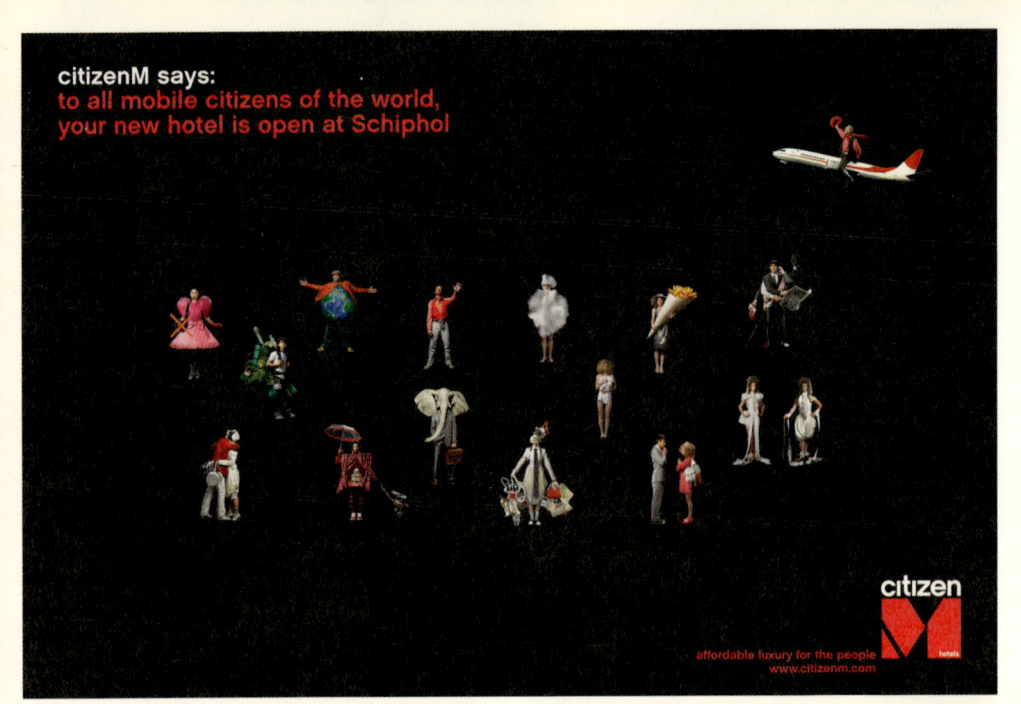

citizenM says:
to all mobile citizens of the world,
your new hotel is open at Schiphol

affordable luxury for the people
www.citizenm.com

to all party citizens:
citizenM is open at Schiphol

to all cultural citizens:
citizenM is open at Schiphol

citizenM, poster campaign
These images were created to announce the arrival of citizenM at Amsterdam's airport. citizenM is a hotel designed for a new breed of traveler – the mobile citizens of the world. These citizens take many forms, including those motivated by culture, business and good times. To celebrate this diversity, a different type of mobile citizen was shown in each execution.
citizenM／ポスター・キャンペーン：これらの画像は、シチズンMが、アムステルダム空港に到着した（オープンした）ことを知らせるためのもの。シチズンMは、新しいタイプの旅行者たち—世界中のモバイル・シチズン—のためのホテル。文化、ビジネス、趣味など、モバイル（移動・旅）の目的とタイプは幅広い。この点に着目し、各作品ではさまざまなタイプのモバイル・シチズンが紹介された。

2.23364 kilo

to all fashion citizens:
citizenM is open at Schiphol

citizen
M
hotels
jan plezierweg 2
1118 bv amsterdam
www.citizenm.com

citizenM, hotel
citizenM is a global chain of hotels offering affordable luxury. A holistic solution was taken to brand, launch and communicate it, one where its guests took central role. All aspects from packaging to signage accorded with the 'Citizen Mobile' strategy, an idea based on the observation that a new type of traveller is emerging, one who travels more, travels smarter, stays shorter at their destination and wants to pay only for what they need. citizenM identified them by their travel purpose, whether it be for culture, business, fun or fashion.
citizenM／ホテル：シチズンMは、手ごろな値段で贅沢に過ごせるグローバル・ホテル・チェーン。ゲストが中心的役割を果たすこのホテルのブランディング、オープニング、広告宣伝には、さまざまなメディアを相互に関連させるホリスティックな方法がとられた。パッケージングからサイン制作にいたる、あらゆる分野が「シチズン・モバイル」戦略に沿って開発されたのだ。「シチズン・モバイル」とは、どんどん旅行に行きたいと考えていたり、旅行慣れしていたり、目的地に短期間しか滞在しなかったり、必要なものにしか料金を払いたくないと考える、新タイプの旅行者が増えている、という観察に基づいたコンセプト。同ホテルは、文化から、ビジネス、楽しみ、ファッションまで内容を問わず、目的ごとに旅行者を認識している。

citizenM, packaging
Shower packs for in-room at citizenM divided into AM and PM. In AM we see a short story relating to the type of person who loves mornings. Conversely, PM embraces those who live for the night.
citizenM／パッケージング：シチズンMの客室に用意されるバスルーム・アメニティは午前と午後で異なる。午前のシャンプーのボトルには、朝が好きな人に関する説明が、午後は夜行型の人についての説明が記されている。

citizenM, extra materials
Examples of citizenM's total communication approach for both inside and outside the hotel, including business cards, menu cards, character design, bathroom amenities, even travel socks.
citizenM／そのほかのツール：名刺、メニュー・カード、キャラクター・デザイン、バスルーム・アメニティから旅行用靴下まで、シチズンMのホテル内外で利用される総合的な広告宣伝ツール。

8

2.24533 kilo

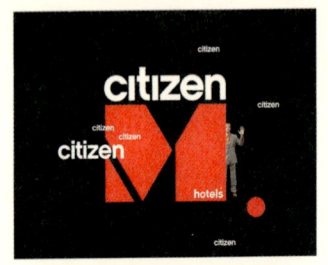

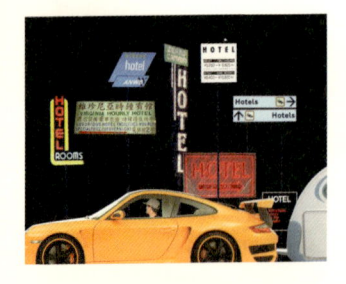

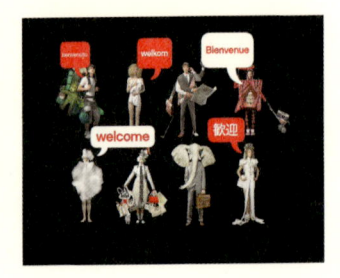

citizenM, hotel interior and online film
KesselsKramer's involvement with citizenM was all-pervasive. Top right, some of KK's contributions to the building itself. Above on this page, stills from a brand film explaining the philosophy of the hotel.
citizenM／ホテル内装、インターネット・ビデオ：全面的に、シチズンMのプロジェクトに携わったケッセルスクライマーは、建物自体のデザインにも協力した（右上）。上図は、ホテルの哲学を説明するブランド・ビデオのスチール写真。

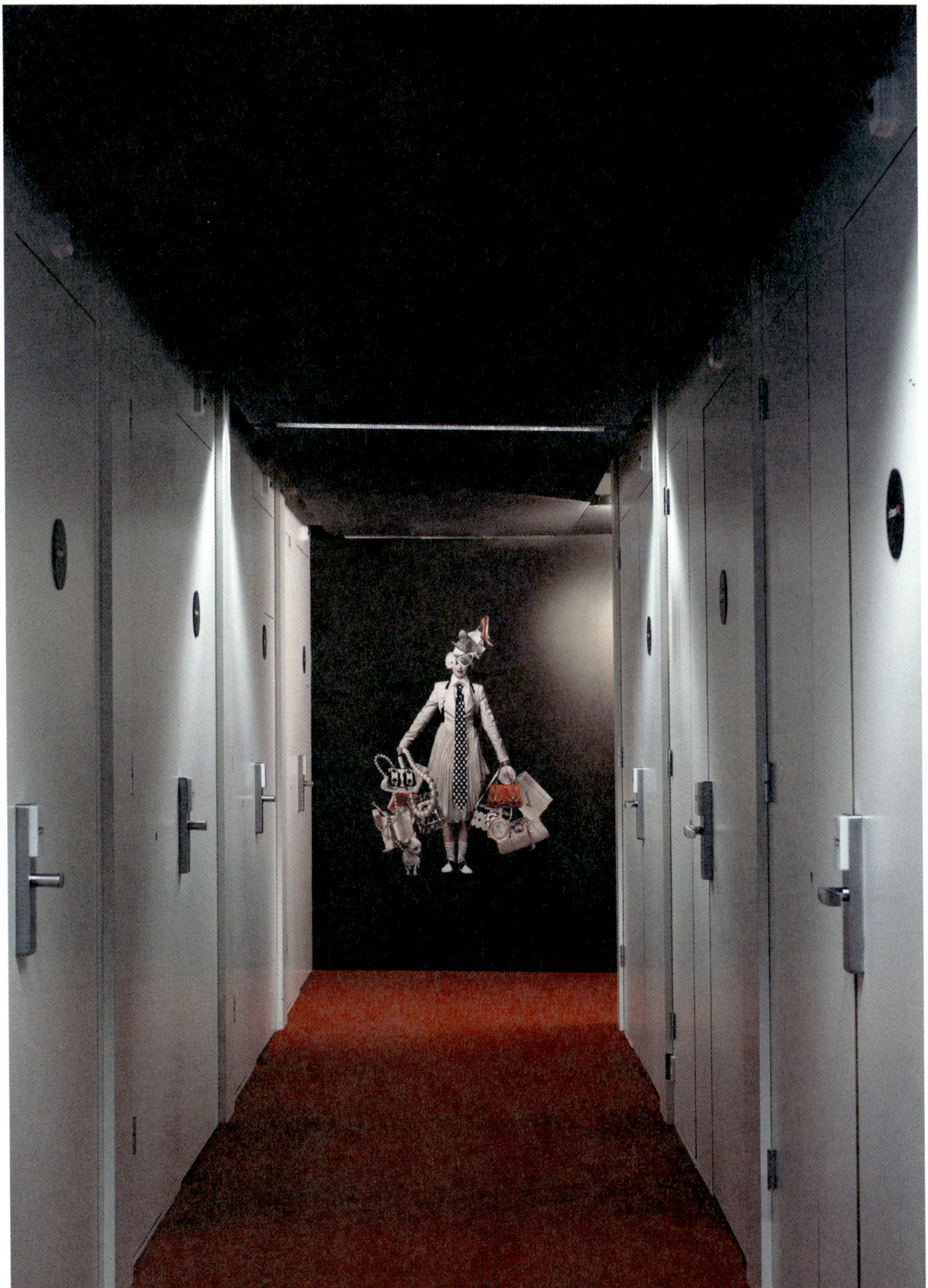

citizenM, website
Online, citizenM sat the public down for the virtual equivalent of a chat and a nice cup of tea. Rather than preaching from the brand pulpit, its digital incarnation spoke to people one-on-one, allowing them to get a feel for the down-to-earth character of this hotel for high-flyers, culture seekers and other diverse travellers. Of course, the practical business of booking a room was kept front and centre at all times.
citizenM／ウェブサイト：インターネットにおいては、おいしいお茶を飲みながらお喋りするように、訪問者をもてなすシチズンM。デジタルの場でも、ブランドについて説教をするのではなく、訪問者に一対一で語りかけるのがモットー。高級志向の顧客や、文化を探求する顧客など、顧客のタイプ数あれど、すべてに対して安心できるホテルであることを、実感させたのである。もちろん、客室予約という実用的サービスは、つねに、最も目立つ中心的な位置に掲載された。

citizenM hotels

welcome citizen

hotel locations
hotel concept
reservations
specials & packages
citizen community
become a citizen
citizenM eshop
about citizenM

check availability	citizen login

check-in-date: dd/mm/yyyy
total nights: 1
location: Choose Hotel

check now

affordable luxury for the people

citizenM says:
the world's a big beautiful place...

faqs | roll out | citizenM jobs | contact citizenM | keep me posted | privacy | site map

Experimenta, poster campaign
Experimenta is a cutting-edge exhibition that explores new themes in architecture and society. In 2008, the organizers showed how cities could become urban play spaces for their inhabitants. These posters showed a literal translation of this concept, with dancers and acrobats using the city as their playground.
Experimenta／ポスター・キャンペーン：エクスペリメンタは建築と社会の新しいテーマを探る最先端の展覧会。2008年、主催者は、どうすれば都市が住人にとっての遊び場になるのかを提示した。これらのポスターは、このコンセプトを文字通りに解釈して表現したもの。ダンサーと曲芸師が街を遊び場にしている。

SPACE AND PLACE
EXPERIMENTADESIGN AMSTERDAM 2008
18 September – 2 November
OPENING WEEK 18–21 SEPT

2.25935 kilo

Experimenta, poster campaign
Another poster in the Experimenta campaign, celebrating new themes in architecture and society.
Experimenta／ポスター・キャンペーン：エクスペリメンタ・キャンペーンのそのほかのポスター。建築と社会の新しいテーマをたたえている。

SPACE AND PLACE
**EXPERIMENTADESIGN
AMSTERDAM 2008**
18 September – 2 November
OPENING WEEK 18–21 SEPT

Dutch Funeral Museum, poster
Tot Zover is the Dutch funeral museum. KesselsKramer was involved throughout its creation, from naming to branding. The name means 'Until Now', a reflection on life as much as a reference to death. To raise awareness for the project, a poster was produced reading 'open due to circumstances', a play on the Dutch phrase 'closed due to circumstances', traditionally seen in situations where a death has occurred.
Dutch Funeral Museum／ポスター：オランダ葬儀博物館Tot Zover。ケッセルスクライマーは名称の考案からブランディングまで、その立ち上げプロジェクトに全面的に参加した。Tot Zoverは「今まで」を意味し、人生と死を示唆している。本プロジェクトへの注目を高めるため、ポスターには「場合によっては開けます」というメッセージが記された。これは、だれかが亡くなったときに昔からよく使われる「場合によっては閉めます」を意味するオランダの慣用表現をもじったもの。

Dutch Funeral Museum, stunt
Accompanying the poster, a grave was dug in the middle of Amsterdam's famous Museumplein.
Dutch Funeral Museum／大胆なプロジェクト：アムステルダムの有名な博物館街の真ん中で、ポスターの脇に墓が掘られた。

POËZIE IN HET PARK

GERBRANDYPARK EN SLOTERPARK
2, 3 EN 6 SEPTEMBER 2008
MEER INFORMATIE OP WWW.AMSTERDAMWERELDBOEKENSTAD.NL

Citaat uit 'Ja Zuster, Nee Zuster'. Annie M.G. Schmidt, 1966.

DOE WAT JE 'T LIEFSTE DOET

Amsterdam World Book Capital, poster campaign
A poster celebrating Amsterdam's status as world book capital, and announcing a poetry reading in the city's parks. The text is a quote from writer Annie M.G. Schmidt and reads: 'Do what you love to do'.
Amsterdam World Book Capital／ポスター・キャンペーン：アムステルダムがワールド・ブック・キャピタル（世界の本の首都）となったことをたたえ、公園で詩の朗読会が開催されることを告知するポスター。掲載されているフレーズ「心からしたいと思うことをせよ」は作家アニー・M・G・シュミットの作品からの引用。

2.27103 kilo

Amsterdam World Book Capital, bags
A small selection of the carrier bags produced for various events and book markets during the World Book Capital program. Shoppers were invited to create their own stories and phrases on the street with other bag carriers.
Amsterdam World Book Capital／手さげ袋：ワールド・ブック・キャピタル中に開催される、さまざまなイベントや書籍市のための手さげ袋の例。買物客は街で、ほかの手さげ袋のユーザーとともに、独自のストーリーやフレーズを作るよう促された。

Amsterdam World Book Capital, poster campaign
Amsterdam's status as World Book Capital is celebrated with work springing from the idea
'A city full of stories'. Each execution featured a quote from a famous literary work appearing
in everyday situations all over town. Here, the Spinoza quote 'Out of nothing comes nothing'
appears on and around a delivery man in the city.
Amsterdam World Book Capital／ポスター・キャンペーン：アムステルダムが
ワールド・ブック・キャピタルになったことをたたえる作品。コンセプトは「物語
に満ちた都市」。すべての作品において、街の日常風景のなかに有名な文学作品
の引用句が登場する。上図では、スピノザの言葉「まかぬ種は生えぬ」を街中の
宅配業者が身に着けている。

Amsterdam World Book Capital, poster campaign
Annie M.G. Schmidt, Ernest Hemingway and Leo Tolstoy are all quoted in the continuing series to promote the World Book Capital series of events in Amsterdam, while Amsterdam locals are seen creating their own quotes with carrier bags on the streets of the city.
Amsterdam World Book Capital／ポスター・キャンペーン：アムステルダムで開催された、ワールド・ブック・キャピタル関連のイベントを宣伝する、一連のシリーズでは、アニー・M・G・シュミット、アーネスト・ヘミングウェイ、レオ・トルストイなどの言葉が引用された。一方、街中の通りでは、自分自身で引用句をつけた手さげ袋を手にしている、アムステルダム市民の姿が見られた。

2.27804 kilo

do camouflage, product
do camouflage continues KesselsKramer's do range, a series of products which ask consumers to participate in their creation or completion. This particular manifestation is a puzzle that functions as a plea for world peace... and a means to while away a Sunday afternoon.
do camouflage／商品：消費者に、商品の創作や仕上げに参加するよう求める、ケッセルスクライマーのdoシリーズ。今回の商品は「doカモフラージュ（カモフラージュ＝偽装する、迷彩柄にする）」という名のパズル。世界平和への嘆願を主張しつつ、日曜の午後をだらだらと過ごすことができるツールでもある。

Vanishing trades, bus posters
Advertising spaces on buses were offered to KesselsKramer for any client it wished.
They were instead given to small – and potentially dying – trades in Amsterdam.
These examples show a 'doll doctor' and a family-run butcher.
Vanishing trades／バスのポスター：バスの広告スペースが、どんなクライアントに使ってもよいという条件でケッセルスクライマーに提供された。そこで、このスペースはアムステルダムの小規模で──ともすれば潰れそうな──商売の顧客に使われた。上図は、「人形のお医者さん」と家族経営の肉屋の広告。

J&B, billboards, online and event
For J&B whisky, KesselsKramer helped create a mammoth series of parties all around Spain. The above billboards advertised these events, collectively entitled The Party Project. Imagery reflected the concept behind the gatherings: a party of constant change, evolving throughout the evening and inviting guest participation.

J&B／ビルボード、インターネット、イベント：ケッセルスクライマーは、スペインじゅうでJ&Bウィスキーの大規模パーティーの開催を手伝った。上図のビルボードはそのイベントを宣伝したもの。すべてに「ザ・パーティー・プロジェクト」という見出しがつけられている。写真はパーティーのコンセプトである「夜の間中進化し続け、ゲストを招待し続ける、つねに変化するパーティー」を表現。

THE PARTY PROJECT

&

reet, Lond

NA | LA CORUÑA | MÁLAGA

THE PARTY PROJECT

&

reet, Lond

NA | LA CORUÑA | MÁLAGA

Hans Brinker Budget Hotel, poster campaign
During the crest of the often dubious eco-friendly brand wave, The Hans Brinker noticed something peculiar: it had been saving the planet for years. Granted, this wasn't intentional. In fact, it was entirely accidental. Nevertheless, the hotel's lack of facilities meant a huge amount of energy saved in both electricity and water. Examples of this were shown in posters, and explored in greater depth in film and a specially published newspaper.

Hans Brinker Budget Hotel／ポスター・キャンペーン：たいてい胡散くさいのに大流行した「エコ・フレンドリー＝環境にやさしい」ブランド。これについて、ハンス・ブリンカーは面白いことに気づいた。「うちこそは長年、地球を守ってきてるじゃないか！」確かに、同ホテルはわざとらしくない方法で地球環境に貢献していた。本当にまったく偶然に‥‥。といっても、設備の貧弱さが電気と水の大きな節約につながっていた、というだけの話なのだが。その例はポスターで紹介され、さらにビデオや新聞の特別号で掘り下げた内容が説明された。

ECO-TOWEL

HANS BRINKER BUDGET HOTEL.
ACCIDENTALLY ECO-FRIENDLY.

KERKSTRAAT 136-138 – AMSTERDAM – TEL +31 (0)20 622 0687 – FAX +31 (0)20 638 2060 – WWW.HANS-BRINKER.COM

Hans Brinker Budget Hotel, online film
As part of the Brinker's 'Accidentally Eco-Friendly' campaign, KesselsKramer produced an informative film that sought to demonstrate the great depth of its eco-friendly credentials. This included eco-staff, who conserve energy at the front desk and eco-beer, little more than beer recycled from the bar towel.

Hans Brinker Budget Hotel／インターネット・ビデオ：ハンス・ブリンカーの「偶然にエコ・フレンドリー」キャンペーンの一環として、ケッセルスクライマーは同ホテルが環境にやさしい証拠を掘り下げて説明しようとビデオを制作。フロント・デスクでエネルギーを節約するエコ・スタッフや、バーの台ふきんからリサイクルされたビールとほとんどいっしょの飲み物、エコ・ビールなどを紹介した。

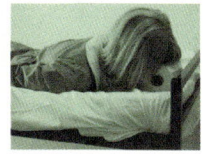

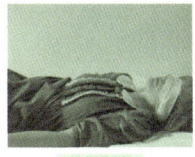

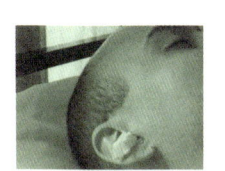

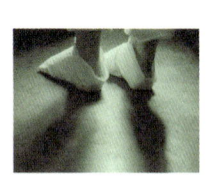

Hans Brinker Budget Hotel, toilet roll
The toilet roll provided the perfect medium to print a manifesto on the world's impending doom through collective eco-stupidity. Again, the message concerned the Brinker's own entirely accidental contribution to saving the planet.
Hans Brinker Budget Hotel／トイレット・ペーパー：エコな愚行をまとめて紹介し、迫り来る世界の破滅に対するマニフェストを印刷するにうってつけの媒体、トイレット・ペーパー。ここでも、ハンス・ブリンカー・バジェット・ホテルの地球保護への、まったく偶然な貢献に関するメッセージが主張された。

2.29673 kilo

Hans Brinker Budget Hotel, newspaper
This newspaper explored the Hans Brinker's accidental eco-commitment which manifested itself in room, bar, lobby and even signage. The image of the hotel sign with only one letter lit (making it much more energy efficient) acted as the initial inspiration for the campaign. Hans Brinker Budget Hotel／新聞：ハンス・ブリンカーの、エコへの偶然な取り組みを探った新聞。同ホテルは、客室、バー、ロビーはもちろんサイン・システムでも努力しているとうたっている。たった一文字しかライトがつかない（ホテルのエネルギー効率を大きく高めている）看板の写真は、本キャンペーンを思いつくきっかけになった。

ECO-FACT:
OUR ECO-SIGN USES 20% OF THE ENERGY OF ORDINARY 'HOTEL' SIGNS. THE HANS BRINKER BUDGET HOTEL IS COMMITTED TO DOING AS LITTLE AS POSSIBLE TO ACCIDENTALLY HELP OUR PLANET AS MUCH AS POSSIBLE.

KERKSTRAAT 136-138 – AMSTERDAM – THE NETHERLANDS – TEL +31 (0)20 622 0687 – FAX +31 (0)20 638 2060 – WWW.HANS-BRINKER.COM

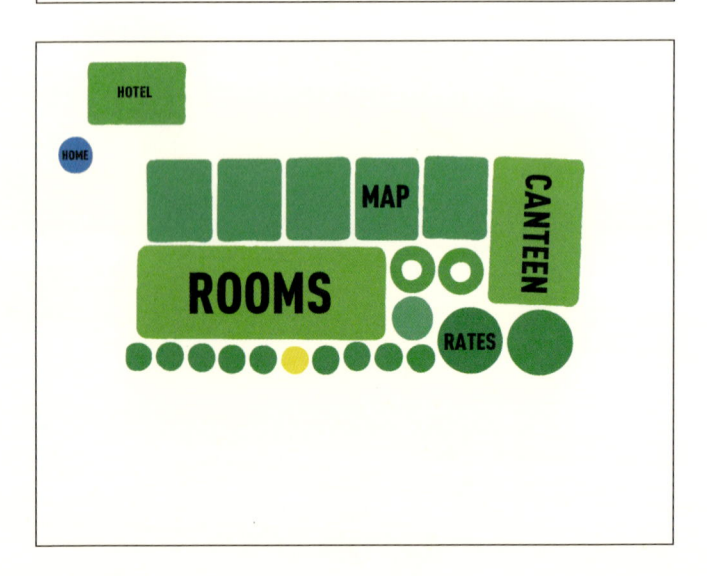

Hans Brinker Budget Hotel, website
The regular booking site for the world's worst hotel. Here, stickers are used as the cheapest of cheap design inspiration, in keeping with the Brinker's perennial lack of class.
Hans Brinker Budget Hotel／ウェブサイト：世界最悪のホテルの正規予約サイト。長年にわたり客室に等級がないことから、究極に安っぽい演出としてシールを使ったデザインが着想された。

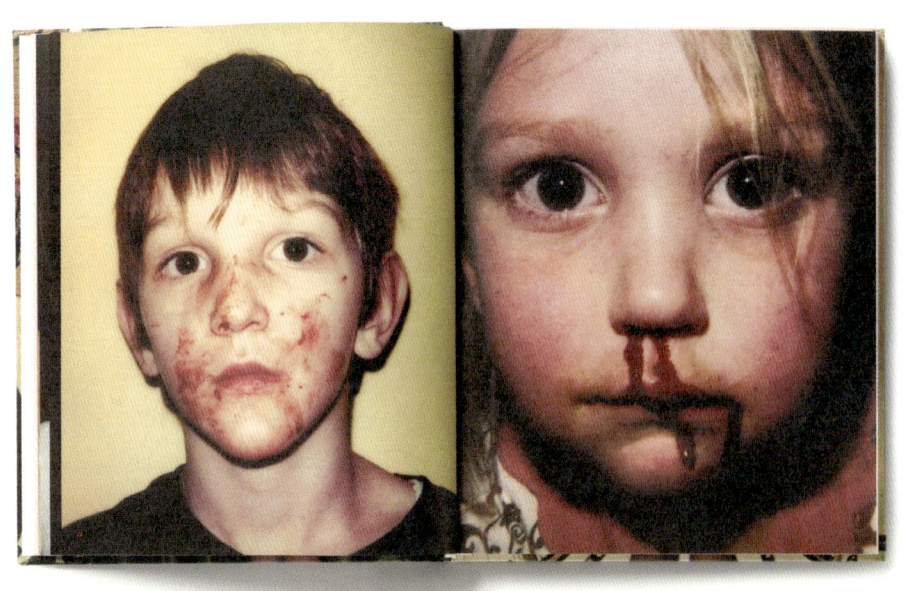

On Show, book
A book based on a lecture given by Erik Kessels. These pages contain photos all taken from Kessels' personal archive. The pictures are unified by their intention: each was made to exhibit its subject to others. Included here are the author's own children showing their bumps and bruises and a pose from an amateur model in St. Petersburg.
On Show, book／書籍：エリック・ケッセルズの講演をベースにした書籍。これらのページに掲載されているのはケッセルズの個人的なストックから選ばれた写真。被写体を他者に披露するために撮影されたという点が共通している。上図では、著者の子どもたちが傷やあざを見せ、セント・ピーターズバーグのアマチュア・モデルがポーズをとって見せている。

2.30841 kilo

Polar Bear Memorial Candle, product
The polar bear is the largest land carnivore on Earth. Only a precious few remain, a fact marked by these memorial candles.
Polar Bear Memorial Candle／商品：北極グマは地球最大の肉食動物。もう残り少なくなってしまった種だが、その事実を記念キャンドルが表現している。

REAAL Insurance, poster campaign
This campaign is based on the chances of various (sometimes seemingly unlikely) desires being fulfilled, for REAAL, the 'realists in insurance'. The concept has a great deal of flexibility, allowing individual executions to be very targeted. Here, for instance, the chances of school pupils cycling in groups, pigeons damaging your car and your wanting to cross the street in a given year are all revealed for REAAL's car-insurance campaign.

REAAL Insurance／ポスター・キャンペーン：（一見あり得なさそうな）さまざまな望みがかなう可能性をベースにした、「保険の現実主義者」REAALのキャンペーン。このコンセプトは非常に柔軟で、それぞれにかなり特殊な望みが取りあげられている。たとえば、小学生が数人で一台の自転車をこいでサイクリングする可能性、ハトが車にダメージを与える可能性、ある年にあなたが通りを渡りたくなる可能性など、すべてがREAAL自動車保険キャンペーン向けに提示されたものである。

REAAL Insurance, poster campaign
Four further examples of the REAAL campaign. Top left: 2% chance that you'll live with your parents when you're 40. Bottom left: 25% chance that you want to live closer to work. Top right: 52% chance that you're sick of traffic jams. Bottom right: 68% chance that you want to live in nature.

REAAL Verzekeringen
52% KANS DAT
U DE FILES
SPUUGZAT BENT
DE OPSTAPHYPOTHEEK VAN
REAAL. REALIST IN VERZEKEREN
reaal.nl

REAAL
68% KANS
DAT U IN DE NATUUR
WILT WONEN

REAAL Insurance, stunt
A stunt inspired by the statistic that there's a 66% chance that you want a house with a bath. This was brought to life with a bathtub-shaped boat floating on Amsterdam's canals.
REAAL Insurance／大胆なプロジェクト：「お風呂付の家が欲しくなる可能性：66％」という統計データに着想を得た大胆な広告。アムステルダムの運河に浮かべられたバスタブ型のボートがこの可能性のリアリティを強めている。

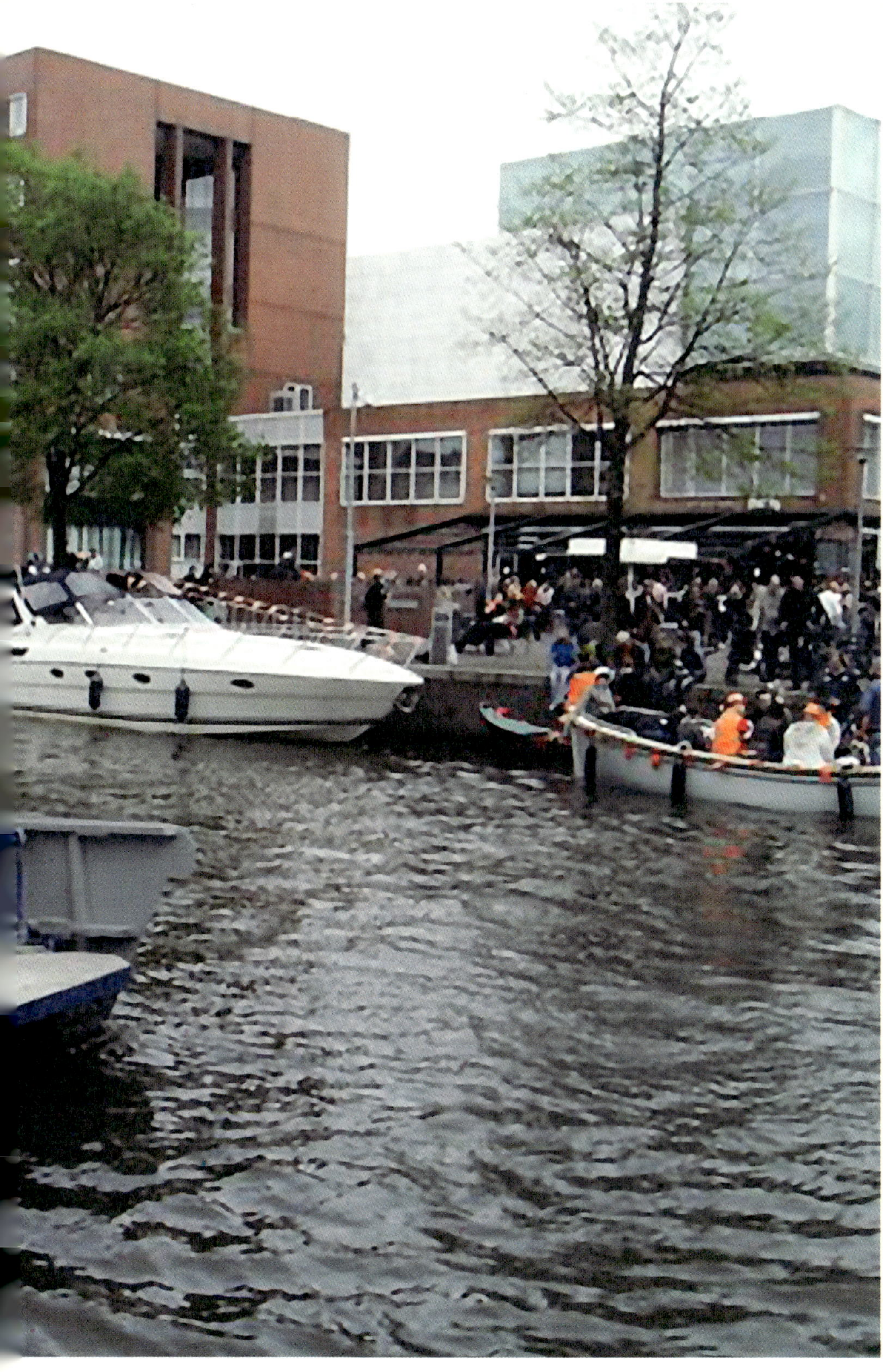

Arnold van Velzen, Teamleider Contact Center Universal Life (AXA/Winterthur) & Maartje Stroomer, Acceptant Leven (REAAL)

REAAL Verzekeringen

REAAL Insurance, print campaign
An internal campaign that took place after the insurance company merged with another organization, thus doubling in size. The images featured one person from the old team together with someone from the new one. Together, they form a new 'Realist'.
REAAL Insurance／紙媒体キャンペーン：REAALがほかの企業と合併した際に実施された社内キャンペーン。Tシャツのサイズが2倍なのは合併を表すため。写真は、合併した企業と合併された企業の社員を組み合わせて撮影されている。彼らはともに新しい「Realist=現実主義者」を形成している。

2.32477 kilo

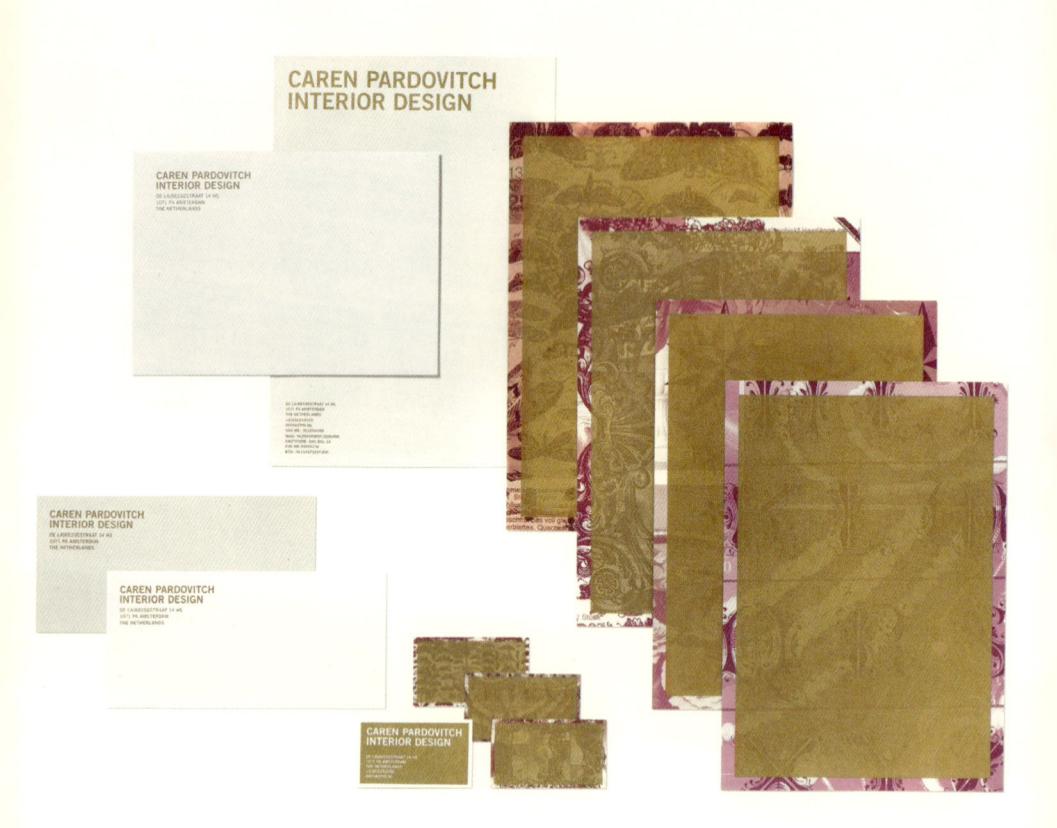

Caren Pardovitch Interior Design, house style
This interior designer with a love for classic creations had her worldview reflected in stationery and business cards: elaborate borders overlaid with bronze acted as a metaphor for Caren overlaying her experience on clients' buildings.
Caren Pardovitch Interior Design／自社ツール：クラシックな作品を愛するインテリア・デザイナー、カレン・パルドビッチの世界観が反映されたステーショナリーと名刺。ブロンズ色が重ね塗りされた手の込んだデザインの縁飾りは、カレンがクライアントの建物に施した自らの経験を暗喩するもの。

Anonymous, book
A book that investigates a trend in found imagery: people who strike others out of their photographs. Each photo herein has been deliberately damaged in some way in order to make its subjects anonymous. Spouses, friends, lovers have all been altered for personal, unidentified reasons.

Anonymous／書籍：ファウンド・フォトに見られる傾向のひとつである「写真から、その被写体となった他人を抹殺した人々」を調査した書籍。掲載されている写真はすべて、被写体を匿名にするために、なんらかの方法で故意に傷つけられている。配偶者、友人、恋人などあらゆる人物が、未確認の個人的な理由で変えられてしまっているのである。

2.32944 kilo

puC

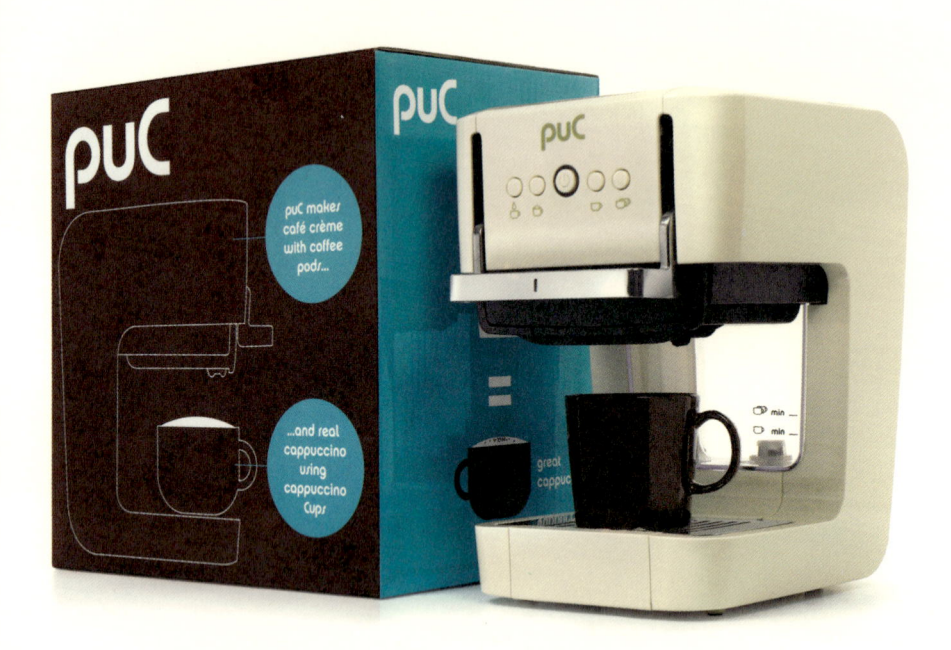

puC, brand identity and packaging
A new generation of coffee-pod machines was christened by KesselsKramer. puC is a multifunctional coffee device which cunningly uses pods and milk cups to cater for all your caffeine needs. The versatility of the machine led to the reversal of Cup in the brand name.
puC／ブランド・アイデンティティ、パッケージング：ケッセルスクライマーが名づけた新世代のコーヒー・ポッド・マシン、puCは、ポッドとミルク・カップを使って、カフェインが欲しくなったときにいつでもコーヒーが用意できる多機能コーヒー・マシン。ブランド・ネームでCupが逆になっているのはマシンの多彩な機能を表現するため。

puC, print and poster campaign
Communication for the cheekily monikered puC tells us that 'The secret is in the cup'.
puC／ポスター・キャンペーン：面白い名前のpuCの宣伝が伝えようとしているのは、「秘密はカップの中にある」ということ。

Het Wapen Van Geldrop, poster campaign
The Weapons of Geldrop is a Dutch road movie concerning three individuals who travel to the small town of Geldrop with gruesome results. These posters feature some of Holland's most famous actors with their faces obscured by images from the trip.
Het Wapen Van Geldrop／ポスター・キャンペーン：「The Weapons of Geldrop＝ゲルドロップの武器」は、小さな街ゲルドロップを目指して旅する3人が身の毛もよだつ結末を向かえるオランダのロード・ムービー。そのポスターでは、オランダの有名な俳優たちの顔が旅の写真で覆われている。

- THIJS RÖMER -
HET WAPEN VAN GELDROP
EEN HARTSTOCHTELIJKE ROADMOVIE
DISKY ENTERTAINMENT & PRINCESS ENTERTAINMENT presenteren een COLUMN FILM productie in samenwerking met AVRO en COBO
KATJA SCHUURMAN TARA ELDERS THIJS RÖMER in "HET WAPEN VAN GELDROP"
director of photography THOMAS KIST editor MEREL NOTTEN licht EMILE GROENEWOUD art director DIMITRI MERKOULOV geluid MARTEN NEGENMAN sound design GIEL VAN GELOVEN
muziek RAINER HENSEL haar & make-up CAROLINA LEENDERS styling JACQUELINE STEIJLEN regie-assistent DOESJKA VAN HOOGDALEM uitvoerend producent ELLEN HAVENITH
executive producers KEES HERMANS AAD OUBORG co-producent JUSTINE PAAUW producent GIJS VAN DE WESTELAKEN scenario & regie THIJS RÖMER

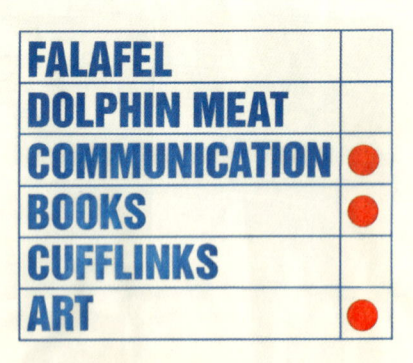

KK Outlet, brand identity
KK Outlet is KesselsKramer's combined agency/shop/exhibition space in London's East End. The thought behind these day-to-day materials at KK Outlet was to show what the company could and couldn't offer. Communications, not clothing accessories. Art, not Middle Eastern fast food.
KK Outlet／ブランド・アイデンティティ：KKアウトレットは、広告代理店、ショップ、展覧会スペースを組み合わせた、ロンドンのイーストエンドにあるケッセルスクライマーの拠点。上図で日常的な事柄が並んでいるのは、同社がなにができて、なにができないかを伝えるため。たとえば、宣伝は大丈夫だけど、アクセサリーは無理。アートはOKだけど、中東のファースト・フードは作れない、ということが分かる。

2.34112 kilo

0

KK Outlet, office
KK Outlet is KesselsKramer's London incarnation. It's a space with multiple personalities, being a communications agency, shop and gallery. The interior was designed by the architectural practice FAT, also responsible for KK's original Amsterdam office/church.
KK Outlet／ブランド・アイデンティティ：KKアウトレットは、ケッセルスクライマーのロンドン拠点。広告代理店、ショップ、ギャラリーと複数の顔をもつ。内装を設計したのは、ケッセルスクライマーのアムステルダム事務所兼教会も設計した建築事務所FAT。

USEFUL PHOTOGRAPHY #008

Useful Photography #008, magazine
This edition of the magazine celebrating utilitarian imagery features the scenarios prior to the action in porn movies. Unlikely pizza-delivery girls and unconvincing driving instructors appear in scenes often skipped in favour of more popular moments of sexual gymnastics. For once, however, this publication gives actors not normally noted for their acting a chance to shine.

Useful Photography #008／雑誌：実用写真をたたえる雑誌『ユースフル・フォトグラフィ』の第8号は、ポルノ映画で出演者たちがコトにおよぶまでのシナリオを特集。ポルノ映画においては、現実にはいそうもないピザのデリバリー・ガールや説得力に欠ける自動車教習所の教官たちのシーンは、より人気がある性の体操シーンを早く見るためとばされがちである。しかし同号は、普段は演技を見てもらえない俳優たちに、一度ぐらいは、と輝くチャンスを与えた。

2.34579 kilo

2.34813 kilo

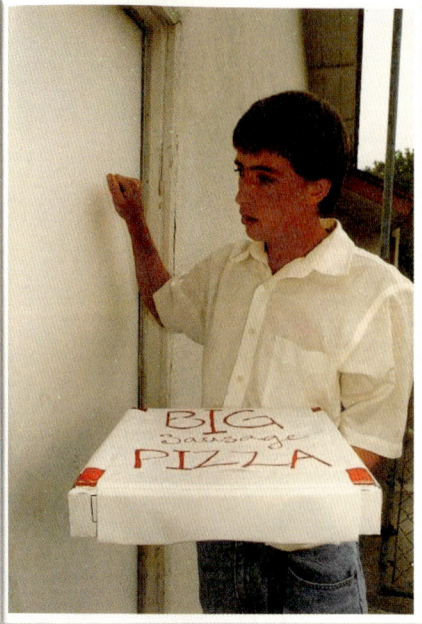

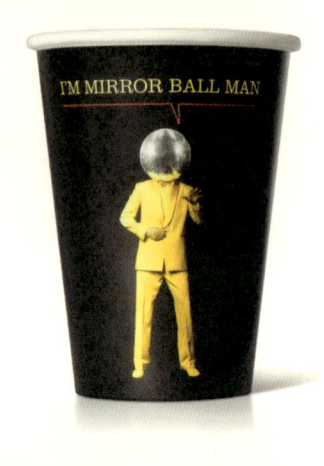

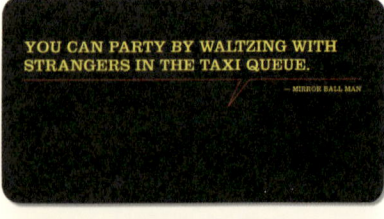

J&B, extra materials
A wealth of materials for J&B whisky over and above the normal channels of press, posters, TV and online. Some of those materials include responsible drinking water cups and a sponge that encourages people to start a party in their shower. The book (top right) was made to tell the full story of the whisky brand's astonishing history, involving epic journeys, broken hearts, prohibition and Rat Pack legends Dean Martin and Frank Sinatra.

J&B／そのほかのツール：出版物、ポスター、テレビ、インターネットといった通常のチャネル以外の、J&Bウィスキーの豊富な宣伝媒体。なかには、専用の水飲みコップや、シャワーを浴びながらパーティーを始めたくなるようなスポンジなどもあった。書籍（右上）は、大旅行、失恋、禁酒法、ラット・パック（50−60年代にこう呼ばれた一団）の伝説的人物ディーン・マーティンとフランク・シナトラなど、このウィスキー・ブランドの驚くべき歴史の全貌を伝えている。

THE MANY STORIES OF THE WORLD'S #1 PARTY WHISKY
RARE
J&B
THE MANY STORIES OF THE
WORLD'S
#1 PARTY
WHISKY

I'M HERE TO TELL YOU THAT THERE'S AN INFINITE NUMBER OF WAYS YOU CAN START A PARTY ANYTIME, ANYWHERE AS LONG AS YOU ENJOY IT RESPONSIBLY. SO CALL YOUR FRIENDS, RELATIVES, PASSERSBY AND HANGERS-ON. USE EVERY PLACE AND OPPORTUNITY, EVEN IF THAT MEANS A BUS-STOP ON A RAINY MONDAY. REMEMBER, GREAT PARTIES JUST NEED YOU, THE RIGHT ATTITUDE AND A LITTLE MODERATION. IF YOUR PARTY INVOLVES ALCOHOLIC DRINKS, REMEMBER TO ALSO SIP LOTS OF WATER. A CUP MIGHT HELP. THAT YOU'LL REMEMBER ALL TOMORROW'S PARTIES THE DAY AFTER TOMORROW AND THE DAY AFTER THAT.
START A PARTY

START A PARTY
START A PARTY
I'M HERE TO TELL YOU THAT YOU CAN START A PARTY ANYTIME, ANYWHERE- AS LONG AS YOU ENJOY IT RESPONSIBLY. SO CALL YOUR FRIENDS, RELATIVES, PASSERSBY AND HANGERS-ON. USE EVERY PLACE AND OPPORTUNITY, EVEN IF THAT MEANS A BUS STOP ON A RAINY MONDAY. REMEMBER, GREAT PARTIES JUST NEED YOU, THE RIGHT ATTITUDE AND A LITTLE MODERATION. A CUP MIGHT HELP.
IF YOUR PARTY INVOLVES ALCOHOLIC DRINKS, REMEMBER TO ALSO SIP LOTS OF WATER. THAT WAY YOU'LL REMEMBER ALL TOMORROW'S PARTIES THE DAY AFTER TOMORROW AND THE DAY AFTER THAT.
— MIRROR BALL MAN
STAGGERING SHOULD BE A WAY OF DRINKING NOT A WAY OF WALKING.
— MIRROR BALL MAN

THIS IS A:

☐ **BROKEN LETTER H** ☐ **CHAIR UPSIDE DOWN** ☐ **NUMBER FOUR**

GRAPHIC DESIGN MUSEUM, BREDA, THE NETHERLANDS
WWW.GRAPHICDESIGNMUSEUM.COM

Graphic Design Museum, poster campaign
The world's first museum dedicated exclusively to graphic design opened in the Dutch town of Breda in 2008. For its launch, posters hinted at the different ways in which various designers can view the same graphic object.
Graphic Design Museum／ポスター・キャンペーン：オランダの街ブレダに2008年に開館した世界初のグラフィック・デザイン専門美術館。そのオープニング用に制作されたポスターは、同じグラフィック・オブジェクトでも、デザイナーによって見方がさまざまであることを示唆している。

THIS IS A:

☐ SOLAR ECLIPSE   ☐ PUPIL OF AN EYE   ☐ END OF A SENTENCE

B Graphic Design Museum

GRAPHIC DESIGN MUSEUM, BREDA, THE NETHERLANDS
WWW.GRAPHICDESIGNMUSEUM.COM

THIS IS A:

☐ GHOST   ☐ CUMULUS CLOUD   ☐ SHEEP IN THE DARK

B Graphic Design Museum

GRAPHIC DESIGN MUSEUM, BREDA, THE NETHERLANDS
WWW.GRAPHICDESIGNMUSEUM.COM

Graphic Design Museum, poster campaign
More posters exploring how the same object can be interpreted from different perspectives.
Graphic Design Museum／ポスター・キャンペーン：同じ物体でも、いかにさまざまな視点から解釈されうるかを探ったポスターのほかの例。

Graphic Design Museum, campaign book
A guide was produced to help designers and other creatives keep to the Museum's look and feel.
Graphic Design Museum／キャンペーン・ブック：美術館のルック＆フィールを保つために、デザイナーやクリエイター向けに作成されたガイド。

Graphic Design Museum, opening event
The world's first museum dedicated to graphic design celebrated its opening with the European Championship of Graphic Design, in which eleven top designers from eleven countries came together to create spontaneous works of art. Among these happenings was a punk ensemble called The Fisters, who performed exclusively for her Majesty the Queen of Holland. Other participants included Anna Szilit, Anthony Burrill, Antoine+Manuel, Browns Design, Cum*, Dennis Eriksson, Happy Pets, Fons Hickmann, Pixelgarten and Scott King.

Graphic Design Museum／オープニング・イベント：世界初のグラフィック・デザイン専門美術館がオープニングを祝して「グラフィック・デザイン欧州選手権」を開催。11カ国から11人のトップ・デザイナーが集められ、それぞれが自由に芸術作品を制作した。なかでも特筆すべきは、オランダ女王陛下にすべての演奏を捧げたパンク・ユニット、ザ・フィスターズ。ほかにもAnna Szilit、アンソニー・バリル、アントワーヌ+マヌエル、ブラウンズ・デザイン、カム*、デニス・エリクソン、ハッピー・ペッツ、フォンス・ヒックマン、ピクセルガーテン、スコット・キングが参加した。

2.36449 kilo

8

2.36682 kilo

At home with the Eames Aluminium Chair.

The original classic in a variety of contemporary colours, designed to fit perfectly in your home.

Vitra is the only authorised manufacturer of all Eames furniture designs for Europe and the Middle East. ©Vitra ®® Tueraessed tis augueril nonsent lortio ea alit adignis corem nit iusto dit ad ea ad magna con exero ea core tem euis augiam, conullamet nit velismo doluptat ad tissi te dunt lutpatie veliquis num quis ea nulla commy nibh exeril irit ulla feugueraesse velent utatem volorti scipsum doluptat praessi. Iquis dolor sit la facillaorper sum digna core tatie dolorerit landre dolobor peraessis nit illaorem adit iriusto commolo rtismol oborem duisl dignibh ex ea alis nulluptat, con utat la faccumm olobore Non vercip et dionum san ut autpatue facincipsum veniam volobortie molobore corperatet luptat. Ut aute core facin is duis niatum zzrilit lore min vel dolobore modolent vel irit lore

---

Vitra, print and poster campaign

Vitra's classic Eames aluminium chairs were originally designed for home use. Over the years, this original purpose changed as customers spontaneously began using them for the office. These images were designed to help bring Eames' timeless pieces back to people's houses. Press ads show Vitra chairs surrounded by all kinds of colour-coordinated household objects.

Vitra／紙媒体、ポスター・キャンペーン：ヴィトラの傑作、イームズ・アルミニウム製チェアは、もとは家庭用に設計されたもの。長年のあいだに、なぜかこれをオフィスで使う人が増え、本来の目的が変化していった。上図は、イームズの不朽の名作を家庭に戻すことを目指したキャンペーン。この紙媒体の広告では、カラーコーディネートされたあらゆる種類の家庭用品が、ヴィトラ・チェアを取り囲んでいる。

vitra.

At home with the Eames Aluminium Chair.

The original classic in a variety of contemporary colours, designed to fit perfectly in your home.

Vitra is the only authorised manufacturer of all Eames furniture designs for Europe and the Middle East. ©Vitra *® Tuerbessed tis augueril nonsent lortio ea alit adignis corem nit iusto dit ad ea ad magna con exero ea core tem euis augiam, conullamet nit velismo doluptat ad hsi te dunt lutpatie veliquis num quis am nolla commy nibh exernit ulla feugueraesse velent utatem volorh scipsum doluptat praessi. Iquis dolor sit la facillaoiper sum digna core tahe dolorerit landre dolobor peraessi nit illaorem adit inusto conmolo rtismol oborem duisl dignibh ex ea alis nulluptat, con utat la faacurrit olobore Non verciper dionumsan ot autpatue facincipsum veniam volobortie molobore corperatet luptan. Ut aute core facinis duis niatum zzrilit lore min vel dolobore modolent vel irit lore

Vitra, print and extra materials
A final ad in the Vitra campaign showing just how well the Eames chair can fit in your life. On the facing page, a booklet helps demonstrate the Eames chair's great ability to be at home in your home and included a transparency printed with the classic chair to allow consumers to size it up in their own home.

Vitra／紙媒体、そのほかのツール：イームズ・チェアが生活にどのくらいフィットするかを示す、ヴィトラ・キャンペーンの広告。右側の写真は、イームズ・チェアが家庭でどのくらいすばらしい能力を発揮するのか、を説明する小冊子。顧客が自宅にあわせてサイズを調整できるよう、この傑作のポジフィルムが同封されている。

**At home with the
Eames Aluminium Chair.**

The original classic in a variety
of contemporary colours, designed
to fit perfectly in your home.

DAG, extra materials
DAG was the name of a free newspaper and online and mobile news service christened by KesselsKramer. The name means both 'Hello' and 'Day' in Dutch. On these pages, we see the news service's breadth of communication materials demonstrated, including diaries, delivery bags and wooden crates for displays highlighting the newspaper's fresh content.
DAG／そのほかのツール：DAGはケッセルスクライマーが名づけた無料新聞兼インターネット/モバイル・ニュースサービス。名前の「DAG」は、オランダ語で「こんにちは」や「日にち」を意味する。上図は、このニュース・サービスのさまざまなツール。ダイアリー、配達用かばん、木箱などが同紙のコンテンツの新鮮さをアピールしている。

DAG
HET
LEUKSTE
T-SHIRT
VAN DE
DAG
DAG
DAG
LUDOLF
RASTERHOF
DAG
BAPTIEST
COOPMANS
DAG
ED
BONTEKOE
DAG
DAG
DAG
ZIE IK JE
ZATERDAG?
DAG 2007
ZIE IK JE
ZATERDAG?
DAG 2007
VERJAARDAG

 2.38084 kilo

LORD OF THE RINGS De erven Tolkien willen geld zien voor de 'Lord of the Rings'-films. De rechtszaak brengt ook de verfilming van 'The Hobbit' in gevaar **21** Beroemd

GRATIS SMS-ALERTS VAN DAG Ontvang het grootste nieuws voortaan gratis in een sms-bericht. Sms 'dag aan' naar 1333

JAMIEDAG. 13.02

24 uur online, mobiel en op papier / www.dag.nl

'Je moet wat dóen voor jongeren'

DAG kiest deze maand wekelijks een held. Vandaag is dat Jamie Oliver, de eerste kok die iets deed aan overgewicht bij kinderen. En die zich afzet tegen de uitwassen in de bio-industrie **4**

2 Vandaag
Militairen in gevaar door uranium
Nederlandse veteranen zijn mogelijk wandelende tijdbommen. De munitie die in Irak en Afghanistan wordt afgevuurd, bevat uranium. Steeds meer soldaten worden ziek.

6 Nieuws
Rapport: Nederlanders lijden aan islamofobie
Uit angst voor de islam slaan Nederlanders aan het discrimineren, zegt de Raad voor Europa. Op het rapport wordt met verbazing gereageerd.

10 Nieuws
Ruilhandel bij tv-programma's heel normaal
Peter R. de Vries werd giftig omdat hij niet uitvoerig over zijn boek kon praten. Zijn gastheer was verbaasd, maar elke talkshow maakt deals.

14 Zaken
Doek valt definitief voor de Polaroid-camera
Fabrieken stoppen met het maken van Polaroid-films. De camera werd vorig jaar al niet meer gemaakt. Daarmee is het Polaroid-tijdperk voorbij.

20 Het weer
Vandaag veel laaghangende bewolking. De grootste kans op zon hebben het zuiden en oosten van het land.

DAG, newspaper
DAG was designed primarily as a highly visual newspaper. Often KesselsKramer and the editorial team played with the flexible title, sometimes naming issues after particular people. Above a special edition draws attention to crusading chef Jamie Oliver.
DAG／新聞：DAGは、ビジュアルのレベルが高い新聞としてデザインされることに、主眼がおかれた。ケッセルスクライマーと編集チームは、ある程度自由に変えられるタイトルを題材に遊び心を発揮。場合によっては、特定の人物の名前をタイトルにもってくることも。上図の特別号は、活動家シェフ、ジェイミー・オリヴァーを大きくフィーチャーしている。

DAG, TV commercial
The free newspaper wanted to reduce waste while increasing readership. This film, shot in reverse, encouraged its audience to share the newspaper with friends, colleagues and strangers.
DAG／TVコマーシャル：無料新聞DAGが、無駄を削減しつつ購読者数を増やすことを求めた。逆回転で撮影されたこの動画は、視聴者に、友人、同僚、見知らぬ人と同紙を共有して一緒に読むようすすめるもの。

2.38551 kilo

in almost every picture #7, book
The seventh edition of in almost every picture collected the photography of amateur sharpshooter Ria van Dijk. These Polaroids are taken at the shooting galleries of travelling funfairs. Every time Ria hit the target she'd win her own portrait in return. The collection began in 1936 and seventy years later, her work was published. The series became the first amateur photos to be acquired by Amsterdam's world famous Stedelijk Museum.
in almost every picture #7／TVコマーシャル：『in almost every picture＝ほとんどどの写真にも』の第7号は、アマチュアの射撃名手リア・ヴァン・ダイクの写真をコレクション。これらのポラロイド写真は巡回型遊園地の射的場で撮影されたもの。リアは的に命中させるたびに、賞品として自分の顔写真を獲得。このコレクションは1936年に始まり、その70年後に彼女の作品集が出版された。同シリーズは、世界的に有名なアムステルダム市立近代美術館の最初のアマチュア写真コレクションになった。

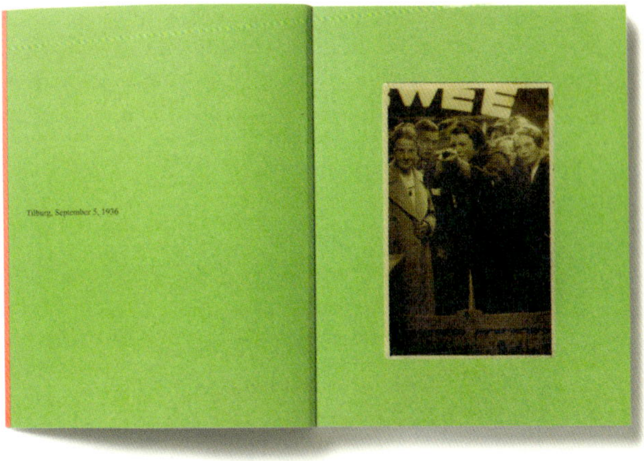
Tilburg, September 5, 1936

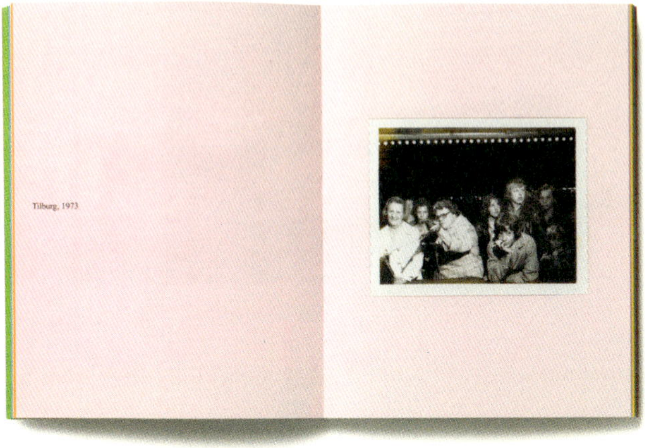
Tilburg, 1973

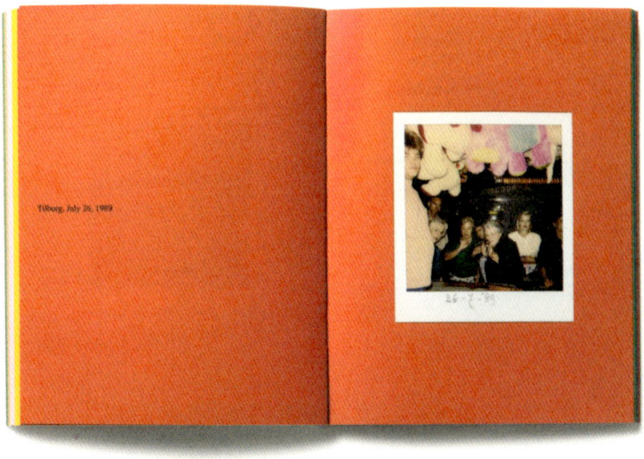
Tilburg, July 26, 1989

artoons, book
A book about overlooked details. Comic panels often contain tiny sketches of great artworks in their backgrounds. So while most readers see stories of giant mice and ducks there's a hidden narrative of Picasso and Van Gogh-like masterpieces behind the anthropomorphized creatures.
artoons／書籍：見過ごされがちな細部についての本。マンガのコマの背景には偉大な芸術作品が小さなスケッチで入っていることが多い。読者が大きなネズミやアヒルの物語を読んでいるときに、これらの擬人化された動物たちのうしろに、ピカソやバン・ゴッホのような名作の隠れた物語が展開しているのだ。

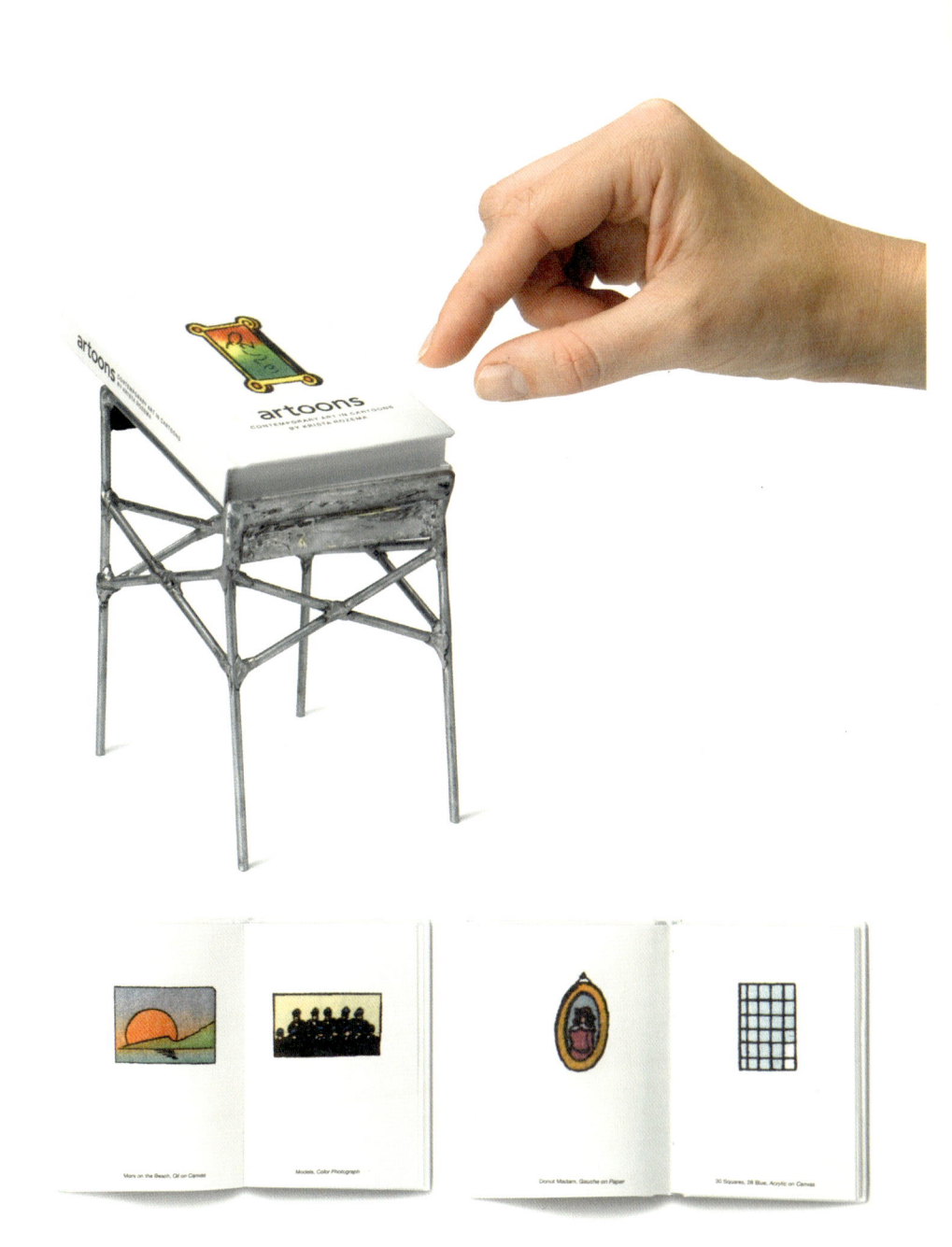

artoons, display
artoons was the smallest art book ever. As a reference to this status, a tiny stand was made as a display (which some might say resembles a certain sumo-sized coffee-table book). artoons／ディスプレイ：『アートンズ』はかつてない極小な本。これにあわせて、ディスプレイ用に小さなスタンドも作られた。（どこかの相撲取りサイズのコーヒー・テーブル・ブックみたいだと言われるかもしれないが。）

2.39486 kilo

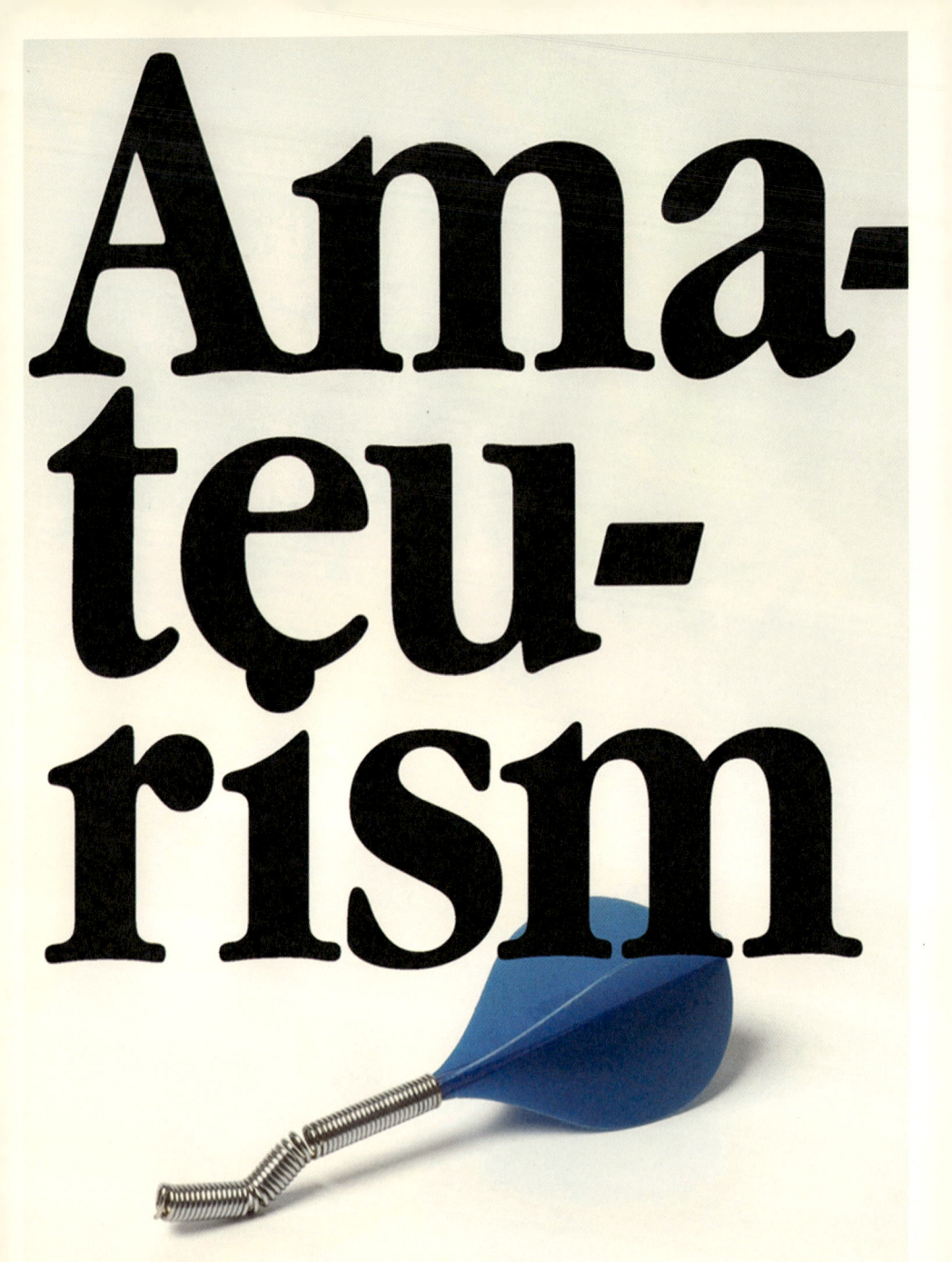

Ama-teu-rism

Amateurism, book
The book of an exhibition about amateur art. It was the result of a workshop for architectural students who became amateurs for a week. Amateurism's argument is that non-professional work is often more alive and inventive than the slick, over-produced creations of established artists.
Amateurism／書籍：アマチュア芸術に関する展覧会の本。一週間にわたってアマチュアである建築を学ぶ学生向けに行ったワークショップの結果がこの書籍。きれいだけど作り込まれすぎたプロの作品よりも、プロではない人の作品の方が、活き活きとしていて発想力豊かな場合が多い、と『アマチュアリズム』では主張している。

2.39953 kilo

Platform 21, poster campaign
Communication for an exhibition at Amsterdam's design, fashion and creation gallery space. This particular show explored the blurred boundaries between real and virtual worlds. In these images, we see real people juxtaposed with their computerized alter egos.

Platform 21／ポスター・キャンペーン：アムステルダムにあるデザイン、ファッション、創作物のためのギャラリー・スペースの広告。このユニークな展覧会は、現実世界と仮想世界とのあいまいな境界を探るためのもの。上図では、現実の人間に、デジタル化されたもうひとりの自己が並置されている。

PLATFORM21 = CHECKING REALITY

18 MAY – 10 AUGUST 2008   WWW.PLATFORM21.COM
A REAL SHOW ABOUT THE VIRTUAL. CHECK PLATFORM21 AND THE BEATRIXPARK.

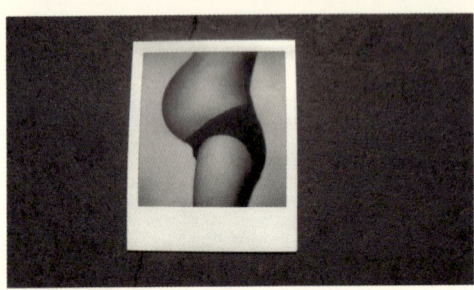

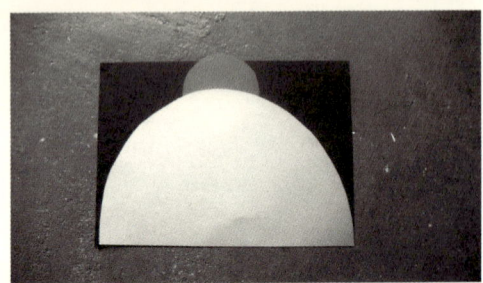

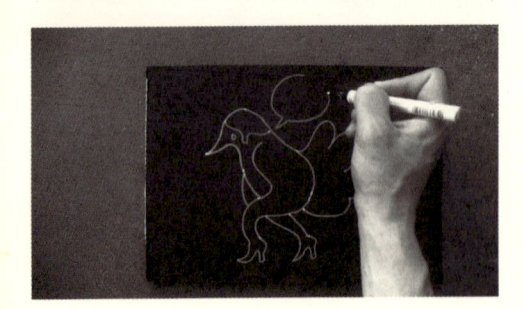

LeLe, music video
Renowned illustrator Parra is also part of electronic music group LeLe, an act that experiments with tracks in Dutch, French and German. This video featured Parra's trademark drawings brought to life with found photos and footage in a mix of surreal, frenetic visuals.
LeLe／音楽ビデオ：有名なイラストレーター、パラは、オランダ語、フランス語、ドイツ語で実験する電子音楽グループLeLeのメンバーでもある。このビデオは、パラのトレードマークともなっているイラストをフィーチャーしたもの。ファウンド・フォトと、騒々しくシュールなビジュアルがミックスされたシーンが、イラストの印象をさらに高めている。

2.40888 kilo

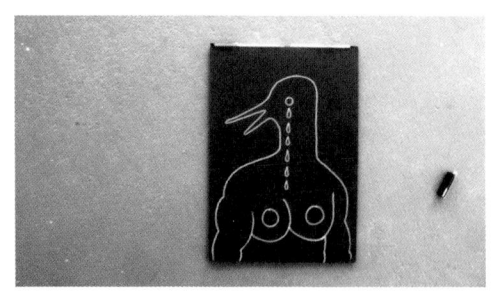

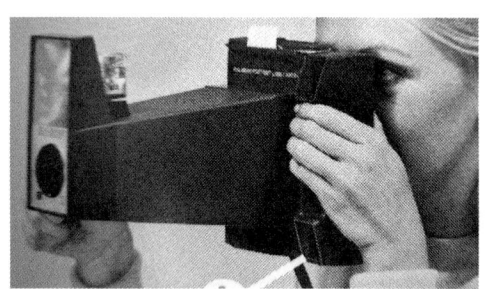

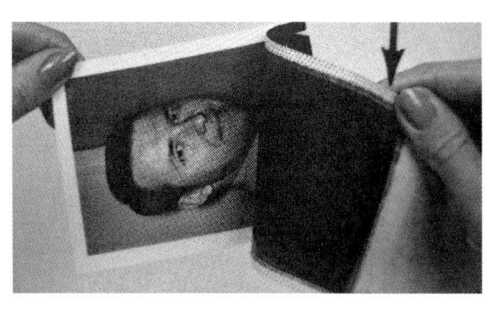

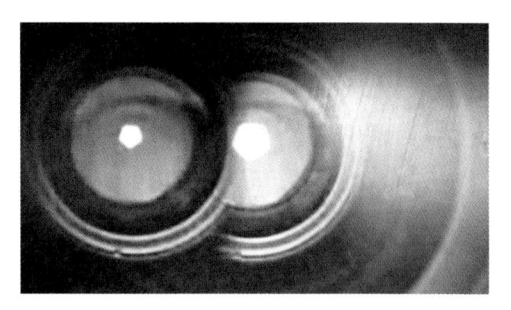

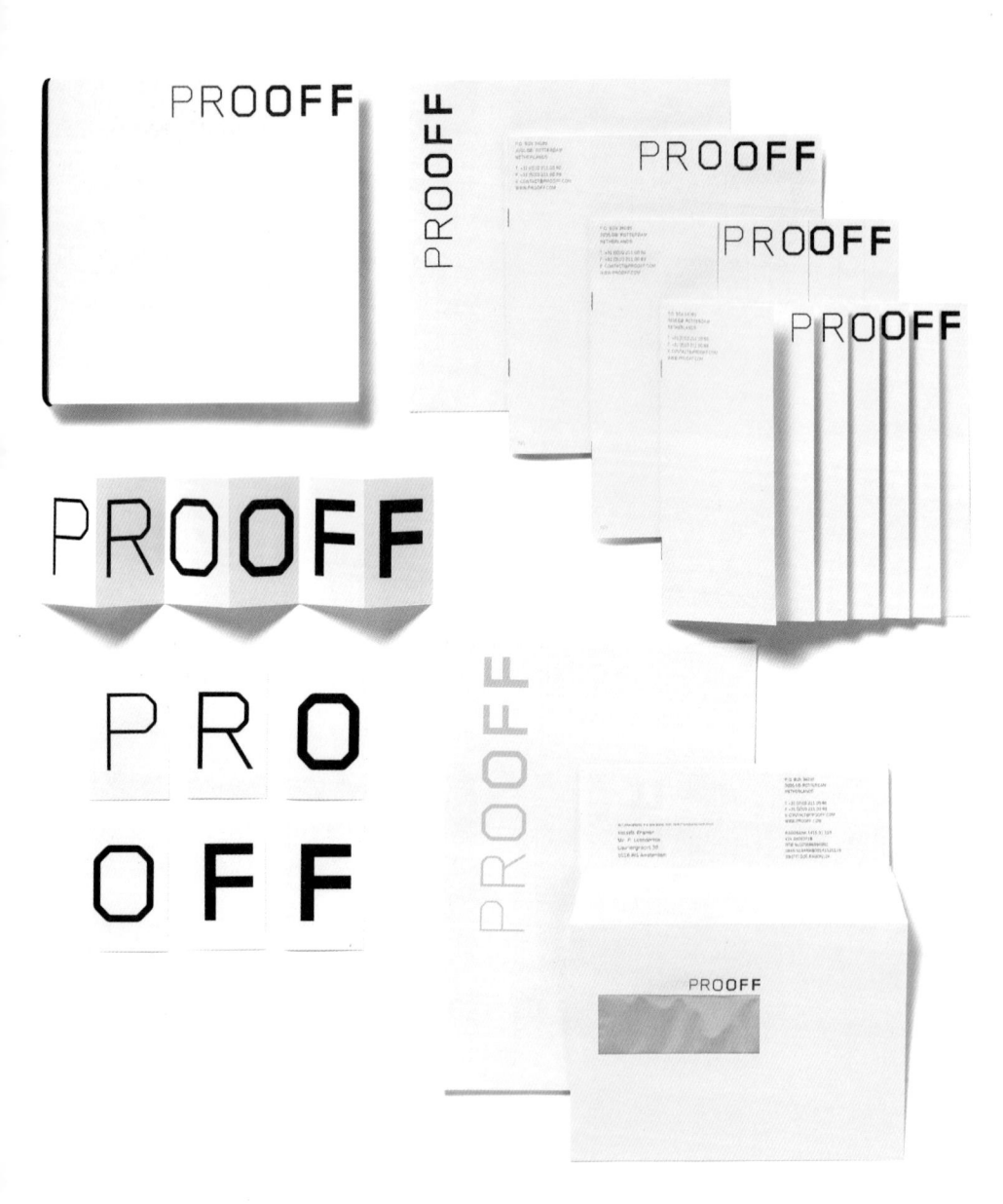

Prooff, brand identity
Prooff is a team of ground-breaking architects and designers including Jurgen Bey. The name stands for product development for the progressive office. This logo design, house style and accompanying booklet help to explain their unique vision.
Prooff／ブランド・アイデンティティ：Prooffはユルゲン・ベイをはじめとする、革新的な建築家やデザイナーで構成されるチーム。チーム名は、進歩的なオフィスのための商品開発を表している。このロゴ・デザイン、自社ツール、小冊子で、そのユニークなビジョンを知ることができる。

NPS, brand identity
NPS is one of the most respected broadcasters dedicated to cultural programming in Holland. This brand identity celebrates its diversity and reach with an ever-changing logo using the backdrops of freeze-framed images from the broadcaster's diverse programming output.
NPS／ブランド・アイデンティティ：NPSはオランダ屈指の文化番組専門放送局。そのブランド・アイデンティティでは、NPSの多様性と放送内容の広範さをたたえ、採用されたロゴはつねに変化しつづけるよう、同局の多彩な番組からフリーズフレーム技法で書き出された画像が背景に使われた。

2.41355 kilo

NPS, extra materials
A continuation of the Dutch cultural channel's rebranding. Here, its ever-evolving (but always coherent) logo is presented in action across material for internal and external use including letterheads, business cards and DVD packages.
NPS／そのほかのツール：オランダの文化チャンネル再ブランディングのそのほかの例。進化し続ける（ただし一貫性のある）ロゴが、レターヘッド、名刺、DVDパッケージなど社内外で使われる素材のすべてに使われている。

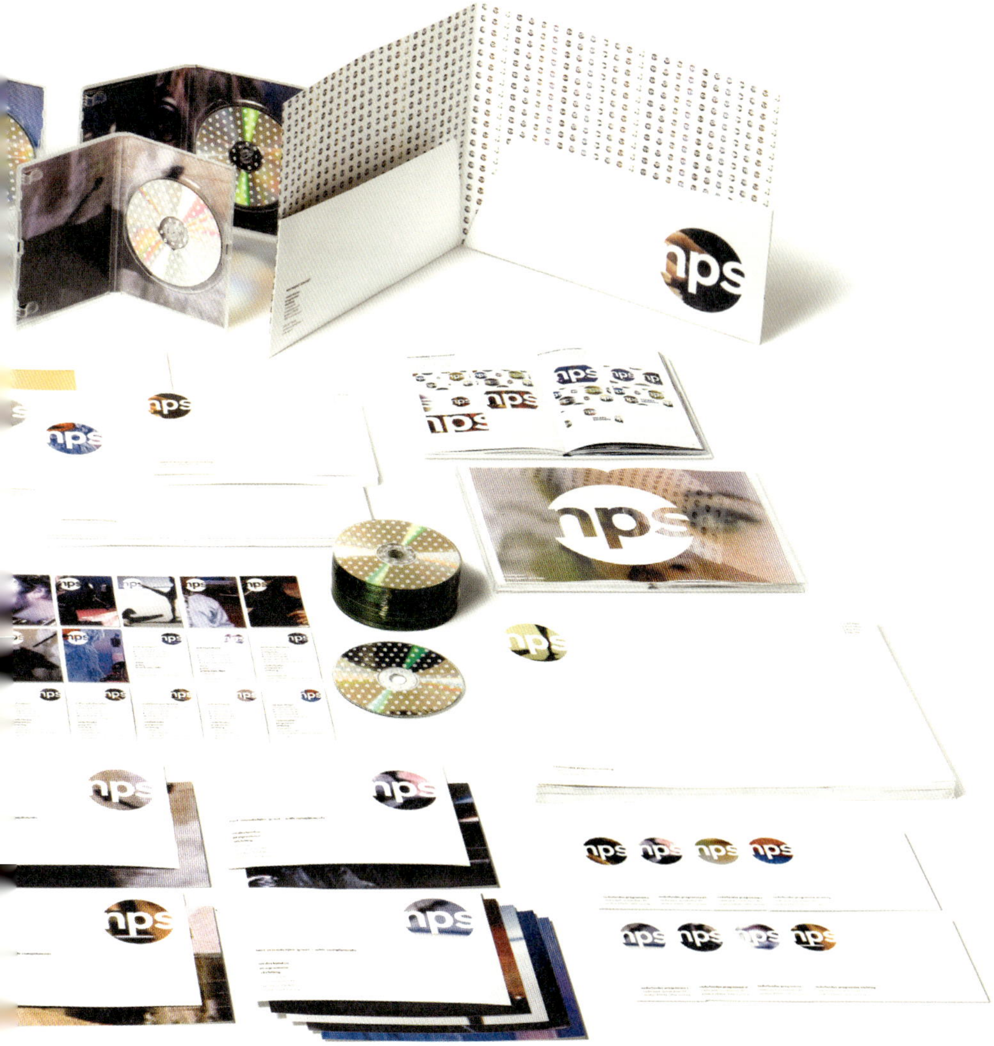

SNS Bank, poster campaign
Dutch bank SNS launched this poster campaign that asked 'What is your savings plan?'- a question designed to stimulate consumers into putting some cash aside for the days to come. The accompanying images suggested people's dreams for the future: from a cocktail-fuelled life of leisure to one of wedded bliss.
SNS Bank／ポスター・キャンペーン：オランダの銀行SNSが「あなたの貯金計画はどうなっていますか？」とたずねるポスター・キャンペーンを開始。この質問は、消費者に将来のためにお金を取っておこうと思わせることを意図したもの。付随する写真は、カクテルを手にしたゆったりとした生活から、結婚の喜びまで、人々の将来の夢を表している。

Wat is jouw spaarplan?

SNS Maxisparen
4,75%* rente als je een vast bedrag per maand spaart

* Rente per 7 november 2008, rentewijzigingen voorbehouden.
Vraag naar de voorwaarden.

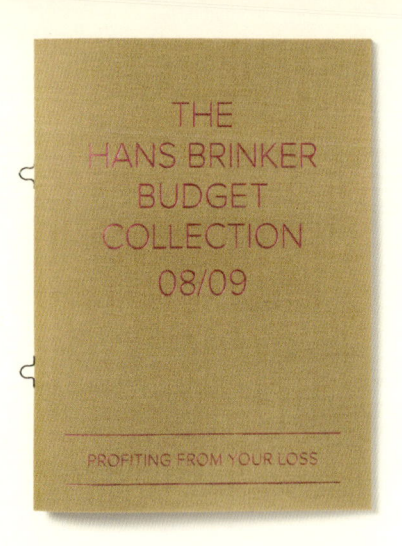

Hans Brinker Budget Hotel, POS
A range of designs created from the leftovers at the Hans Brinker lost-and-found department. The Hans Brinker Budget Collection is a catalogue presenting a selection of fashionably unfashionable knick-knacks made to draw attention to the Brinker for an international hotel fair in New York.
Hans Brinker Budget Hotel／配布物：ハンス・ブリンカー・バジェット・ホテルの遺失物取り扱い部にある残り物で作られたさまざまなデザイン。「ハンス・ブリンカー・バジェット・コレクション」は、ダサかっこいいガラクタのセレクションを紹介するカタログ。ニューヨークで開催された国際ホテル・フェアでハンス・ブリンカーに注目を集めるために制作された。

Madre Perla, poster campaign
Images made in collaboration with Diana Scheerer for a new kids-fashion brand.
Madre Perla／ポスター・キャンペーン：新しいキッズ・ファッション・ブランドのために、写真家ダイアナ・シェラーとのコラボレーションで制作された画像。

S1ngletown, exhibition materials
For the prestigious architectural biennale in Venice, KesselsKramer created S1ngletown in association with Droog Design. The exhibition was made to raise awareness of the growing impact of single-living on urban society, and to explore the issues raised by this: from urban planning to environmental cost. The town featured archetypal single citizens and was supported by a newspaper exploring the issue in greater depth.
S1ngletown／展示物：有名なベネチアの建築ビエンナーレで、ケッセルスクライマーはドローグ・デザインと協力して「S1ngletown」を制作。この展示は、都市社会において高まり続けている独身者の影響に関する認識を高めることと、「都市計画から環境コストまで」というテーマが提起する問題を探求することを目指している。典型的な独身者をとりあげたS1ngletownは、この問題を詳しく調査する新聞が後援した。

2.42991 kilo   0

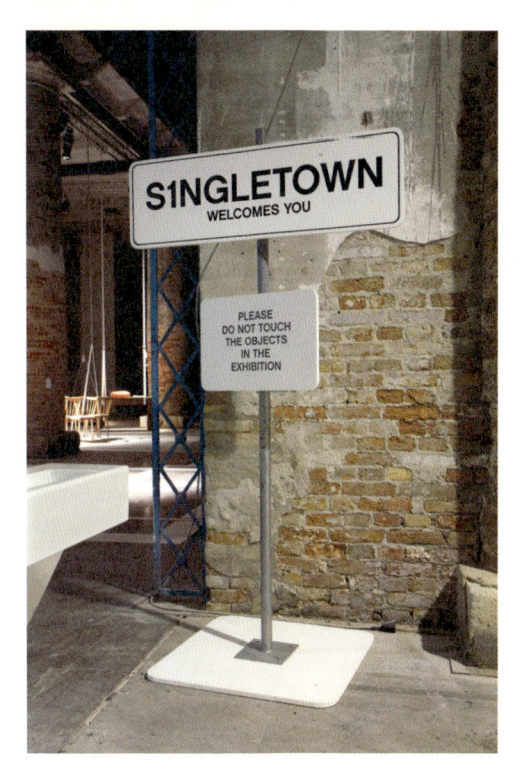

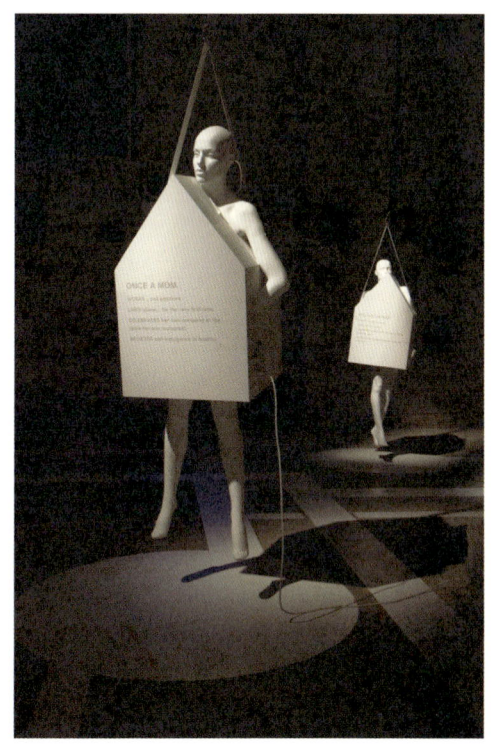

8

2.43224 kilo

S1ngletown, exhibition
An overview of S1ngletown for the Venice Biennale. The exhibition illustrated the rise of single life in the developed world and took the form of an abstract interpretation of a possible future habitation for single people.
S1ngletown／展覧会：ベネチアビエンナーレに展示されたS1ngletownの概観。展示物は、先進国世界における独身者の増加を描写するのと同時に、予想される彼らの将来の住まいの抽象的解釈を表現している。

2.43692 kilo

Kind, poster campaign
Posters for the quirky, super-luxury knitwear label, Kind and its Fall/Winter collection. The campaign showed how wearers might best enjoy their outfits.
Kind／ポスター・キャンペーン：奇抜だが、非常に高級なニットウェア・レーベル「カインド」とその秋冬コレクションを紹介するポスター。最高に楽しめそうな着こなしを披露している。

2.43925 kilo

KIND
ROYAL FLUSH - COLLECTION F/W 07/08

7

2.44159 kilo

Theatre Academy Maastricht, print campaign
Maastricht's academy of theatre and performing arts needed to attract new students. This simple concept asked potential applicants whether they saw themselves as a future actor, performer or director.
Theatre Academy Maastricht／紙媒体キャンペーン：マーストリヒトの演劇アカデミーが生徒を募集することになった。キャンペーンのコンセプトはシンプルで、自分を未来の俳優、パフォーマー、監督のどれだと考えているかを入学希望者にたずねるというもの。

FUTURE ACTOR?
TONEELACADEMIE MAASTRICHT

Theatre Academy Maastricht, print campaign
More images suggesting what it took to become a future actor.
Theatre Academy Maastricht／紙媒体キャンペーン：未来の俳優になるためにはなにが必要かを示す、そのほかの画像。

Theatre Academy Maastricht, online films
Online films, each showing extreme examples of performers in the making. This example portrays a future actor in a toilet cubicle reciting the famously intense speech of Robert de Niro in 'Taxi Driver'. Made in collaboration with the students of the Academy.
Theatre Academy Maastricht／インターネット・ビデオ：制作中のパフォーマーたちの極端な例を示すインターネット・ビデオ。上図は、映画「タクシー・ドライバー」におけるロバート・デ・ニーロの有名な激しい語りを暗唱しながらトイレの便器に立つ未来の俳優を描いたもの。アカデミーの生徒たちの協力を得て制作。

2.45093 kilo

Uitmarkt, poster campaign
The start of the cultural season in Holland is pointed out by these posters, using the theme 'the cultural season breaks loose' and draws on the winds around one of Amsterdam's main concert buildings for inspiration.
Uitmarkt／ポスター・キャンペーン：オランダの文化シーズンの始まりを伝える ポスター。テーマの「文化シーズンが爆発」にのっとり、アムステルダムの有名な コンサート・ホールの周辺に風を起こすことで刺激的に演出。

UIT MARKT

AMSTERDAMS UIT BURO

HET CULTURELE SEIZOEN BREEKT LOS

24 / 25 / 26 AUG 2007

OOSTELIJK HAVENGEBIED / AMSTERDAM

REAAL Insurance, poster campaign
An example of REAAL's long-running campaign using the lighter side of risk calculation as its theme and relating the percentages in the headline with the size of the objects in the photography. This headline reads: 89% chance that you've got enough going on in your head. Copy continues: The collective pension plan from REAAL. Realist in insurance.
REAAL Insurance／ポスター・キャンペーン：保険会社のロングラン・キャンペーンの一例。リスク計算の面白い面をテーマとして使い、見出しのパーセンテージを写真内の囲みのサイズと関連づけている。見出しは「頭に浮かべたことがらを十分に理解している確率：89%」と記され、次に「REAALの共同年金プラン。保険の現実主義者」と続けられている。

**NS DAT U AL MEER DAN
AAN UW HOOFD HEEFT.**

PENSIOENVERZEKERINGEN VAN REAAL.
KEREN.

Verzekeringen

REAAL Insurance, TV commercial
Film in which images representing statistics literally change size according to whatever percentage is described.
REAAL Insurance／TVコマーシャル：統計データを象徴するモノのサイズが、
説明されたパーセンテージどおりに変わる映像。

2.46262 kilo

0

REAAL Insurance, booklet
A booklet on the philosophy of REAAL, entitled The Realism of REAAL. In form, it consists of a list of possibilities and the chances of those possibilities occurring. At the end, with the 100% score, was the chance that you will die.
REAAL Insurance／小冊子：「REAALの現実主義」と題された当社の哲学についての小冊子。可能性のリストと、それらが現実に起こる可能性で構成されている。最後に記された100％は、あなたが死亡する可能性。

2.46495 kilo

Uitburo Rotterdam, poster campaign
The culture department for Rotterdam suggests you leave your comfort zone and discover the city's more interesting happenings.
Uitburo Rotterdam／ポスター・キャンペーン：ロッテルダム市の文化部門が、快適な場所から離れて、市内で起こっているもっと面白い出来事を探すよう促したポスター。

UIT?

ROTTERDAMS UITBURO

INFORMATIE EN KAARTVERKOOP
VOOR UITGAAN IN ROTTERDAM
UITBURO.NL

DE FEITEN OVER VOLLE MAAN

Volle maan spreekt al eeuwenlang tot de verbeelding. Weerwolven genieten nog steeds een aardige populariteit. En een paar honderd jaar geleden kregen misdadigers in Engeland zelfs strafvermindering als ze hun delict tijdens volle maan gepleegd hadden. Dan was er namelijk sprake van *lunacy*, de middeleeuwse variant van ontoerekeningsvatbaarheid. Terecht? Neen, helaas. Uit een door REAAL Verzekeringen gehouden onderzoek, afgelopen maandagnacht was het weer zover, blijkt dat een nacht met volle maan niet noemenswaardig verschilt van een willekeurige andere nacht. Geen romantische conclusie misschien, maar wel een realistische.

REAAL. REALIST IN VERZEKEREN

0,002%
MEER KANS OP EEN BEVALLING
Gemiddeld worden er op dagen van volle maan 588 kinderen geboren, precies eentje meer dan tijdens een willekeurige andere dag. Het Waterlandziekenhuis in Purmerend registreerde maandagnacht vier geboorten, waarvan maar één spontaan. Geen overtuigende cijfers dus.
Bron: SVB

1%
MINDER KANS OP RUZIE
Mocht u maandagavond met het verkeerde been uit bed zijn gestapt, dan is dat vervelend. De kans dat dit te wijten was aan volle maan, lijkt echter vrij klein. Alle verhalen over onrust, agitatie en sneller stromend bloed ten spijt: de kans op ruzie lag gisteravond lager dan gemiddeld: 1%.
Bron: Motivaction

24%
MEER KANS OP EEN INBRAAKMELDING
Uit onderzoek blijkt dat het aantal inbraakmeldingen tijdens volle maan stijgt: van 1,07 gemiddeld naar 1,33. Misschien dat de heren inbrekers dankbaar gebruik maken van het licht. Onduidelijk is of het aantal inbraken tijdens een onbewolkte nacht hoger is dan bij een bewolkte. Voor 2 mei, de volgende volle maan, in ieder geval de deuren goed op slot.
Bron: REAAL Verzekeringen

11,1%
MINDER KANS OP LETSEL DOOR GEWELD
Goed nieuws voor romantici: de kans dat u tijdens een volle maan na een onzacht treffen met een medemens op de afdeling spoedeisende hulp van het ziekenhuis belandt, is 11,1% lager dan gemiddeld. Of het de gunstige uitwerking van de volle maan zelf is, durven we echter niet te zeggen.
Bron: Letsel Informatie Systeem, Stichting Consument & Veiligheid

0,0%
MEER KANS OP EEN HONDENBEET
De kans dat u maandagnacht een weerwolf tegen het lijf gelopen bent, is vrij klein: 0,0%. Zelfs de kans op een hondenbeet steeg niet. Het aantal geregistreerde hondenbeten bleek namelijk exact gelijk aan dat van een willekeurige andere nacht: zo'n 20 stuks. Wel even opletten voor de dwergpapegaai: van de ondervraagden gaven twee personen aan maandagavond gebeten te zijn.
Bron: Letsel Informatie Systeem, Stichting Consument & Veiligheid

5,8%
MEER KANS OP EEN LAGERE OPENINGSKOERS
Uit onderzoek blijkt dat volle maan een ongunstige uitwerking heeft op de openingskoers van de beurs. De kans dat deze na een volle maan lager opent dan hij de avond ervoor sloot, is 5,8%. Opmerkelijk is dat, geheel tegen deze trend in, de beurs dinsdagochtend 2,66 punten hoger opende.
Bron: AEX

5%
MINDER KANS DAT U GAAT DRINKEN
Blijkbaar hebben niet meer mensen van de gelegenheid gebruik gemaakt om een goed glas wijn in de hand van de werkelijk schitterende volle maan op maandagnacht te genieten. Het aantal alcoholische consumpties was tijdens de volle maan 5% lager dan gemiddeld. Ook het percentage mensen dat helemaal geen alcohol dronk, steeg licht: 4%.
Bron: Motivaction

8,26%
KANS OP MINDER REGEN ALS HET REGENT
Uit onderzoek blijkt dat er ruim 8% minder kans op regen is, gesteld dat het tijdens een nacht met volle maan regent. Valt er gemiddeld 2,18 millimeter, tijdens een nacht met volle maan is dat 'slechts' 2 millimeter. Helaas net niet genoeg om droog de hond uit te laten.
Bron: KNMI

7%
MEER KANS OP KORTE NACHT RUST
Nachten met volle maan zijn berucht vanwege het vermeende slaapgebrek. Niet geheel ten onrechte, zo blijkt. Ruim 7% van de ondervraagden gaf aan een stuk korter geslapen te hebben. Vier personen gaven aan zelfs helemaal geen oog dicht gedaan te hebben. Ai. Bovendien blijken de effecten bij vrouwen groter te zijn dan bij mannen.
Bron: Motivaction

3%
MINDER KANS OP SEKS
Voor de vuurwormen bij de Bermuda-eilanden was het feest maandagavond. In tegenstelling tot de Anchistioides-garnaal die alleen bij nieuwe maan paart, doet de vuurworm dit bij volle maan. De meeste mensen, zo blijkt, er rustiger aan. De kans dat u maandagavond seks heeft gehad, lag zelfs 3% lager dan gemiddeld.
Bron: Motivaction

REAAL Verzekeringen

REAAL Insurance, print
A press ad providing the true story behind myths relating to the full moon. Does it statistically increase your chances of turning into a werewolf? Will you get in more fights? And are you less likely to get laid? The ever-intrepid insurance company seeks to find out.
REAAL Insurance／紙媒体：満月にまつわる神話に隠された実話を伝える新聞広告。満月によって、あなたがオオカミ人間になる可能性は、統計的に高まるのだろうか？ケンカの回数は増えるのだろうか？セックスは減るのだろうか？かつてない大胆な保険会社がその答えを探る。

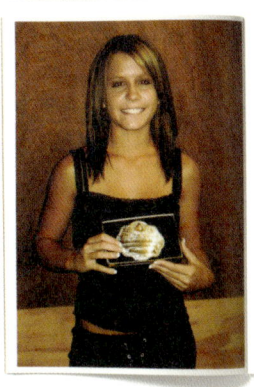

Useful Photography #007, magazine
In this edition of the magazine celebrating utilitarian photography, all images are culled from the generally overlooked world of amateur award ceremonies.
Useful Photography #007／雑誌：実用的用途のために撮影された写真をたたえる『ユースフル・フォトグラフィ』の第7号が掲載した写真はすべて、一般にあまり注目されないアマチュア向けの授賞式から選んだもの。

do box, product
A do product that encourages environmentally friendly violence and comes in the form of a punch bag waiting to be filled with newspapers and other recyclable materials. Also relieves office stress.
do box／商品：今回の do 商品は、環境にやさしい暴力を奨励する、新聞などのリサイクル素材を詰め込んで使えるサンドバッグ。オフィスでたまるストレスも解消できる。

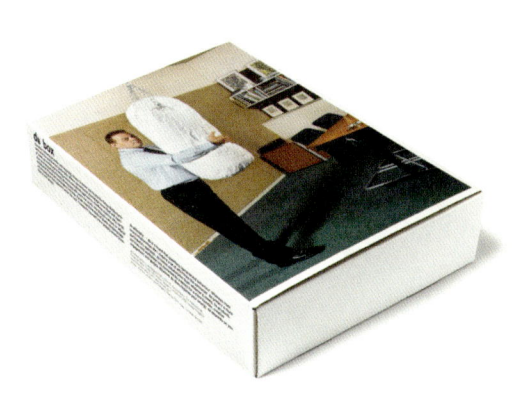

do box, exhibition
50 of these eco-punch bags were hung at the Utterubbish exhibition in Singapore for visitors to test both their punching and garbage collecting skills.
do box／展覧会：シンガポールで開催された「アターラビッシュ展」で、do のエコ・サンドバッグは50本も吊るされた。目的は、訪問者のパンチ力とゴミ収集能力の両方を試すこと。

2.47897 kilo

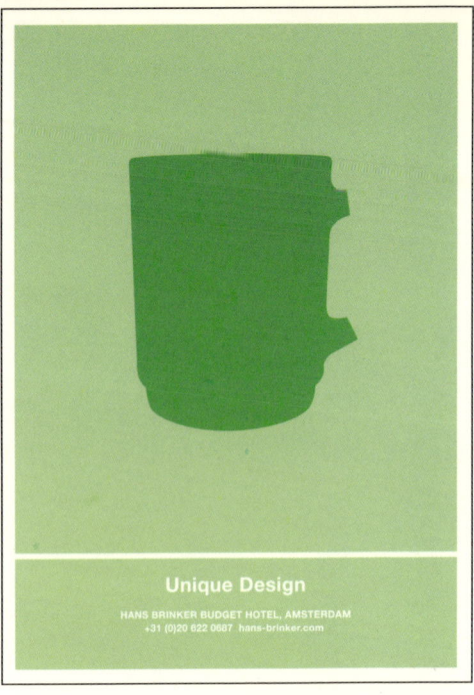

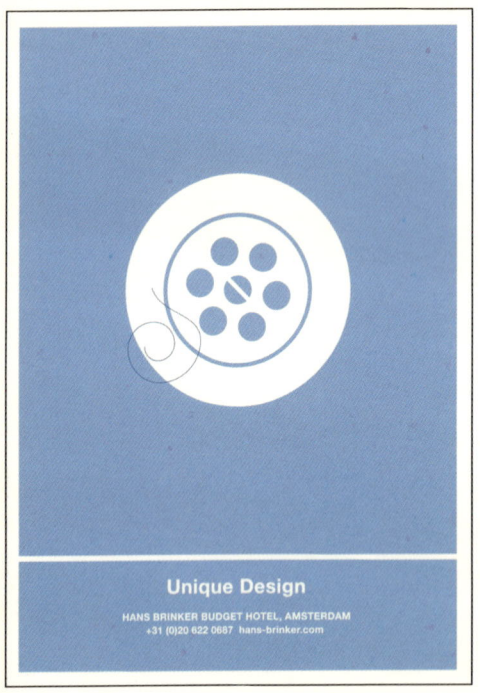

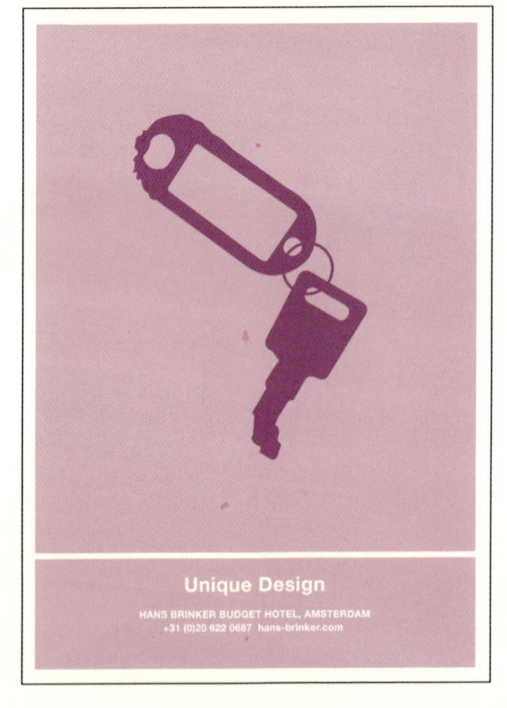

Hans Brinker Budget Hotel, poster campaign
At a time when boutique hotels were popping up wherever there was space to build them, the Hans Brinker Budget Hotel wanted to remind the universe that unique designer furniture, artefacts and objects had, in fact, been sitting gathering dust in its halls for many decades already.
Hans Brinker Budget Hotel／ポスター・キャンペーン：場所さえあればブティック・ホテルがそこらじゅうに建てられていたころ、ハンス・ブリンカー・バジェット・ホテルは、もう何十年も前から、個性的なデザイナー家具、芸術品、オブジェがほこりにまみれながらホールに陳列されていたことを世間に知らせようとした。

Unique Design

HANS BRINKER BUDGET HOTEL, AMSTERDAM
+31 (0)20 622 0687 hans-brinker.com

2.48364 kilo

Hans Brinker Budget Hotel, clothing
To support the Hans Brinker's bid for design-hotel fame, a line of ultra-fashionable clothing was produced. Each item featured a different example from the Brinker's catalogue of designs, including this must-have item, a unisex designer vest.
Hans Brinker Budget Hotel／洋服：ハンス・ブリンカー・ホテルのデザイン・ホテル・ブームへの参入をサポートしようと、超おしゃれな洋服ラインがプロデュースされた。各アイテムには同ホテルのデザイン目録からさまざまな作品をフィーチャー。たとえば、このおしゃれさん必携アイテムはユニセックスなデザイン・ベスト。

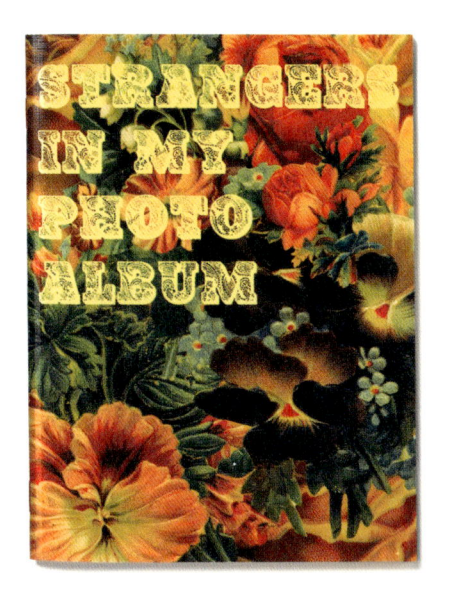

Strangers In My Photo Album, book
A photobook dealing with the appearance of complete strangers in the background of personal snaps. Here, these mysterious unwanted guests were foregrounded for the first time.
Strangers In My Photo Album／書籍：個人的なスナップ写真の背景に写りこんだまったく見知らぬ人ばかりを集めたフォトブック。本書により、ミステリアスな招かれざる客たちが初めて最前面に押し出された。

Helmut Dick, The Rising Dog, 2003

De HOND van Mr MOTLEY

Lees meer over Mr Motley in Mr Motley en op mistermotley.nl

Mr Motley, poster campaign
Mr Motley is a magazine for contemporary arts. A world around the mysterious Mr Motley was created using the artworks featuring in the magazine. Here we see details from that character's life, including Mr Motley's dog, drum kit and hobbies. As a result of this small scale campaign, subscriptions went up 30%.

Mr Motley／ポスター・キャンペーン：『ミスター・モトリー』は現代美術誌。掲載された芸術作品がミステリアスなミスター・モトリー・ワールドをつくりだしている。上図はミスター・モトリーの犬、ドラム・セット、趣味など、ミスター・モトリーというキャラクターの生活を詳細にレポートしたもの。この小規模なキャンペーンが功を奏し、定期購読者数が30％も上昇した。

2.49065 kilo

De NICHTJES van Mr MOTLEY
Lees meer over Mr. Motley in Mr. Motley en op mistermotley.nl

Het DRUMSTEL van Mr MOTLEY
Lees meer over Mr Motley in Mr Motley en op mistermotley.nl

De IMPRESARIO van Mr MOTLEY
Lees meer over Mr Motley in Mr Motley en op mistermotley.nl

De HOBBY van Mr MOTLEY
Lees meer over Mr Motley in Mr Motley en op mistermotley.nl

J&B, TV and cinema campaign
A series of commercials announcing J&B's intention of becoming the number one party whisky. To do so it enlisted the help of a giant mirror ball as its icon to persuade the world to Start a Party. The commercials showed party-goers rolling their own huge mirror balls through cities to prepare for celebrations on a fishing boat, a car-park roof and other unusual places.

J&B／テレビ、映画キャンペーン：パーティー用ウィスキーとしてナンバー・ワンになることを宣言するコマーシャル・シリーズ。シンボルとして巨大なミラーボールの力を借り、世界に「パーティーを始めよう」と説得するもの。コマーシャルでは、漁船や駐車場の屋根などのユニークな場所で開催される祝賀パーティーに備え、パーティー参加者が自分の巨大なミラーボールを転がしながら街を歩く。

J&B, print and poster campaign
The launch of the global Start a Party campaign continued on posters and billboards.
Each displayed the start of a party in unusual or spectacular locations, signalled by the arrival of a massive mirror ball.
J&B／紙媒体、ポスター・キャンペーン：ポスターやビルボードにも展開された、グローバルな「パーティーを始めよう」キャンペーンの立ち上げ。各広告が、ユニークかつ壮大な場所で巨大なミラーボールの到着を合図にパーティーが始まるようすを表現している。

START A PARTY

HOWEVER YOU START A PARTY
PLEASE ENJOY IT RESPONSIBLY

J&B, print and poster campaign
Another launch execution in the worldwide campaign for J&B. The campaign was developed to help own a specific area in the crowded market of night-time spirits brands – the start or anticipation before a party. An accompanying website, startapartyhere.com, used the digital possibilities to create a more user-generated party world, including a global agenda of the best parties to attend.

J&B／紙媒体＆ポスター・キャンペーン：グローバル・キャンペーン開始時のそのほかの広告例。このキャンペーンは、競争が激しいナイト・タイム・スピリッツ市場においてある特定の領域──パーティーの開始時、または、パーティー前の期待感──を確保することを目指したもの。そのウェブサイトstartapartyhere.comでは、デジタルの可能性が駆使され、参加すべき世界のベスト・パーティーといった、世界共通のテーマとなるコンテンツにより、ユーザー主導型のパーティー・ワールドが展開された。

2.50000 kilo

STARTAPARTYHERE.COM

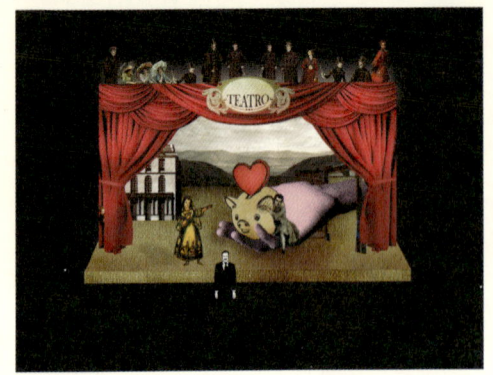

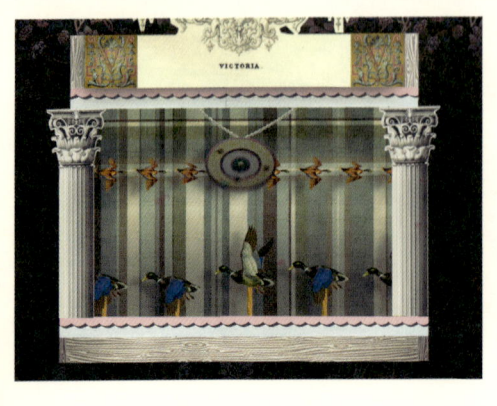

J&B, DVD
The heritage of J&B whisky consists of many surprising stories, including nights with the Rat Pack, evenings with Queen Victoria and a host of other monarchs and well-known figures. In this animated film, J&B's history is brought to life from 1749 to present times, for online viewing enjoyment.
J&B／DVD：J&Bウィスキーの歴史は、ラット・パック（＝50〜60年代に一世を風靡したフランク・シナトラなどの一団）やビクトリア女王など、数多くの王族やセレブの夜のお供になったという、驚くべき逸話で構成されている。インターネットで楽しめるこのビデオは、1749年から現在までの、同社の歴史を活き活きと描いている。

2.50467 kilo

J&B

42

J&B

JUSTERINI
&
BROOKS
STRICTLY SHOWBIZ

DESAYUNO
CON
DIAMANTES

LIQUOR
STORE
J&B.

INVENTIVE
SINCE
1749

YOU CAN PARTY BY WALTZING WITH
STRANGERS IN THE TAXI QUEUE.

— MIRROR BALL MAN

START A PARTY

HOWEVER YOU START A PARTY
PLEASE ENJOY IT RESPONSIBLY

J&B, print and poster campaign
Responsible drinking is a key message for J&B. It's so important that J&B created its own character, the Mirror Ball Man, to represent this vital function in a user-friendly way and without resorting to negative or off-putting messages. Posters showed the man with the mirror ball head giving tips on ways to party responsibly without losing out on the fun.
J&B／紙媒体、ポスター・キャンペーン：「責任をもって酒を飲むこと」はJ&Bにとって主要なメッセージ。ネガティブな印象や不快感を与えず、ユーザーに分かりやすい形でこの重要な命題を表現するために、「ミラーボール・マン」というキャラクターがつくられた。ポスターでは、ミラーボール頭の男が、楽しさをそこなわずに、責任をもってパーティーに参加するためのヒントを伝えている。

J&B, online films
The crusade of Mirror Ball Man continues digitally as he suggests different styles of responsible partying including 'partying with strangers, the stranger the better' above.
J&B／インターネット・ビデオ：ミラーボール・マンの改革運動はデジタル・メディアでも展開され、責任をもってパーティーに参加するためのさまざまなスタイルが提案された。上図のメッセージは「見知らぬ人とパーティーする。知らなきゃ知らないほどよい」

J&B, product
The Start a Party campaign's iconic mirror ball becomes yours to own, along with a branded party T-shirt and a bottle of the golden Scotch liquid which began it all.
J&B／商品：「パーティーを始めよう」キャンペーンのシンボルであるミラーボールがあなたのものに。オリジナルのパーティーTシャツと、すべての始まりの源である金色のスコッチ酒一瓶もついてきた。

2.51636 kilo

Claro, print campaign
The refreshingly clear brew from Dutch beer brand Bavaria took product over-selling as its theme, in a campaign that sought to include – contrary to the wishes of most communication agencies – as many logos as possible in a single image.
Claro／紙媒体キャンペーン：オランダのビール・ブランド、ババリアのすきっとクリアなビール「クラロ」のマーケティング・テーマは、商品を過剰に売り込むこと。そこでキャンペーンでは、ほとんどの広告代理店の意に反して、一点の画像にできるだけ多くのロゴをつめこむことが求められた。

Claro!
Claro!
Claro!
Refreshingly Clear
Claro!
By
Bavaria
Claro!
Claro!
hingly Clear

Bavaria, print campaign
The metrosexual man was once again shown the error of his aloe vera loving ways in this press campaign for the Dutch brewery. On consecutive pages, real men were depicted doing what real men do best. Above, the guy you always wanted to be wrestles a giant squid before barbecuing his vanquished foe. Bavaria beer provides satisfaction after the action.
Bavaria／紙媒体キャンペーン：オランダのビール会社の紙媒体キャンペーンは、アロエをスキンケアに使っているメトロセクシャルな男（＝外見などへの美意識が強く、スキンケアやファッションなどに時間と金を費やす男性）が間違っていることを再び見せつけた。「真の男」が、成すべきことをする男の中の男として、数ページにわたり、描かれたのである。上図では、理想的な男性が巨大なイカと格闘したあとに、打ち負かした敵をバーベキューにしているようすが描かれている。ババリア・ビールが、ひと仕事終えたあとの満足感を喚起している。

Zo.
Nu
eerst
een
Bavaria

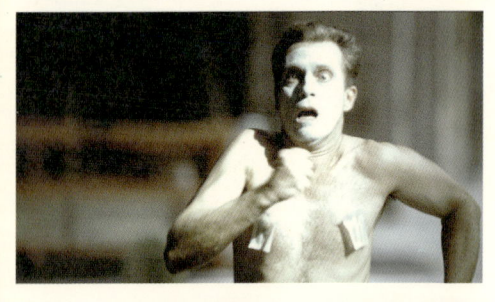

Bavaria, TV commercial
The Bavaria beer brand prides itself on a celebration of traditional masculinity (albeit in a rather tongue-in-cheek way) and in its fight against the onslaught of metrosexuality. This large-scale ad showed the power of the man's man to overcome all that crossed his path, from big mountains to emotions.
Bavaria／TVコマーシャル：バパリア・ビールは伝統的な男らしさをたたえること（といっても、どうも茶化している風ではあるが）と、メトロセクシュアリティの襲来と戦うことを、誇りとしている。その大規模広告キャンペーンでは、大きな山脈から自らの感情まで、行く手をはばむあらゆる障害を克服する、男の中の男のパワーが描かれた。

FEAR

Bavaria

Zo. Nu eerst een Bavaria.
Alcohol onder de 16, nog even niet.

Coffee Company, posters and cup designs
The Netherlands is largely coffee franchise-free. In their place is the home-grown Coffee Company, offering all kinds of coffee in all kinds of neighbourhoods. In this campaign, 'the shortest way to the tastiest coffee' is pointed out with maps on posters and takeaway cups so you can find your way to the next caffeine fix.
Coffee Company／ポスター、カップ・デザイン：オランダにはコーヒー・フランチャイズはほとんどない。その代わりとなるのが、地元の店、コーヒー・カンパニー。地元のあらゆるご近所向けに、あらゆるタイプのコーヒーを販売している。このキャンペーンでは、ポスターやテイクアウト用のカップに印刷された地図が「最高のコーヒーへの近道」を示し、コーヒーを飲みたくなったらどこへ行けばよいかがわかるようになっている。

Coffee Company
JACOBIJNERSTRAAT
OUDE EBBINGENSTR
19-31
MARTINI TOREN
GROTE MARKT
WAAGPLEIN
ZWANESTRAAT
GULDENSTRAAT
TUSSEN BEIDE MARKTEN
VIS MARKT
GRONINGEN
de kortste weg naar de lekkerste coffee

ROTTERDAM
Coffee Company
2
NIEUWE BINNENWEG
Metro
de kortste weg naar de lekkerste coffee

Coffee Company
RIJNSTRAAT
TURFMARKT
AMMUNITIEHAVEN
Coffee Company
BOTERINGESTRAAT
OUDE EBBINGENSTR
GROTE MARKT
ZWANESTRAAT
GULDENSTRAAT
TUSSEN BEIDE MARKTEN
VIS MARKT
MARKT
Coffee Company

Held, poster campaign
Everyone can be a hero in this campaign for the art exhibition Held (or 'Hero'). Posters featured ordinary folk in heroic poses, while plinths (like those seen here) were erected around the city so people could jump up and experience instant nobility.
Held／ポスター・キャンペーン：美術展「Held ＝ヒーロー」のキャンペーンでは、だれもがヒーローになれた。だれでも上に飛び乗って、手軽に崇高な気分が味わえるよう、街のあちこちに台座が設置されたのだ。ポスターは、英雄的なポーズを取る一般人の姿をフィーチャー。

7 2.53972 kilo

Ursus, TV commercial
Ursus is a flavoured vodka once big in Greece. In this large-scale commercial designed to revive the brand, a fantastical journey was undertaken to find 'nights less ordinary'. Mysterious baroque line-painting machines, red-suited mad hatters and a forest full of giant women in revolving dresses all pointed the way.

Ursus／TVコマーシャル：アーサスはかつてギリシャで大流行したフレーバー付きウォッカ。同ブランドの人気復活を目指した大規模なコマーシャル・キャンペーンでは、「不思議な夜」を探し求める幻想的な旅が展開された。神秘的なバロック調のライン塗装車、赤いスーツ姿のおかしな帽子屋、回転するドレスを着た大女だらけの森が道を教えてくれる。

7

2.54439 kilo

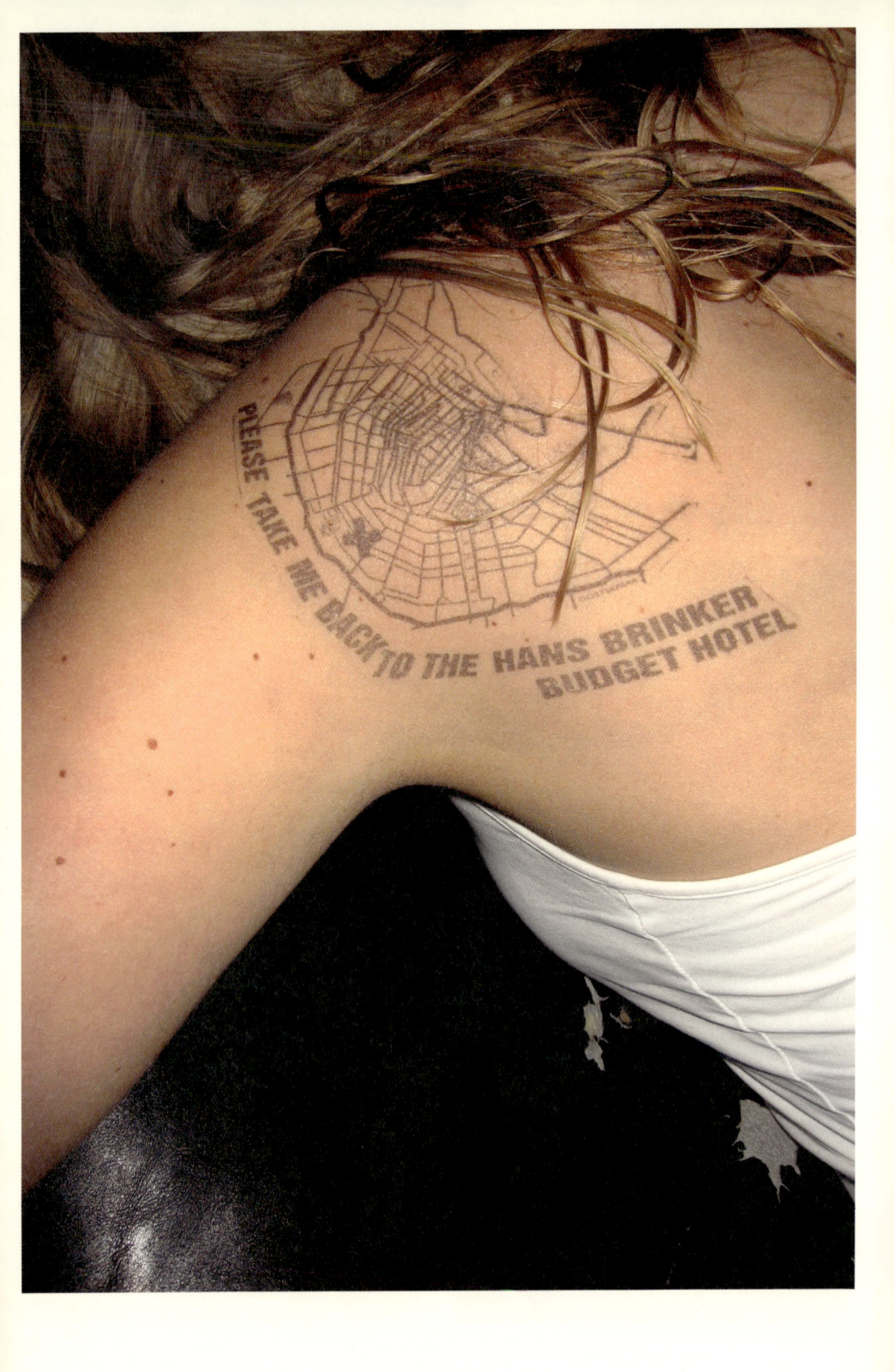

Hans Brinker Budget Hotel, stamp
The Brinker's often inebriated guests were offered a handy map-like stamp, allowing them to be returned to the grimy hostel after various substances had rendered their capacities of speech and orientation worthless.
Hans Brinker Budget Hotel／スタンプ：ハンス・ブリンカー・バジェット・ホテルでは、よく酔っ払う宿泊客の身体に地図のスタンプを押す。そのおかげで、こうした客は、さまざまな物質でろれつが回らなくなったり、方向感覚がなくなってしまっても、ほこりだらけのホステルに帰ってくることができるのである。

REAAL Insurance, stunt
Copy reads: '38% chance that someone will sit on your glasses'. Beneath this poster, the bus-stop bench has been turned into a giant pair of specs.
REAAL Insurance／大胆なプロジェクト：キャッチコピーは「あなたの眼鏡の上にだれかが座ってしまう可能性：38%」。ポスターの下では、バス停のベンチが大きな眼鏡に変わっている。

DAG, newspaper
One of the early issues of the Dutch free newspaper DAG, part of a news service that also offered 24-hour online and mobile reports. DAG translates as 'Day', 'Hello' or 'Goodbye'. Each meaning was put to good use in the masthead of the newspaper as well as communication. The paper, designed by Lava, made maximum use of a clean design and colourful imagery.

DAG／新聞：インターネットと携帯電話でニュースの24時間配信サービスも提供する、オランダの無料新聞の創刊間もないころの号。DAG には「日にち」「こんにちは」「さようなら」の意がある。それぞれの意味は、新聞などの題字で効果的に活かされた。ラヴァがデザインした上図の号は、すっきりしたデザインとカラフルな写真が最大限に活かされている。

DAG, brand manual
A guide to working with DAG, plus its philosophy explained, in the form of a Dagboek, or diary.
DAG／ブランド・マニュアル：「Dagboek＝ダイアリー」の形になっている DAG の作業ガイド。その哲学も説明されている。

2.55374 kilo

2.55607 kilo

Waater, product design and branding
Waater is a brand of table water from Bavaria, the Dutch brewery known in other communication as the beer for real men. Bavaria wanted to communicate its high quality, something which could be attributed to the pure water obtained from its own spring, but without encroaching on its butch image.
Waater／プロダクト・デザイン、ブランディング：男の中の男のためのビールの宣伝で有名なババリアのミネラルウォーター・ブランドWaater。ババリアが求めたのは、同社のマッチョなイメージを損なわずに、自社所有の泉からとれる純水にふさわしいハイクオリティなイメージを宣伝することだった。

0

Waater, product design and branding
Instead of an ad campaign, the beer brand was persuaded to take the unusual step of introducing water as a product, to feed the information in an alternative way to consumers. Waater was first launched at the best restaurants and later at all good supermarkets nationwide. The unique bottle, complete with water rippling effect, was designed by Frank Tjepkema.
Waater／プロダクト・デザイン、ブランディング：このビール・ブランドは、ミネラル・ウォーターを商品としてデビューさせる際に異例の手順を踏むことになった。それは、広告キャンペーン以外の方法で消費者に向けて情報発信するという戦略。Waaterは、はじめに高級レストランでデビューしたのちに、国中の高級スーパーマーケットで売り出された。さざ波を模したユニークなボトルは、フランク・ティプケマのデザインによるもの。

2.55841 kilo

2.56075 kilo　バンコクに出場した女性たちの写真コレクション。右図はハンカチにプリントされた写真をおさめた限定版のボックス・セット。

bangkok beauties

Bangkok Beauties, book
A photography book collecting images discovered in Bangkok featuring women from a long-forgotten beauty contest. The right-hand image is a limited-edition boxset in which the images were printed on handkerchiefs.
Bangkok Beauties／書籍：バンコクで見つけた、遠い昔に開催された美人コンテストに出場した女性たちの写真コレクション。右図はハンカチにプリントされた写真をおさめた限定版のボックス・セット。

2.56075 kilo　　　　　　　　　　　　　　　　　　　　　　　　　　0

bangkok beauties

erik kessels

Queen, Bitch, Queer, poster
Poster advertising a show from drag-queen legend Vera Springveer. Its call to action appealed to those with an appreciation for both rocking and male genitalia.
Queen, Bitch, Queer／ポスター：伝説のドラッグクイーンのショーを宣伝するポスター。ショーへの参加を呼びかけるそのデザインは、ロック音楽＆男性生殖器というコンセプトを深く理解する観客にアピールした。

Concreet, branding
House style for Concreet, an independent company offering marketing strategy advice.
Concreet／ブランディング：独立型マーケティング戦略コンサルティング企業、コンクリートの自社ツール。

Dutch Theatre, poster, print and TV campaign
Campaign by a syndicate of The Netherlands' finest theatres persuading individuals to leave behind their daily routines and lose themselves in front of the stage. A TV commercial showed various empty and desolate scenes including a tennis court and shopping mall.
Dutch Theatre／ポスター、紙媒体、TVキャンペーン：オランダ最高レベルの劇場で構成された組合によるキャンペーン。人々に日常から離れて、舞台の前で我を忘れるよう呼びかけている。TVコマーシャルでは、テニス・コートやショッピング・モールなどがもぬけの殻になっているようすが描かれた。

7 2.57243 kilo

Dutch Theatre, poster, print and TV campaign
A continuation of the campaign for The Netherlands' theatres with advice especially targeted at homebound families. It shows images of abandoned situations, deserted as everyone involved has decamped to the theatre.
Dutch Theatre／ポスター、紙媒体、TVキャンペーン：オランダの劇場キャンペーンのそのほかの例。家族のなかでも特に家から離れられない層をターゲットにしている。上図は、関係者がそっと劇場に向かってしまったため、家事が放棄されているようすを表したもの。

2.57710 kilo

CUT BY SHAMPOO PLANET

PRINSENGRACHT 489 AMSTERDAM +31204206412

Shampoo Planet, poster
The long-running campaign for local hairdressers, Shampoo Planet, continues. In this case, a yeti-like creature with a perfectly chopped mane helps explain the extreme nature of the cuts on offer.
Shampoo Planet／ポスター：地元の美容院、シャンプー・プラネットのロングラン・キャンペーン。ふさふさした毛を完璧に切り刻まれたイエティのような生物が、おすすめカットの特徴の説明に一役買っている。

On Hold at KesselsKramer, CD
Callers to KesselsKramer occasionally find themselves put on hold. When this occurs, they are treated/subjected to a range of helpful/bizarre recordings featuring pool-cleaning services and pizza-delivery advertisements (amongst others). This CD allowed those whose calls were answered immediately to enjoy the advantages of being On Hold at KesselsKramer.
On Hold at KesselsKramer／CD：ケッセルスクライマーに電話してくる人はときどき電話口で待たされることがある。そんなとき、役に立つ（けれどヘンテコな）録音がそんな人々をもてなしてくれる（無理やり聞かされる）。その内容は、プール清掃サービスや宅配ピザの広告など、さまざま。このCDは、電話口で待たされなかった人のために、「ケッセルスクライマーに電話して待たされた」ときのすばらしさをすぐに味わえるようにしたもの。

2.58178 kilo

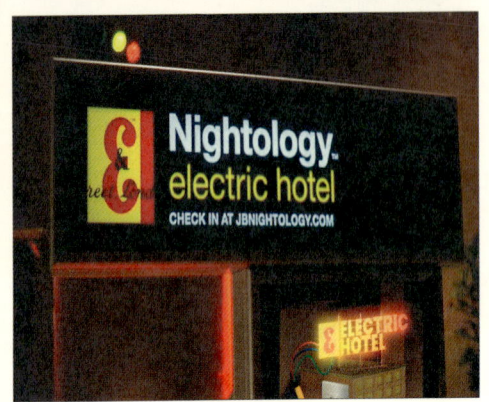

J&B, online films

Filmic invites designed to support the Electric Hotel, a series of parties in Spain hosted by J&B whisky in which the rooms in hotels were given over to acts and live performances. These films demonstrated that the party was powered by the energy of its guests, and showed unlikely contraptions designed to free this power, including a frantic drummer, a young woman on a treadmill escaping from homemade bees or a man in a giant hamster wheel.

J&B／インターネット・ビデオ：スペインでJ&Bが主催したパーティー・シリーズ「エレクトリック・ホテル」を宣伝するビデオ。このパーティーのために複数のホテルがショーやライブ・パフォーマンス用に部屋を提供。これらのビデオでは、パーティーが観客のエネルギーによって盛り上がるようすや、その盛り上がりをさらに高めようと用意された、ありえないような仕掛けが披露された。それはどんなものかというと、狂ったドラマー、作り物のハチから逃げようとルームランナーのベルトの上を走る若い女性、巨大なハムスター用の回し車に入り込んだ男といったもの。

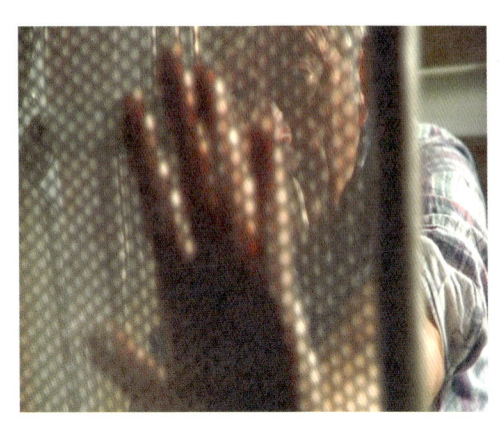

7

2.58645 kilo

TRUE, brand identity
Name, communications, packaging and website for a rose bred to be bigger, more beautiful and long-lasting than any other, available in New York's finest florists.
TRUE／ブランド・アイデンティティ：ニューヨークの高級花店で販売されている、大輪で、美しく、しかも長持ちするバラの品種のための名称設定、宣伝、パッケージング、ウェブサイト制作。

TRUE.

PTT post, poster and stamps
It used to snow in Holland. Nowadays, winter is a continuation of summer, in that it just rains some more. Made for the Dutch postal service, these stamps were an attempt to redress that balance with a letter based snowstorm blanketing the country. They totalled some 20 million, meaning that the man-made blizzard reached every corner of The Netherlands.
PTT post／ポスター、切手：かつてオランダにはよく雪が降った。最近の冬は、雨が増えたという点では夏とそう変わらなくなっている。オランダ郵政局のために制作されたこれらの切手は、手紙という吹雪で国全体をおおうことにより、そのバランスを正そうとする試み。この切手の合計発行枚数は2000万枚ほどに達したが、これは、人口の猛吹雪がオランダの隅々にまで行き渡ったことを意味する。

7

2.59579 kilo

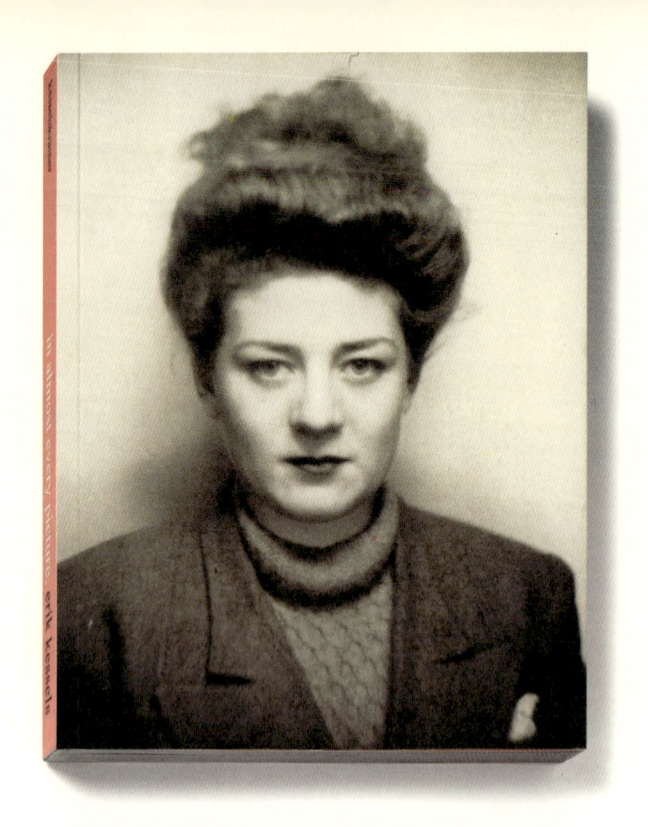

in almost every picture #6, book
The series showcasing found photography continues with a series of self-portraits spanning a lifetime. The woman in this book took passport-style images of herself from the age of sixteen up until her late middle age. Eventually, the story simply ends without explanation, begging the question: what happened to our heroine?
in almost every picture #6／書籍：ファウンド・フォトを紹介するシリーズの第6号では、生涯にわたり撮影された一連のセルフ・ポートレートが取りあげられた。これは、16歳から中年の後半になるまで自分の写真をパスポート・サイズで撮り続けた女性のもの。写真は最後になんの説明もないまま途絶えてしまう。ヒロインになにが起こったのか？という疑問を残したまま。

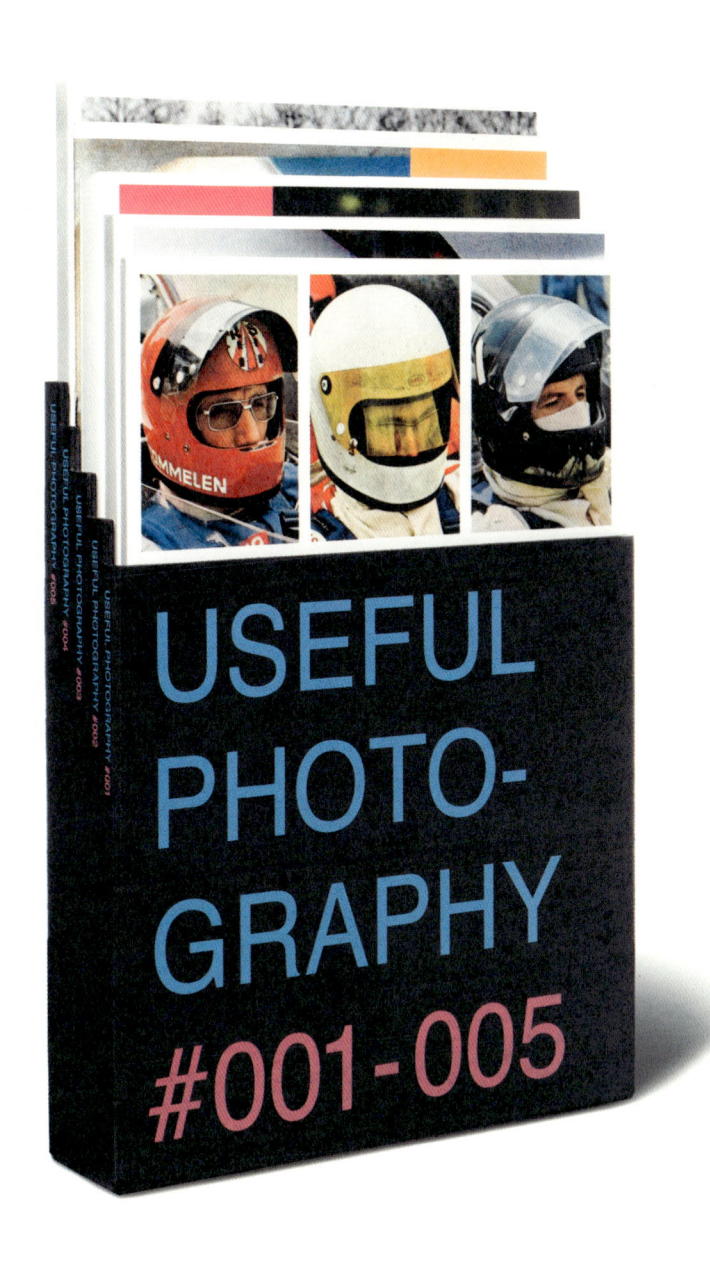

Useful Photography, magazine box set
A collection of Useful Photography, the magazine celebrating generally uncelebrated photography. This limited edition boxset contained all five magazines produced up until 2005.
Useful Photography／雑誌ボックス・セット：無名の写真をたたえる雑誌『ユースフル・フォトグラフィ』のセット。この限定版ボックス・セットには2005年までに制作された1〜5号すべてが入っている。

2.60047 kilo

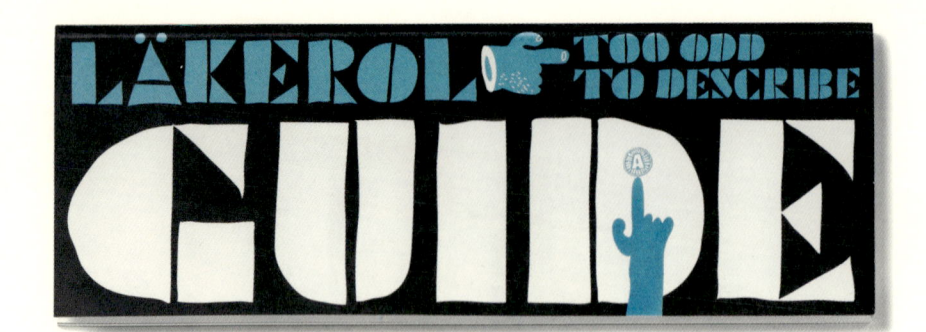

Läkerol, brand book
A brand book for a range of small Swedish sweets whose unusual taste is beyond the power of words to describe.
Lakerol／ブランド・ブック：スウェーデンの小さなお菓子のためのブランド・ブック。このお菓子の味は、言葉では説明できないほど独特である。

Läkerol, poster campaign
How can one categorize the uncategorizable? Läkerol explores the sheer impossibility of defining its product.
Lakerol／ポスター・キャンペーン：カテゴライズできないものを、どうやったらカテゴライズできるというのか？レイクロールは、その商品の定義がまったくできないという点をさらに追求している。

Läkerol, poster campaign
More executions exploring Läkerol's hard-to-pin-down taste.
Lakerol／ポスター・キャンペーン：特定困難なレイクロールの味を探るさらなる試み。

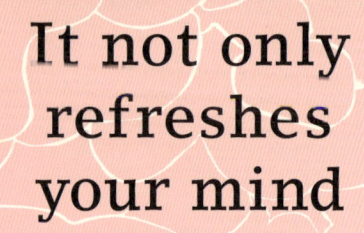

It's not
a candy
and it's
not a mint
Läkerol
SUGARFREE PASTILLES
BLUE FRUITS
LÄKEROL,
TOO ODD
TO DESCRIBE
www.lakerol.com

Läkerol, TV campaign
In television, Läkerol continues to completely avoid any useful description of what the weird little sweet actually tastes like and instead shows what it doesn't taste like – being brushed by a mint for example, or licked by a long-tongued lollipop.

Läkerol／TVキャンペーン：テレビではあいかわらず、この変わった小さなお菓子が実際どんな味がするかについては一切の説明が避けられていた。その代わりに、ミントにブラシをかけられたり、舌の長い棒付きキャンディにベロッとなめられたりして、こういう味はしない、という例が示された。

7

2.61449 kilo

AROMA

DELICATE

J&B, print and poster campaign
In this work for J&B in Spain, the whisky asked artists and illustrators to visualize its most important product claims. The claims appeared in pairs linked by J&B's ampersand, a symbol Spanish people immediately associate with the brand.
J&B／紙媒体、ポスター・キャンペーン：スペインのJ&Bの広告のために、芸術家とイラストレーターに、このウィスキーの最も重要なセールス・ポイントのビジュアル化が依頼された。その後、セールス・ポイントは、スペインの人々がJ&Bブランドをすぐに思い浮かべるシンボルである「&」をはさんでペアで登場した。

TASTE

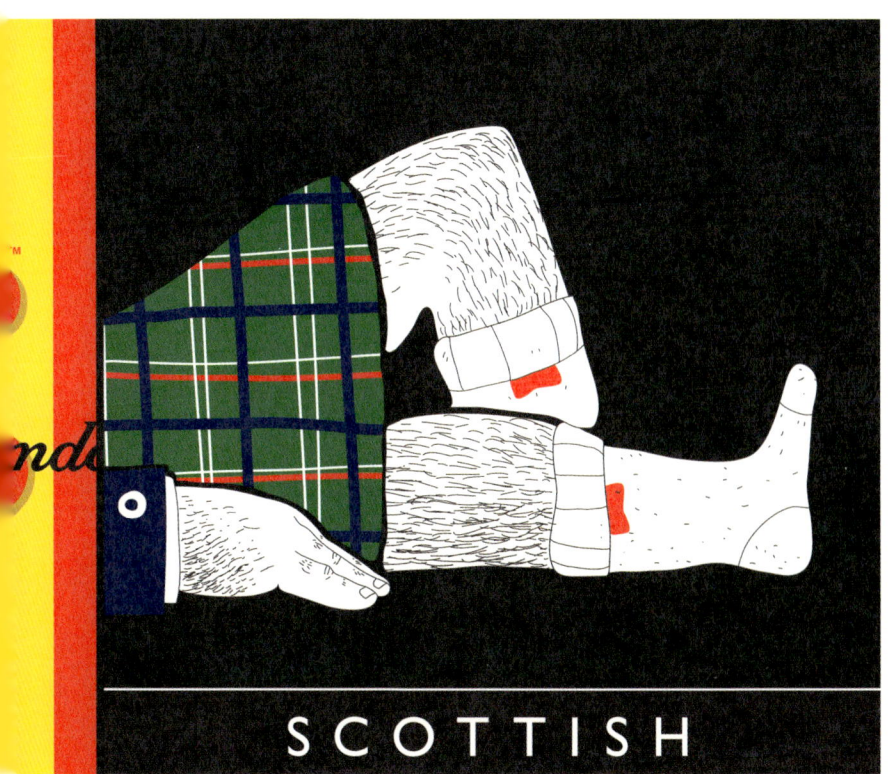

SCOTTISH

SNS Bank, booklet
Produced in order to promote an SNS scheme which encouraged customers to keep their money in a savings account for longer. After one year, interest rates became even more attractive, meaning your money made yet more money. The very honest idea behind this booklet was that keeping your hands off your cash for a year might be tough: in order to make things easier, a series of tongue-in-cheek tips were created.

SNS Bank／小冊子：顧客にむけて、より長期間、口座に預金しておくことを勧める銀行の戦略を推進するための小冊子。この1年後、金利はより魅力的になり、お金がさらにお金を生むこととなった。この小冊子の真のコンセプトは、自分のお金に一年間も手をつけないことは難しいため、一連のおふざけヒントを作って、それをより気楽にできるようにする、というものだった。

zo kan het ook:

geld moet rocken

SNS Bank, print, poster and event
Great bands made the otherwise tedious queue for the cash machine into a live street concert. SNS also sponsored a music festival to continue its theme of money that both rocked and rolled (a play on the Dutch idiom 'money must roll,' meaning 'make the most of your cash').
SNS Bank／紙媒体、ポスター、イベント：すばらしいバンドが、ともすれば退屈しがちなATMの順番待ちを、ストリート・ライブ・コンサート会場に変えた。また当銀行は、お金に関する自社テーマであるロックド&ロールド（「お金は転がすもの」を意味するオランダの熟語をもじったもので「お金を最大限に活かせ」の意）を貫くため音楽フェスティバルも後援した。

2.62617 kilo

Waar begin je in vredesnaam met het oplossen van het klimaatprobleem?

Hier, print campaign
Climate-change is a global problem, yet each of us can make a difference with changes in our daily behaviour. 'Hier' is a campaign from several Dutch foundations who want to encourage climate awareness by asking people to start with themselves. Copy reads: 'Where do you begin to solve our climate problems?'

Hier／紙媒体キャンペーン：気候の変動は世界的な問題だが、我々ひとりひとりが日常の行動を変えることで変化をもたらすことができる。「Hier＝ここ」は、自分から行動を起こすよう人々に呼びかけて気候への意識向上を目指す、オランダのいくつかの基金が実施するキャンペーン。キャッチ・フレーズは「気候問題の解決に向けて、どこで行動を起こしますか？」

Hier, print campaign
The answers to the question on the left-hand page came in the form of these subsequent print ads. Large format stickers show that 'here,' wherever you are, there's something you can do to help. The ads point to the 'hier' website which gave specific examples of ways to help combat climate change.

Hier／紙媒体キャンペーン：左ページで提起された問題の答えは、その次ページに掲載された広告で提供された。大判のステッカーが、あなたがどこにいようとも、あなたが支援に向けてなにか行動できるのは「ここ」であることを示している。また広告にそのアドレスが載っているHierのウェブサイトでは、気候変動と戦うのに役立つ具体的な例をあげている。

2.62850 kilo

Waar kun jij wat doen aan het klimaatprobleem?

hier

Hier, print campaign
Copy reads: 'Where can you do something to solve the climate problem?' The answers are all around: save energy by using your appliances wisely.
Hier／紙媒体キャンペーン：キャッチ・フレーズは「気候変動の問題の解決に向けて、どこで行動を起こしますか？」。その答えは「そこらじゅう」。電化製品を賢く使って、エネルギーを節約しよう。

Het oplossen van een groot probleem begint vaak met kleine dingen. De televisie niet op stand-by laten staan bijvoorbeeld. Maar gelukkig sta je er niet alleen voor. Hier is een initiatief van 45 goede doelen. Op dit moment werken al veel van hen op tientallen plaatsen over de hele wereld aan het klimaatprobleem. Op www.hier.nu lees je wat deze projecten inhouden en wat jij hier nog meer kunt doen.

Hier, extra materials
Stickers for the 'hier' campaign, allowing people to mark the objects in their everyday lives that can help alleviate our planet's pressing problems, from light switches to television standby buttons.
Hier／紙媒体キャンペーン：Hier キャンペーンのステッカーがあれば、照明のスイッチからテレビの待機ボタンまで、日常生活で対象となるものに印をつけることができ、地球の差し迫った問題にわずかながら対処できる。

hier begint het

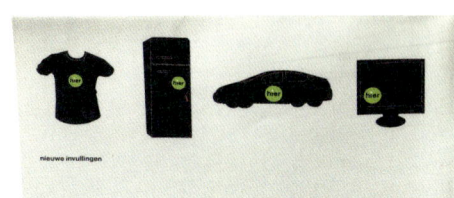

Hier komen we binnenkort overal tegen. Hier is het symbool van iedereen die werkt aan het klimaatprobleem. Goede doelen, bedrijven en overheden. En van jou. Hier laat zien wat we samen kunnen doen. Hier is een beweging, een merk, dat zich als een positief virus over de hele wereld verspreidt.
Het probleem: klimaatverandering. Het klimaat verandert, daar is iedereen het wel over eens. Maar wat is het probleem? Overal op de wereld krijgen we steeds meer te maken met de nadelige gevolgen. Zoals ongebruikelijke droogtes, hittegolven, extreme regenval, overstromingen en zeer krachtige orkanen. Dit leidt weer tot meer armoede, meer ziektes en meer conflicten, bijvoorbeeld over de schaarse vruchtbare grond of over water.
Waar moet je beginnen? Waar ligt de oplossing van dat enorm grote klimaatprobleem? Niet daar ergens ver weg, maar hier. Bij ons. Wij kunnen iets doen. En andere dingen juist laten. Er is nog meer goed nieuws: je staat er niet alleen voor. Hier gaan we samen iets aan dat klimaatprobleem doen. Deels door de oorzaken terug te dringen, bijvoorbeeld door energiebesparing. Deels door ons aan te passen aan de gevolgen, bijvoorbeeld via natuurbescherming en ontwikkelingssamenwerking.
Hier is overal. Het klimaat verandert wereldwijd. Van de Noordpool tot de Zuidzee. Van Nicaragua tot Nepal. En van het rijke Westen tot de arme landen in Afrika. Er lopen al tientallen projecten om in Nederland en in andere landen (de gevolgen van) de klimaatverandering aan te pakken. Zo zijn we hier in Nepal actief met de bescherming tegen smeltende gletsjers. Het Wereld Natuur Fonds realiseert onder meer een 'early warning system' dat waarschuwt bij catastrofale uitbarstingen van volgelopen meren. En hier in Nederland promoot Greenpeace spaarlampen om thuis energie te besparen. En hier op de West-Kaap (Zuid-Afrika) helpen we arme boeren die door de droogte zijn getroffen bij de overstap naar droogtebestendige olijfteelt.
Wat iedereen kan doen. Het klimaatprobleem is enorm groot. Maar als iedereen een paar kleine maatregelen neemt, kunnen we samen grote successen boeken. Ook als 'gewone Nederlander' kun je meedoen. Bijvoorbeeld door spaarlampen en een waterbesparende douchekop te kopen. Door een hybride leasebak te nemen in plaats van een diesel. En door groene stroom te kiezen.
Hier wordt steeds meer zichtbaar. Hier kom je tegen in onder andere advertenties en radiocommercials. En op www.hier.nu vind je onder meer tips, informatie van de goede doelen en links naar andere websites over het klimaatprobleem. Het hier-logo zal ook steeds vaker op straat en in winkels opduiken. Want bedrijven die klimaatvriendelijke producten op de markt brengen, mogen het hier-logo gebruiken.
Meedoen? Neem dan contact op met hier: 030 234 8209 of info@hier.nu

Hier, extra materials
Manifesto for 'hier' explaining how every individual has the power to solve climate problems, by paying closer attention to the way we go about our daily lives.
Hier／紙媒体キャンペーン：日常生活の過ごし方に注意を傾けることによって、いかに個人個人が気候問題を解決する力を発揮できるかを説明する Hier のマニフェスト。

2.63785 kilo

do change

do change, editorial
This manifesto for change from 'do' appeared in a book about the brands of tomorrow. The article put forward an argument for habit-breaking actions including 'use your living-room window instead of the front door' and 'change your name for different occasions'.
do change／エディトリアル：未来のブランドに関する書籍に登場した、変化に関する do のマニフェスト。この記事は「玄関ドアの代わりにリビングルームの窓を使おう」や「状況に応じて自分の名前を変えよう」といった、習慣をくつがえす行為に関する議論をもちかけている。

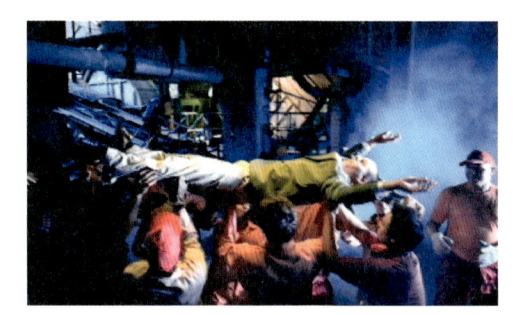

SNS Bank, TV commercial
This commercial for an investment-fund service from SNS Bank used the very unbusinesslike metaphor of crowd-surfing to depict an investor moving easily and swiftly from one fund to another.
SNS Bank／TVコマーシャル：銀行の投資ファンド・サービスのコマーシャル。クラウド・サーフィング（＝客席にダイブしたミュージシャンなどを大勢の観客が手を伸ばして一緒に支え、頭上を移動させること）というあまりビジネス・ライクではないメタファを使って、あちらのファンドからこちらのファンドへとすいすい移動する投資家を表現している。

SNS REAAL
is beursgenoteerd
Dank je wel

De beursgang van SNS REAAL is succesvol verlopen. En dat hebben we aan veel mensen te danken. Niet alleen aan diegenen die de afgelopen maanden zo hard hebben gewerkt aan de voorbereiding van onze beursnotering, maar aan iedereen binnen dit bedrijf. Onze bedrijfsonderdelen laten namelijk op zowel commercieel als financieel gebied goede cijfers zien. Door onze gezamenlijke inspanningen en aansprekende resultaten is dit een bedrijf geworden waar consumenten in durven te vertrouwen. En in durven te investeren. We willen je daarom hartelijk bedanken voor je bijdrage. Nu gaan we met nog meer slagkracht de toekomst in. Met jouw hulp groeien we door. Ga je mee?

Bedankt namens de Raad van Bestuur,
Sjoerd van Keulen

SNS REAAL, print campaign
The Dutch service provider in insurance and banking was being floated on the stock exchange. A wide ranging campaign including, print, TV, radio and outdoor used the colourful metaphor of butterflies to suggest shares being freed up for the public.
SNS REAAL／紙媒体キャンペーン：オランダの保険と銀行業に関するサービス企業が証券取引所に上場。紙媒体、テレビ、ラジオ、屋外などを利用した幅広いキャンペーンで、一般公開株を表現するため、蝶のカラフルなメタファが用いられた。

zaterdag 20 mei 2006 · SNS REAAL Beurs Genoteerd PAGINA 5

HET VOORWERK

Prospectus wordt nachtwerk

Voor elke beursgang wordt een prospectus gemaakt, waarin heel veel informatie staat die voor beleggers van belang kan zijn. Het is dus geen nieuws dat er voor de beursgang van SNS REAAL ook een is opgesteld en gedrukt. Maar dit is wel het dikste prospectus dat tot dusver in Nederland is gemaakt, in de hoogste oplage ooit. En dat mag wel in de krant.

Salesforce briefing groot succes

ZEIST, 2 en 3 MEI – Dinsdag 2 en woensdag 3 mei waren niet alleen zonnige dagen, maar ook zeer informatieve. De verkopers van Rabobank, ABN AMRO en SNS REAAL werden geïnformeerd over de beursgang van SNS REAAL en hun rol daarin.

Kris Kras Klaar

Kris Weltevrede

Tussenpersonen handelen met kennis

SNS REAAL, TV commercial
A ninety-second commercial announces the IPO of insurance and banking group SNS REAAL, marked by the symbolic arrival of thousands of butterflies in a city centre.
SNS REAAL／TVコマーシャル：保険／銀行グループの新規株式公開を知らせる90秒のコマーシャルでは、街の中心に無数の蝶が象徴的に到来した。

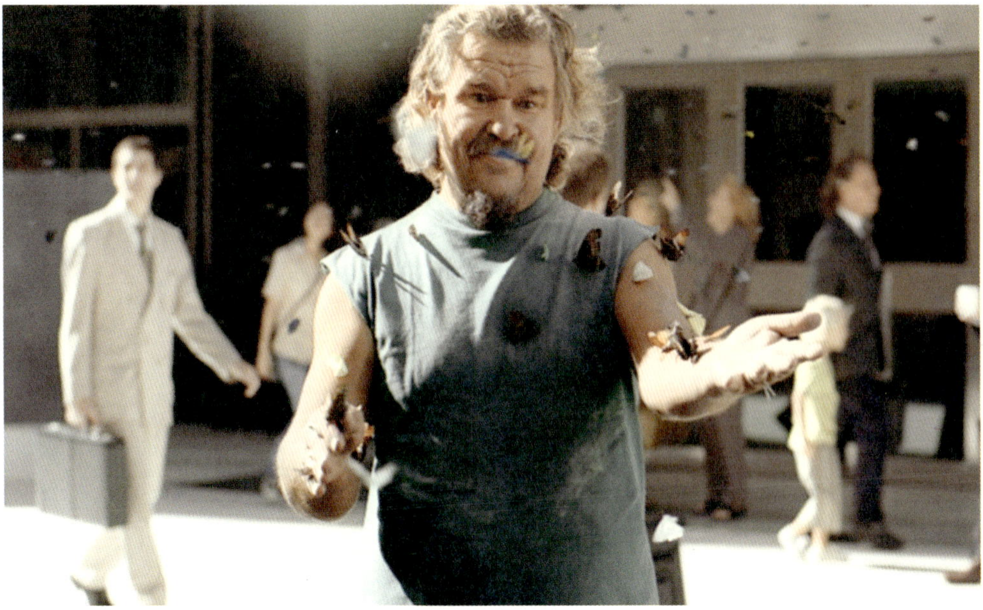

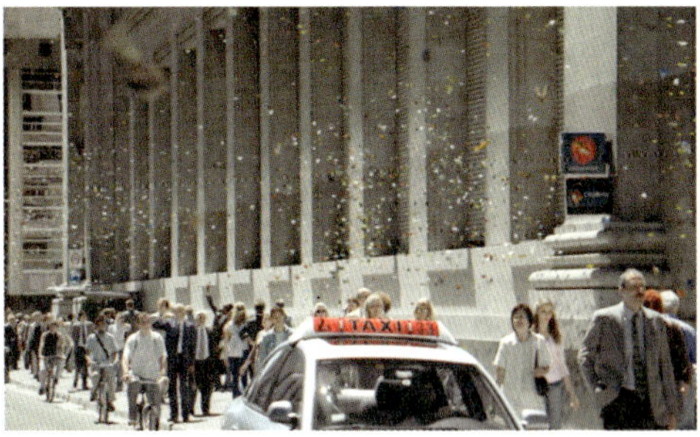

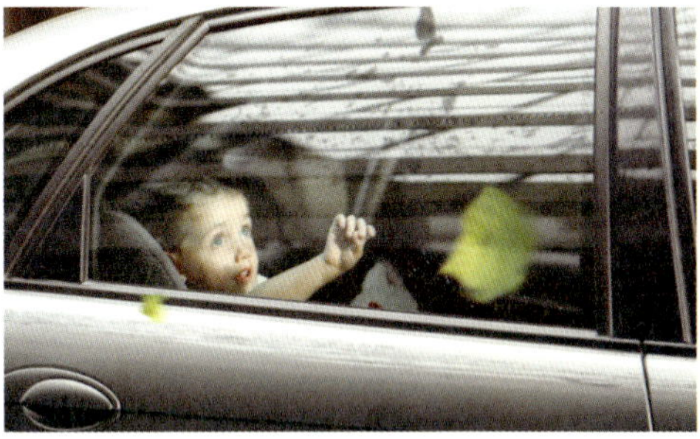

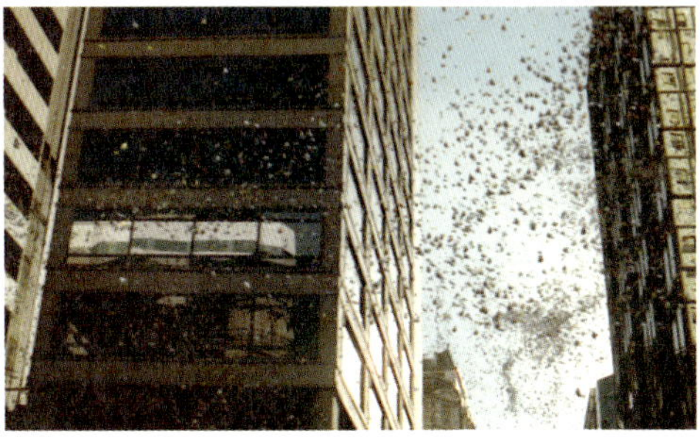

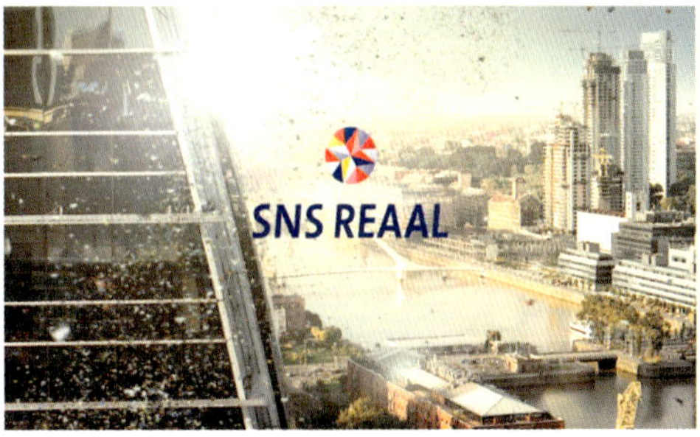
SNS REAAL

in almost every picture #5, book
The fifth edition of the found photography series features a special and photogenic dog. Over the course of many years, the lives of dog and owner are intertwined in a series of homemade shots that illustrate the touching bond between people and pets.
in almost every picture #5／書籍：ファウンド・フォト・シリーズの第５巻はフォトジェニックな特別な犬を取り上げた。自家製の素朴な写真の一枚一枚に人とペットのあいだのしみじみするような絆がにじみでており、長年にわたり、犬と飼い主の人生がつながりあっていたようすが見て取れる。

2.65654 kilo

Wakker Dier, TV commercial
'Wakker Dier' (literally 'awake animal') is a Dutch idiom meaning one who is paying attention. The phrase was borrowed as the name of an organization campaigning for more humane treatment in factory farming. In the films, the comedian who plays the Dutch Ernie presents horrifying facts about animal slaughter while posters back up the campaign's main message: eat at restaurants approved by 'Wakker Dier.'

Wakker Dier／TVコマーシャル：「Wakker Dier＝目覚めた動物」は、「注意を払う者」を意味するオランダの慣用句。この言葉は、工場式の畜産において、より人情味のある処理を行うためのキャンペーンを実施している組織の名に使われた。そのビデオでは、オランダでセサミ・ストリートのアーニー役を務めるコメディアンが動物の食肉処理に関する恐ろしい事実を語る。他方でポスターはキャンペーンの主要メッセージ「Wakker Dierが承認したレストランを利用しよう」を宣伝。

Wakker Dier, poster campaign
Translation of these posters include: 'No factory farming on the menu' and 'Don't eat castrated pigs'.
Wakker Dier／ポスター・キャンペーン：これらのポスターの見出しには「工場式畜産場からの肉はメニューにはありません」「去勢された豚を食べないで」などがある。

2.66121 kilo

Bob Fosko, poster
Image communicating Dutch artist Bob Fosko's tour of the country's theatres.
Bob Fosko／ポスター：オランダのアーティスト、ボブ・フォスコの全国劇場ツアーを宣伝。

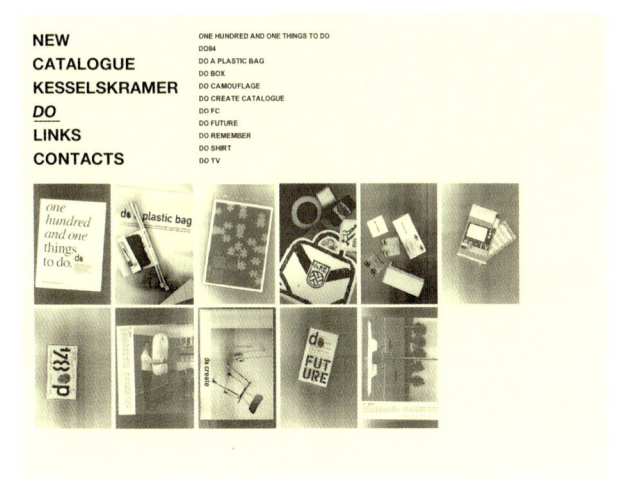

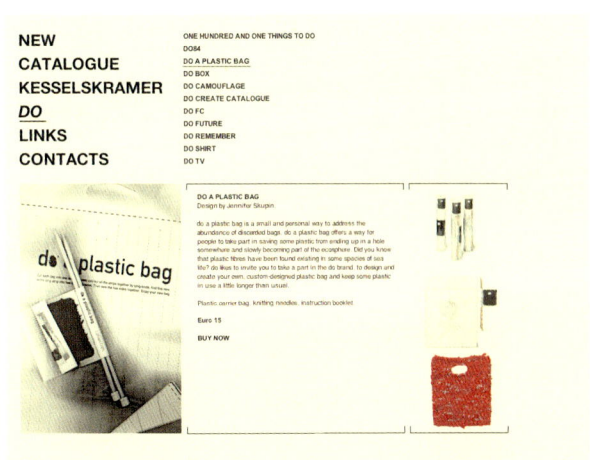

KK Publishing, website
All of KesselsKramer's books and products collected on kesselskramerpublishing.com.
Also contains a webshop for all your photobook needs.
KK Publishing／ウェブサイト：ケッセルスクライマーの書籍や商品はすべてkesselskramerpublishing.comにまとめられている。また、写真集が欲しい人のあらゆるニーズに応えられるよう、ウェブショップも備えてある。

2.66589 kilo

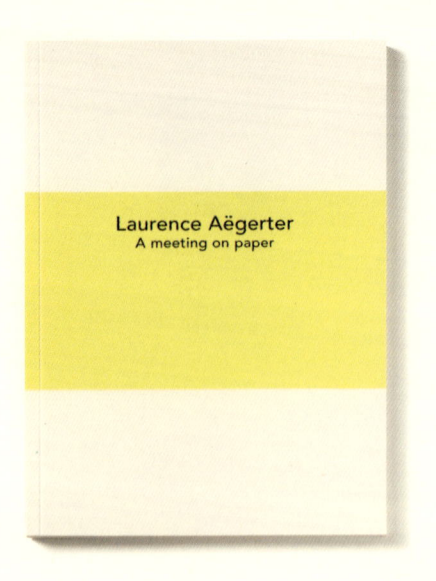

NEROC'VGM, book
The continuation of a series of creative meetings to help explain the world of digital-image management company, NEROC'VGM. In this edition, artist Laurence Aegerter juxtaposes images and words from encyclopaedias, apparently at random, giving both new meaning. For instance, a castle becomes a 'generator' and the coliseum becomes 'communism.'
NEROC' VGM／書籍：デジタル画像管理会社のサービスを説明するための「クリエイティブな出会い」シリーズ。本号ではアーティストのローレンス・エージャーターが百科事典から引いた画像と言葉をランダムに並置することにより、両方に新しい意味を与えている。たとえば、城は「発電機」、コロシアムは「共産主義」に。

NEROC'VGM, book
Another creative meeting, this time from Claude Closky. The book comprises a series of images in which natural objects meet man-made ones. The natural object represents a question, and the artificial one provides an answer.
NEROC' VGM／書籍：「クリエイティブな出会い」シリーズのほかの例。今回とりあげたのは、クロード・クロスキーのチョイス。同書は自然界に存在するものと人工的につくられたものが出会う一連の画像で構成されている。自然界のものが問いを発し、人工的なものが答えを出している。

2.67056 kilo

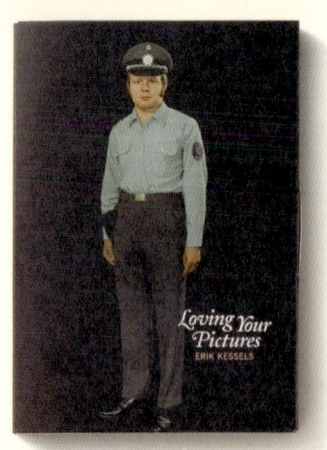

Loving Your Pictures, postcard book
'Loving Your Pictures' was an exhibition encompassing eight photo series of anonymous photographers. This set of thirty postcards allowed visitors to take them home for further inspection.
Loving Your Pictures／ポストカード・ブック：『ラビング・ユア・ピクチャーズ』は匿名の写真家による8つの写真シリーズの展覧会。この30枚のポストカード・セットにより、訪問者は写真を家に持ち帰って、さらにじっくりと鑑賞することができる。

Loving Your Pictures, poster
Poster for exhibition taking place at the Centraal Museum Utrecht, showing images which weren't intended as 'works of art' but which could now be seen in a new context.
The image was taken from the first 'in almost every picture', a book showcasing images found at a Barcelona flea market.
Loving Your Pictures／ポスター：ユトレヒトのセントラール美術館で開催された展覧会のポスター。展示写真は、もともとは「芸術作品」として撮影されたものではないが、今や新しいコンテクストをまとっている。これらの写真は、バルセロナの蚤の市で偶然見つけた写真をまとめた『in almost every picture＝ほとんど、どの写真にも』の第1巻から選ばれたもの。

2.67523 kilo

Loving Your Pictures, exhibition
This scene is taken from the multi-roomed vernacular photography exhibition. This particular space displayed giant-sized photo cubes of various family portraits collected from wildly different sources, all collected and edited by Erik Kessels.
Loving Your Pictures／展覧会：複数の部屋で構成される、日常を撮影した写真展の1シーン。この特別なスペースには、さまざまな家族写真でできた大きな立方体が展示されている。これらの写真はエリック・ケッセルスがあちこちから集め、編集したもの。

2.67757 kilo

2.67991 kilo

Loving Your Pictures, exhibition
This exhibition collects an eclectic variety of images from photo albums and other amateur and semi-amateur sources. Amongst them, a life-sized parade of 70s German police uniforms and projections of deer seen through the lens of a hunter's camera. Taken together they make artworks out of photos never intended to be seen as such.
Loving Your Pictures／展覧会：アマチュアやセミ・アマチュアが撮影した写真アルバムから幅広くコレクションした展覧会。特筆すべきは、70年代にドイツで撮影された制服姿の警官の等身大のパレードや、狩人のカメラを通して見たシカの映写など。総じて、どんなビジュアルにするか意図して撮られていない写真が、芸術作品となっている。

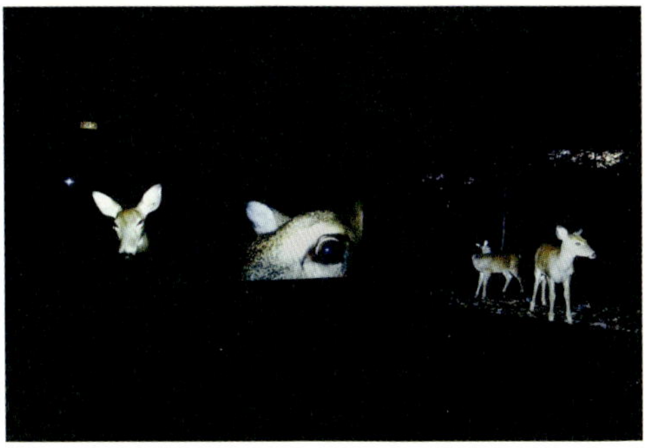
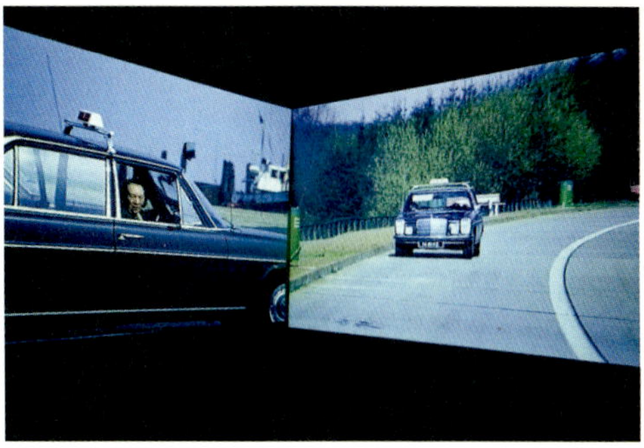
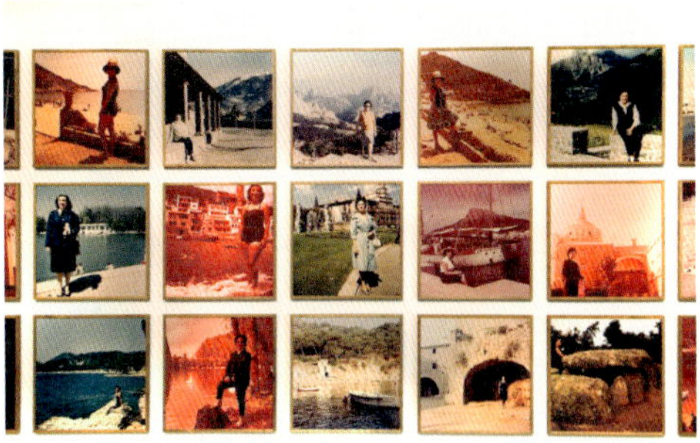
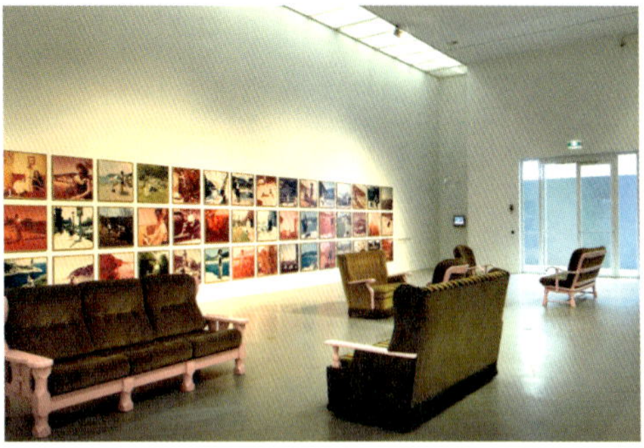
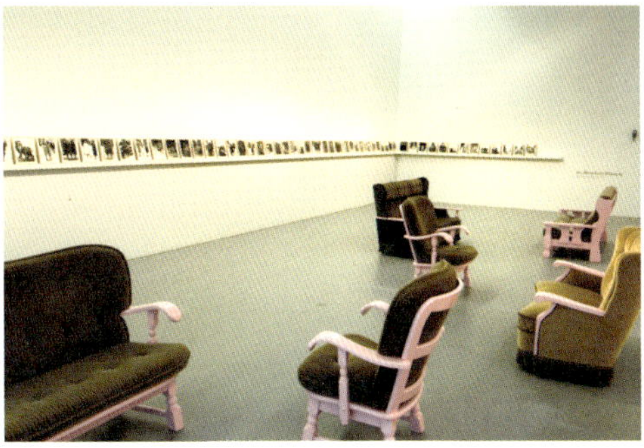
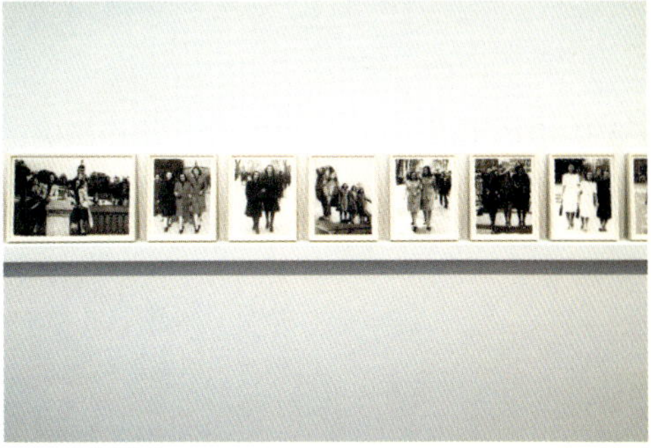
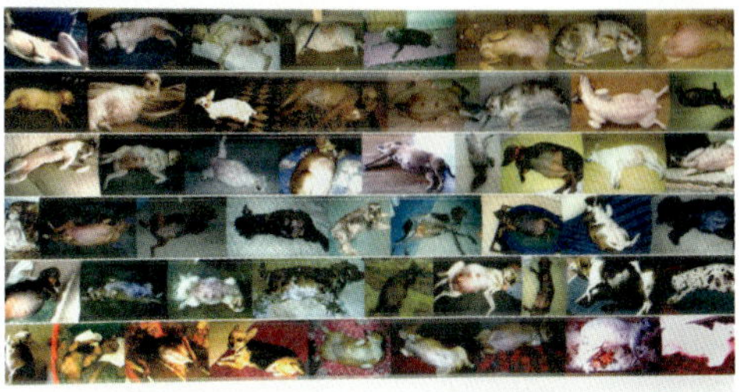
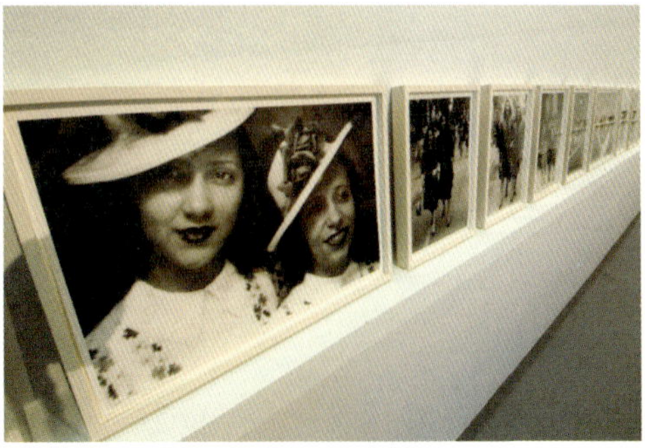

Fruit Shoot, poster
Copy-driven poster in praise of children's boundless imagination. The product, Fruit Shoot, is a drink inspired by kids' complex fantasy lives.
Fruit Shoot／ポスター：子どもたちの果てしない想像力をたたえたメッセージ中心のポスター。フルート・シュートは、子どもたちのにぎやかな空想でいっぱいの生活に着想を得た商品である。

Fruit Shoot, TV commercial
Imagination is the central theme for the launch of this natural fruit juice for children.
A living room is seen through a child's eyes and is transformed into the high seas by means of thousands of balls.
Fruit Shoot／TVコマーシャル：この子ども向けナチュラル・フルーツ・ジュース発売にあたっての中心的テーマは、イマジネーション。子どもの目から見たリビング・ルームが、無数のボールでできた大海原に変わっている。

2.68925 kilo

2.69159 kilo

one hundred and one things to do, book
A collection of the work and the story so far of KesselsKramer's own brand, do. The products herein are alternately useful, pointed and bizarre, but all are underpinned by do's philosophy of asking its consumers to participate in their creation or completion.
one hundred and one things to do／書籍：ケッセルスクライマーのブランド do のこれまでの作品と歴史をまとめた書籍。do の商品には便利なものもあれば、とっぴなものやヘンなものもある。しかし、すべてが一貫した do の哲学に裏打ちされている。その哲学とは、消費者に、商品の創作、あるいは完成までの過程に参加してもらうこと。

0

one hundred and one things to do, book
These spreads show products from do's enormous range, suggested and produced by various contributors from around the world. As well as those featured above, do appeared in the form of a 'green hand grenade', stuffed with seeds designed to fertilize depleted urban areas, and plates made out of other broken plates.
one hundred and one things to do／書籍：世界中のさまざまな協力者から提案・制作してもらった、do の膨大なコレクションの商品を紹介した見開きページ。上図の商品以外にも、都会の枯れ果てた土地を肥沃に変えるための種が詰めこまれた「グリーン手榴弾」や、割れたお皿で作ったお皿などがある。

2.69393 kilo

2.69626 kilo

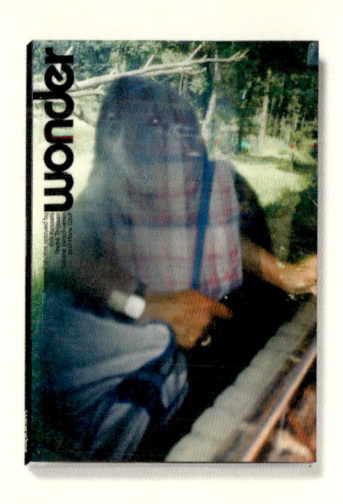

Wonder, book
A book that sees beauty where others see mistakes. In these images, technically flawed photos are showcased for their strange and striking effects. Made in collaboration with Andre Thijssen, Sabine Verschueren and Hans Wolf.
Wonder／書籍：普通は失敗と見られる部分に美を見出すための本。上図では、技術的に問題のある写真が不思議で印象的な効果をかもしている。アンドレ・テイツセン、サビーネ・フェルシューレン、ハンス・ウルフとのコラボレーションで制作。

0

Bad Food Gone Worse, book
Food photography from restaurants and takeaways is given the chance to shine like too much grease in a deep-fat frier. Strangely enough, these images were designed to make your mouth water, but their effect is (more often than not) only to make your stomach turn.
Bad Food Gone Worse／書籍：レストランやテイクアウトの料理写真が、大きい揚げ物鍋にたっぷりと入った油のような輝きを放つチャンスを与えられた。これらの画像は、鑑賞者がよだれをたらすほどおいしそうに撮るはずだったのが、不思議なことに（ほとんどが）げっぷしか出ないような写真に。

Useful Photography, exhibitions
Useful Photography is the magazine that takes pride in photography for practical purposes. It's been exhibited internationally, from Antwerp to Manchester's CUBE gallery (pictured above).
Useful Photography／展覧会：『ユースフル・フォトグラフィ』は実用的な写真をテーマとすることに誇りをもつ雑誌。アントワープから、マンチェスターのキューブ・ギャラリー（上図）まで、国際的な展覧会も開催している。

KK Outlet, poster
Poster communicating the opening of KK Outlet, an exhibition at the Kunsthal Rotterdam
and the name later used for KesselsKramer's hybrid London office. The exhibition showcased
the communication agency's diverse work output over ten years.
KK Outlet／ポスター：ロッテルダムのクンストハル美術館で開催された展覧会「KKアウトレット」のオープニングを宣伝するポスター。この展覧会名は、のちにケッセルスクライマーのハイブリッドなロンドン・オフィスの名として使われた。展覧会では10年以上にわたって制作された、広告代理店としてのさまざまな作品が紹介された。

2.70327 kilo

KK Outlet, exhibition

Two floors of the Kunsthal in Rotterdam were given over to display KesselsKramer's work, the first time a communications agency had the honour of appearing at the renowned museum. Fashion collections, magazine spreads in shelves, giant logos and book-filled vending machines helped turn the gallery space into a one-off outlet for all manner of communication.

KK Outlet／展覧会：ロッテルダムにあるクンストハル美術館の２フロアーがケッセルスクライマーの作品展示に提供された。広告代理店がこの有名な美術館で展覧会を開催する栄誉にめぐまれたのは、初めてのことである。ギャラリー・スペースには、ファッション・コレクション、巨大なロゴ、本の自動販売機が置かれ、棚には雑誌の見開きページが並べられ、あらゆる形態のコミュニケーション・ツールを販売する一度限りの直売所、アウトレットになった。

6

2.70794 kilo

KK Outlet, exhibition
One floor of the Kunsthal Rotterdam exhibition was used to hang an assorted collection of posters. The lower floor felt like a strange and sophisticated pop-up store, with branded boxes displaying old TVs showing commercials, short films and documentaries.
KK Outlet／展覧会：クンストハル美術館の展覧会では、1フロアは種々雑多なポスター・コレクションの展示に使われた。その下のフロアは、洗練されてはいるが、不思議な期間限定ショップのような雰囲気で、ブランド名が付された箱にコマーシャル、ショート・ビデオ、ドキュメンタリーを上映する古いテレビが飾られた。

2.71028 kilo

2.71262 kilo

USEFUL PHOTOGRAPHY #006

Useful Photography #006, magazine
The sixth edition of Useful Photography collects examples of the oldest trick in the advertising book: the before and after shot. Shaving cream, buildings ravaged by warfare and various beauty treatments are all depicted using these simple two-step stories.
Useful Photography #006／雑誌：『ユースフル・フォトグラフィ』の第6号は、広告の手引書で説明される最古の技「ビフォア&アフター写真」の例をコレクション。髭剃りクリーム、戦争で破壊されたビル、さまざまな美容術など、すべてがこのシンプルな2ステップ手法で表現されている。

2.71495 kilo

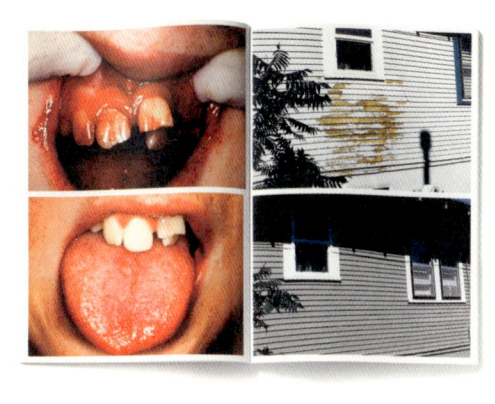

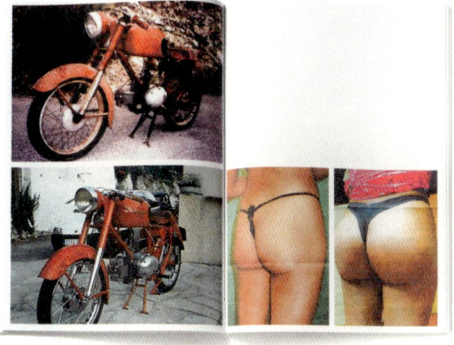

6

2.71729 kilo

Sultana, TV campaign
Sultana is a small biscuit with superior saving powers. Attacks of sudden hunger were declared by small puppets erupting from people's tummies. The creatures would then attempt to entice the individuals towards unhealthy snacks. Sultana Support to the rescue.
Sultana／TVキャンペーン：スルタナは小腹を満たす小さなビスケット。お腹から飛び出してくる小さなパペットが、突然の空腹感が攻撃してきたことを宣言。その後、この生き物は不健康なおやつを食べろ、と人々をそそのかす。そこに、このビスケット、スルタナ・サポートが登場して空腹から救い出した。

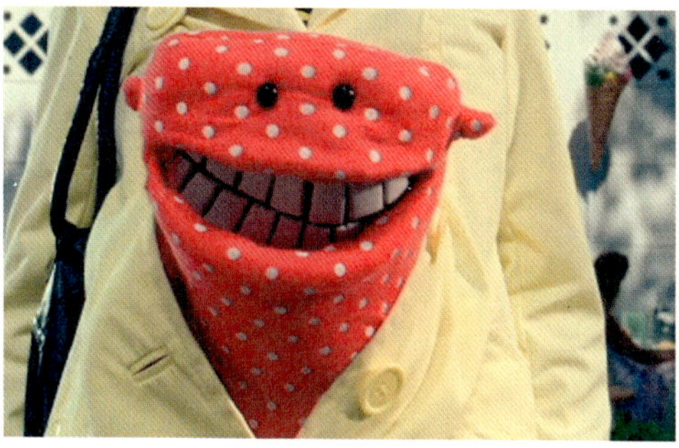

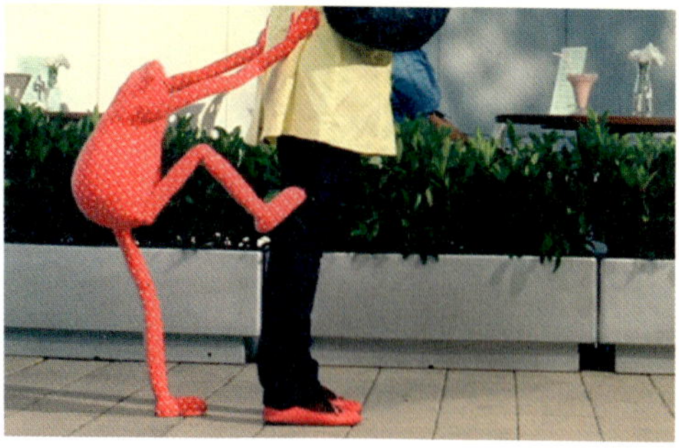

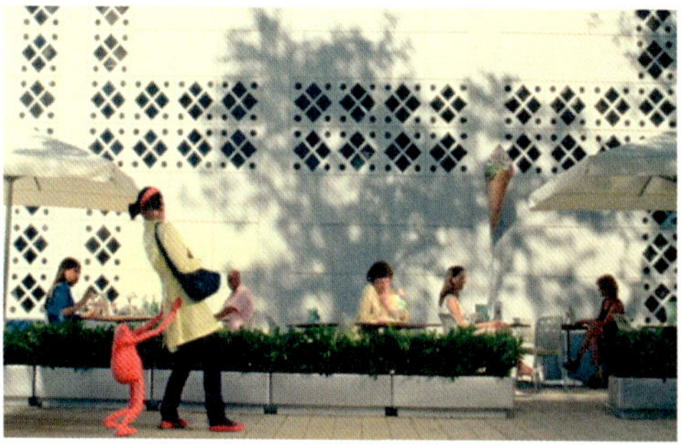

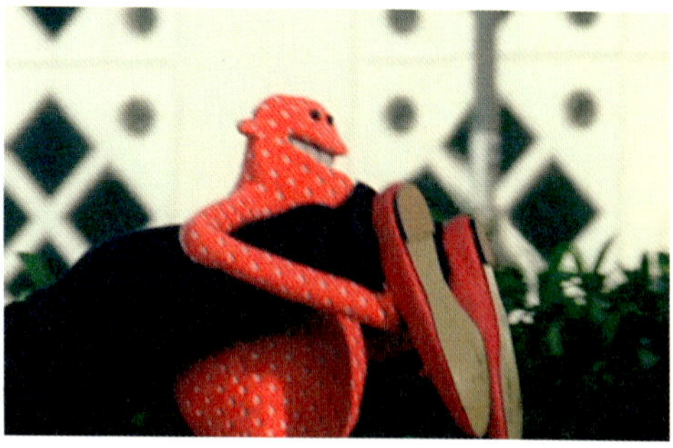

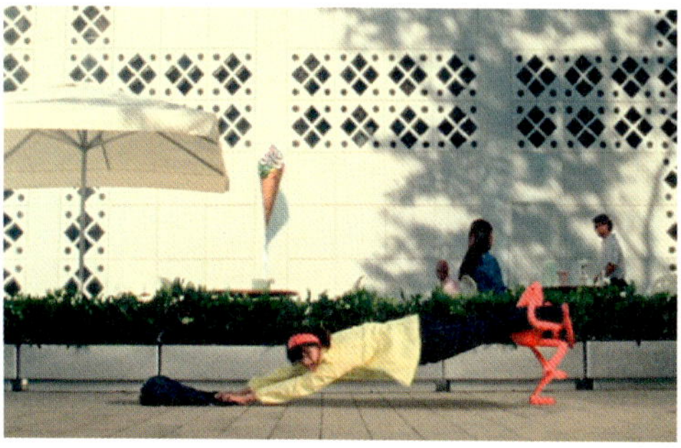

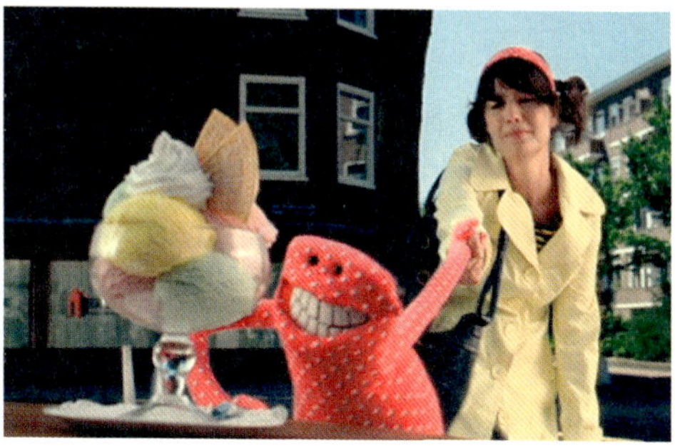

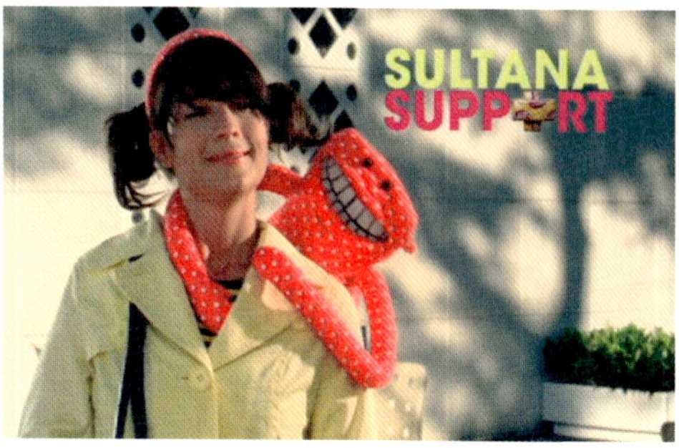
SULTANA
SUPP RT

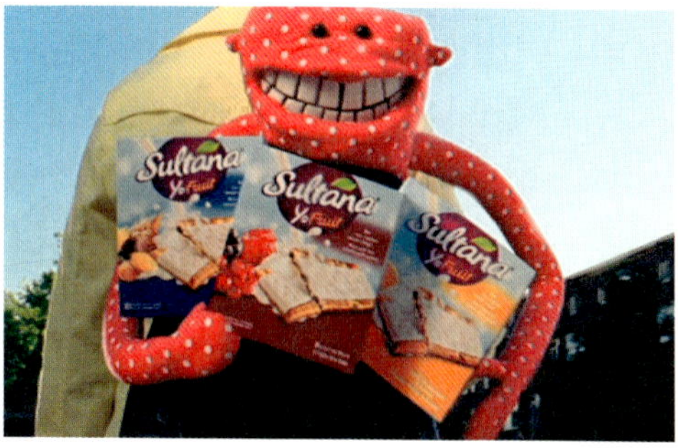
Sultana
Sultana
Sultana

Sultana, poster campaign
New flavours of the Sultana biscuit are presented by strange puppets with mischievous grins.
Sultana／ポスター・キャンペーン：いたずらっぽい笑みを浮かべたヘンテコな
パペットが、スルタナ・ビスケットの新しいフレーバーを紹介。

NIEUW:
SULTANA YOFRUIT VOLKOREN APPEL

mod. 110 "Padre Pio"

mod.118 "Bordo Oro Fiori"

mod. 719 "Orchidea"

Antwerp Photo Museum, editorial
A Useful Photography style spread for another photo magazine whose theme was 'Lost and Found.' The images are from an Italian coffin company who advertised its wares by bringing sex and death closer than may be appealing to the majority of people.
Antwerp Photo Museum／エディトリアル：「失い、見つけること」をテーマに『Useful Photography』風のスタイルで作成した、写真雑誌の見開きページ。この写真はセックスと死を接近させることで商品を宣伝しようとしたイタリアの棺桶メーカーのもの。しかし、接近させすぎて、ほとんどの人にアピールしなかったもよう。

mod. 112 "Viti a scomparsa"

mod. 218 "Love Divi

2.73131 kilo

Radio 1, TV commercial
Radio 1 is the channel for news and sport, including World Cup football coverage.
On the left, the report of a goal being scored by the Dutch national team brings intense and spontaneous joy to a football fan and reluctant dog walker- so much so that he spins the animal skyward during his celebrations.
Radio 1／TVコマーシャル：ラジオ1は、ワールド・カップのサッカー試合などを放送するニュースとスポーツの専門チャンネル。左ページでは、オランダ代表チームがゴールを決めて得点したという報道を聞き、犬の散歩代行の仕事をいやいやしていたサッカー・ファンの男が元気づけられ、大喜びしている。しかし得点を祝っている最中に興奮のあまり犬を空へと吹っ飛ばしてしまう。

2.73364 kilo   0

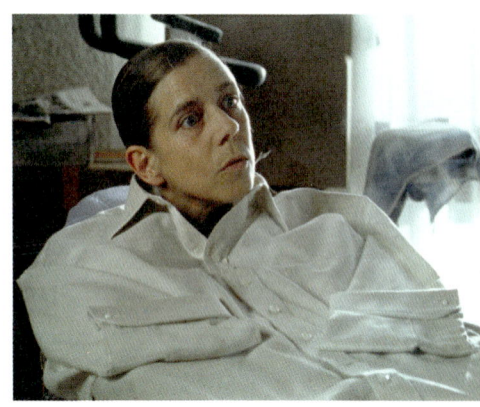

Radio 1, TV campaign
To communicate a new service by Radio 1 – news headlines every quarter hour to keep you constantly up to date – a series of commercials shows listeners being startled by the sudden arrival of the news while attending to their lawn or ironing.

Radio 1／TVキャンペーン：15分ごとに最新ニュースの見出しを流す、ラジオ1の新サービスを宣伝するコマーシャル・シリーズ。芝刈りやアイロンがけをしている最中に突然のニュースに驚かされるリスナーたちを描いている。

6

2.73598 kilo

Absolut, PR materials and underwear collection
A continuation of Absolut Label, the fashion project cementing the vodka brand's commitment to the fashion world. An annual fashion collection was created with a team of up-and-coming designers briefed to produce a single item of clothing – in this case, underwear, based on an Absolut-inspired theme.
Absolut／PR媒体、下着コレクション：ケッセルス・クライマーが長年手がけている、ウォッカ・ブランドとファッションの世界を結びつけようとするファッション・プロジェクト「アブソルート・レーベル」。今回は新進気鋭デザイナー・チームの各人が一点ずつ洋服を制作する、年に一度のファッション・コレクション。テーマはアブソルートから発想した下着だった。

2.74065 kilo

Absolut, PR materials and underwear collection
This particular collection was inspired by 1879, the year of Absolut's inception. The photographs took the theme of a 19th-century masked ball to show off the undergarments, each of which contained a motif, detail or shape from the famous bottle.
Absolut／PR媒体、下着コレクション：アブソルートが誕生した年である1879年に着想を得た特別なコレクション。写真は19世紀の仮面舞踏会をテーマに撮影され、それぞれの下着には有名なボトルのモチーフ、細部あるいは形が取り入れられている。

Absolut, catalogue and underwear collection
Absolut Label took the form of a limited-edition fashion collection, sent to designers, stylists and magazine editors to be used in their own editorials. A guide was completed to help the brand managers in each country get to grips with the concept and throw the appropriate fashion shows.
Absolut／PR媒体、下着コレクション：アブソルート・レーベルは限定版のファッション・コレクションという形態をとり、デザイナー、スタイリスト、雑誌編集者に、担当する媒体でそのファッションを使ってもらおうと情報提供。各国のブランド・マネージャーがコンセプトをきちんと把握して、アブソルートにふさわしいファッション・ショーが開催できるよう、ガイドが作成された。

Tarwebiscuit met echte chocolade

Verkade, poster campaign
Verkade is a Dutch brand of biscuits and chocolate that has been satisfying hunger since the 1800s. During this early period, the term 'de meisjes van Verkade' or 'the girls from Verkade' was used to collectively name the workers at the biscuit factory. This campaign revived the motto as a symbol of power and positive female bonding.

Verkade／ポスター・キャンペーン：フェァカーデは、1800年代から人々の空腹を満たしてきた、オランダのビスケット&チョコレート・ブランド。発売当初は「de meisjes van Verkade＝フェァカーデの女たち」という用語が、そのビスケット工場の作業者たちの総称として使われていた。本キャンペーンでは、この言葉を、パワーと女性の積極的な団結のシンボルとして、現代によみがえらせた。

*Saluti! Stracciatella
met stukjes chocolade*

*Saluti! Cappucino
met stukjes chocolade*

*Saluti! Caramello
met stukjes caramel*

*Filipinos. knapperig
met chocolade*

Verkade, TV campaign
No subject is too taboo or emotional for the girls from Verkade. Commercials show women discussing critical subjects of life, love and cookies with tears, laughter and even anger or frustration.
Verkade／TVキャンペーン：フェァカーデの女たちにタブーはなく、感情表現の激しさもとどまるところを知らない。コマーシャルでは、女性たちが人生、愛、クッキーにまつわる重要なテーマについて、涙を流したり、笑ったり、ときには怒ったりしながら話し合った。

2.75467 kilo

zo kan het ook:

altijd weten waar uw geld is

SNS Zakelijk Internet Bankieren
Als ondernemer wilt u natuurlijk bij de tijd blijven. En dan helpt het als uw bank dat ook is. Daarom verwerkt SNS Bank uw betalingen real time. Uw bij- en afschrijvingen zijn dus direct zichtbaar. Nog meer bijzonders: met SNS Zakelijk Internet Bankieren kunt u al uw rekeningen beheren, ook die bij andere banken. En we hebben ondernemers nog veel meer te bieden. Bel voor meer informatie 0900 – 18 90 (lokaal tarief) of kijk op snsbank.nl/zakelijk

SNS Bank, print campaign
Ads for the Dutch bank that appeared as a two-page set in one magazine. Each highlighted a different aspect of SNS's service. On the first page, the image of a man searching through his briefcase appears under the headline 'It can also be like this: always know where your money is'. On the second, the line reads: 'It can also be like this: the highest interest rates for businesses'.

SNS Bank／紙媒体キャンペーン：一冊の雑誌につき2ページがセットになった、オランダの銀行のための広告。ページごとに、SNS銀行のサービスの異なる局面を説明している。初めのページでは男がブリーフケースのなかを探っている。その見出しは「こんなこともあります：お金がどこに入っているか、いつも把握しておきましょう」。次のページの見出しは「こんなこともあります：事業にとって最も有利な金利です」

zo kan het ook:

de hoogste zakelijke spaarrente

...et Supersparen
...drijf? Precies, geld verdienen.
...eten dat u als ondernemer
...gste zakelijke spaarrente van
... noemen het niet voor niets
... Supersparen. Zo kunt u geld
...g heeft lekker laten groeien.
...nemers nog veel meer te
...er informatie 0900 – 18 90
...op snsbank.nl/zakelijk

SNS Bank

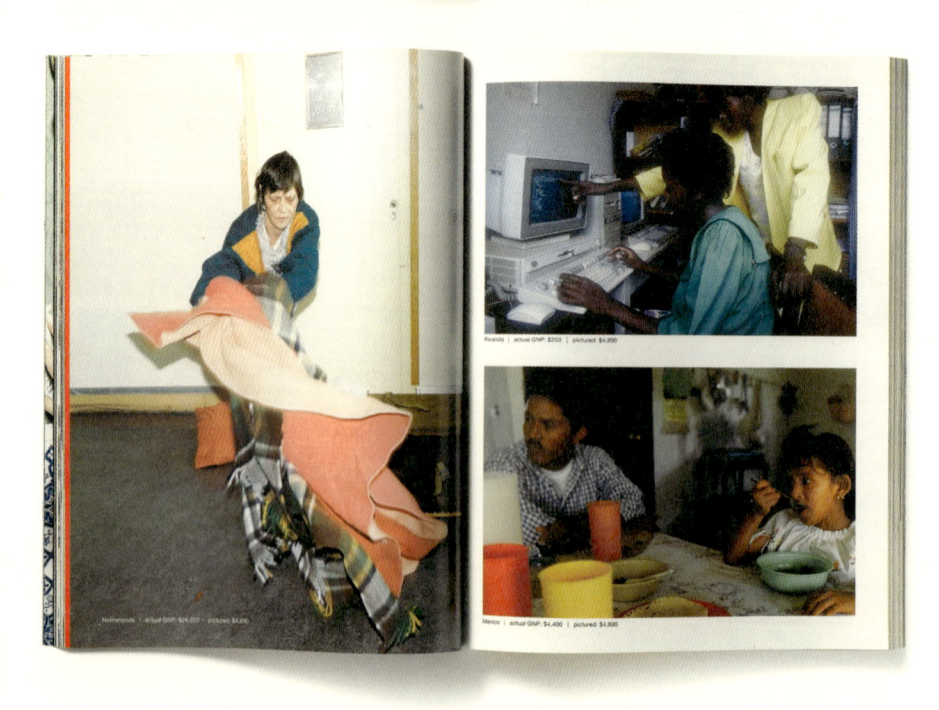

do, editorial
The ever-changing brand 'do' was asked to contribute to a style magazine which gave over its entire issue to the subject of Africa. 'do share' imagined what would happen if the planet's entire GNP was split equally and with every single living person, rich or poor.
do／エディトリアル：つねに変化し続けるブランド do が、1号分まるごとアフリカを特集するスタイル雑誌への寄稿を求められた。「do share＝共有しよう」と題された記事では、地球全体のGNPが、金持ち、貧乏人を問わず、どんな人にも均等に分けられたらなにが起こるかが想像された。

2.76402 kilo

MTV Japan, poster campaign
Campaign for MTV Japan's annual music video awards consisted of music listeners transforming into futuristic instruments as a visual and sonic demonstration of music's ability to impact people in various ways.
MTV Japan／ポスター・キャンペーン：MTVジャパンが毎年開催するミュージック・ビデオ・アワードのキャンペーン。人々にさまざまな形でインパクトを与える音の力を、視覚的、聴覚的に表現するため、未来的な楽器に変身する音楽ファンを登場させた。

TRANSFORM JAPAN FOR THE MTV VMAJ 06

2.76869 kilo

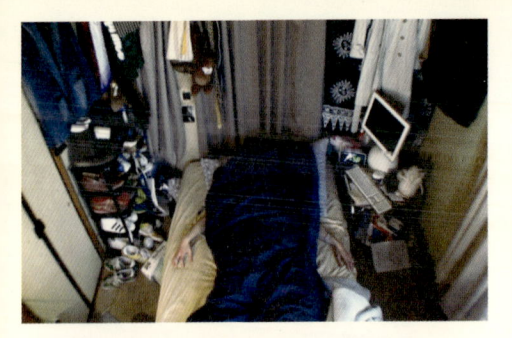

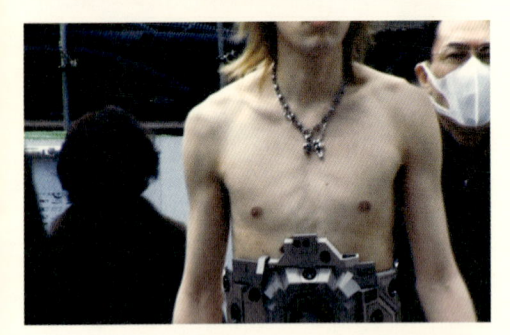

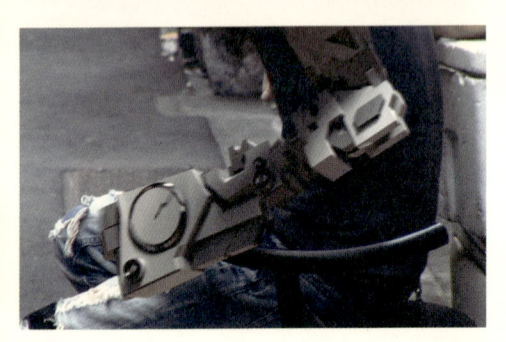

MTV Japan, TV commercial and mobile film
The MTV music awards announcements continue as different characters change into pulsating and gyrating instruments, designed to show that music can inspire people to transform both physically and mentally.
MTV Japan／TVコマーシャル、モバイル・ビデオ：複数の人間が、脈打ち、回転する楽器に変身するMTVミュージック・アワードの告知。これらの楽器は、音楽が人を肉体的にも精神的にも変身させるきっかけとなりうることを表現しようとデザインされた。

MTV Japan, tape and brand book
To help 'Transform Japan for the MTV Music Awards' make use of this handy roll of gaffer tape, or simply read the brand manual with instructions of how to utilize the campaign.
MTV Japan／テープ、ブランド・ブック：キャッチ・フレーズ「MTVミュージック・アワードに向けて日本を変身させよう」を広めるための、便利な粘着テープと、キャンペーンの進め方を説明したブランド・マニュアル。

2.77336 kilo

Bavaria, poster
The spring season is upon you. What better way to enjoy its arrival than with a bottle of Bavaria's fresh but strong Spring Bock beer? Helping to mark the occasion, a Hollywood-style poster campaign starring man and goat (Bock also means 'goat' in Dutch).
Bavaria／ポスター：春がきた！その到来を楽しむときのお供に、さっぱりとしてアルコール度の強い、ババリアのスプリング・ボック・ビール以上のものがあるだろうか？男とヤギ（ボックはオランダ語でヤギの意味もある）を起用した、ハリウッド・スタイルのポスター・キャンペーンがこの状況を際立たせている。

Bavaria, packaging
Packaging for this sequel to Bavaria's popular Hooghe Bock autumn beer, containing one bottle of the spring brew plus two glasses.
Bavaria／パッケージング：人気のあるババリア秋用ビール、ホーグ・ボックの続編となるパッケージング。春用ビール1本とグラス2個のセット。

Claro, brand identity and packaging
Bavaria, the third-largest Dutch brewery, introduced a new summer beer, brewed with rice and a dash of lemon. KesselsKramer named the new beer Claro to highlight its clear taste. Since the word stands for not only refreshment but also for transparency and an attitude (i.e. 'that's clear'), it became the perfect name for both a new beer and the communications surrounding it.
Claro／ブランド・アイデンティティ、パッケージング：オランダで第3位の規模であるビール会社、ババリアが、米と少々のレモンで醸造した新しい夏用ビールを発売。ケッセルスクライマーは、そのクリアな味を強調しようと、このビールにクラロと名づけた。この言葉は爽快感ばかりでなく、透明感やクリアな喉ごしも表しており、商品名として申し分なく広告映えもよいため、非常に効果的だった。

This poster probably won't make you thirsty. But just maybe...

When you get home, you probably won't remember the name at the bottom of this poster.

Refreshingly Clear

Refreshingly Clear

As if you didn't know from the sign, Claro is on sale here.

Claro is a new beer that speaks as clearly as it tastes.

Refreshingly Clear

Refreshingly Clear

Claro, poster campaign
Posters for Claro, demonstrating its clear, no-nonsense approach to addressing the public.
Claro／ポスター・キャンペーン：クラロのポスター。消費者に対するクリアできまじめな姿勢を表現している。

2.78271 kilo

Claro, billboard
Claro tells it like it is with an unapologetically unsubtle approach.
Claro／ビルボード：クラロは堂々と大胆にアプローチする、と語っている。

sing is so Eighties.

BIER
BEER
CERVEZA
BIRRA
BIERE

Claro!

Refreshingly Clear

Bavaria, books
Continuing its tireless crusade against herbal-tea-drinking metrosexuals, Bavaria beer introduced a range of self-help guides. These books contained the one necessary thing to help those who were swayed by moisturizer and tossed salad and helped them return to their manly roots. Available at all tough book stores, on-and offline.
Bavaria／書籍：ハーブティーを愛飲するメトロセクシャルズに対する飽くなき反対運動の一環として、ババリア・ビールは数種類の自己啓発ガイドを発行。これらの本には、保湿クリーム選びに右往左往したり、サラダを手作りしたりする男たちを救済し、男としての本分を回復させるために必要な対策が掲載されている。インターネットでもオフラインでも、このガイドを販売している書店はヤワじゃない。

Releasing
My Inner Man
How to take the man in you out of you
by M.I. Rownd (A.L.C., V.O.L.)
The No. 1 best-seller!*
*in Iceland
Releasing My Inner Man
Bavaria
PREMIUM
PILSENER

Bavaria, TV and cinema commercial
In recent years, social analysts were troubled by the role of man. Research showed that he no longer saw himself as the 'hunter gatherer'. Bavaria, a beer with guts for men with guts, released this anthem to testosterone to help wrestle modern man back to his rough and ready roots.
Bavaria／TV、映画用コマーシャル：昨今の社会アナリストは男性の役割に関して悩んでいる。調査によれば、男性たちは自身を「狩猟採集民」だとはもはや考えていないようである。ガッツのある男のためのビール、ババリアは、無骨で荒っぽいルーツに帰ろうとする現代男性たちの闘争を助けようと、男性ホルモンへの賛歌を発表した。

The film followed a group of men rediscovering their true selves on an epic journey from hair salon and ironing duties back to the wilderness and finally to the epicentre of manhood – the bar.
上図は、ヘアサロンやアイロンがけの家事を離れて荒野へと向かい、最後には男らしさの源、バーへとたどりつく大冒険を通じて、真の自己を見出す男性の一群を追ったビデオ。

2.79673 kilo

1. REAL
2. MEN
3. DON'T
4. DANCE

Bavaria, T-shirts
The rise of the 'spa and salon man' continued, especially in fashion, so Bavaria beer helped to counter the trend by introducing its own spring/summer collection.
Bavaria／Tシャツ:「スパ＆サロン男」的なファッションが増え続けている。そこでババリア・ビールは、オリジナルの春夏コレクションを発表することで、この傾向に歯止めをかけようとした。

2.80140 kilo

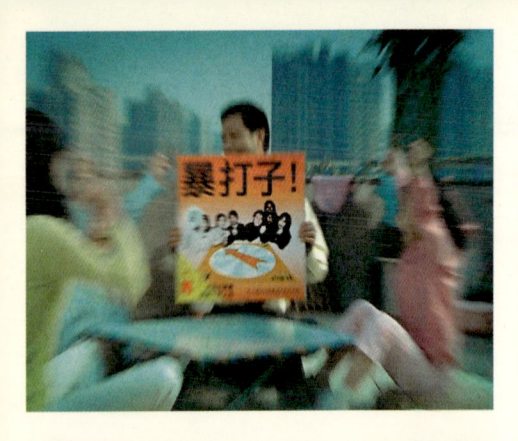

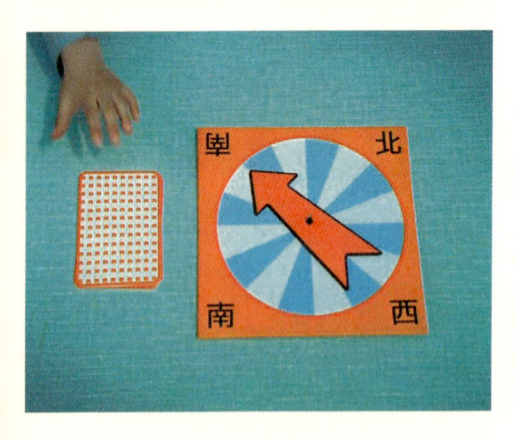

Bavaria, online film
The Bavaria Leeuwenhosen featured as the main component in a fictional new family board game, one that does away with its players in increasingly morbid ways. The film was designed to create further attention and adoration from the Dutch football supporters during the World Cup.

Bavaria／インターネット・ビデオ：ババリアのオレンジ色（オランダのチーム・カラー）のオーバーオールLeeuwenhosen（=オランダ語でライオン・パンツの意。ドイツの民族衣装Lederhosenをもじったもの）が架空の新しい家族用ボードゲームのメイン・キットとして登場。このゲームは負けたプレイヤーの退場の仕方が過激で、その恐怖はどんどんエスカレート。この動画は、ワールド・カップ中にオランダのサッカー・ファンの注意を引き、魅了するために制作された。

Bavaria

Bavaria

Bavaria

www.wangmingco.cn
暴打狮子!
十年中最令人激动的游戏!

Bavaria, product
The Bavaria Leeuwenhosen (translation: lion pants, a play on the German, Lederhosen) hit it big with Dutch football fans during the 2006 FIFA World Cup in Germany, so much so that the organizers banned the garment. Online attention and confusion in equal measure was further stirred with the arrival of a strange Chinese game featuring the bizarre orange outfit. Bavaria／商品：ババリアのLeeuwenhosenは、2006年のドイツW杯開催中、オランダのサッカー・ファンのあいだで大ヒット。W杯主催者がこれを着用して入場するのを禁止したことも、ヒットに拍車をかけた。ネット上の注目と混乱も同様だったが、この奇抜なオレンジ色の服をフィーチャーした奇妙な中国のゲームが登場すると、混乱はさらに深まった。

2.81075 kilo

Bavaria, online films and website
Real men are not the best communicators. How do you ask a friend for dinner without appearing improper? How do you compliment a mate without embarrassment? The Bavaria Stuntmail online service provided the answers with a series of personalized, danger-flavoured films.
Bavaria／インターネット・ビデオ、ウェブサイト：男の中の男は口ベタなもの。無作法にならずに友人をディナーに誘うにはどうしたらいい？相手を戸惑わせずに仲間をほめる方法は？ババリア・スタントメール・オンライン・サービスは、ちょっと危険な個人用ビデオ・シリーズでその答えを用意した。

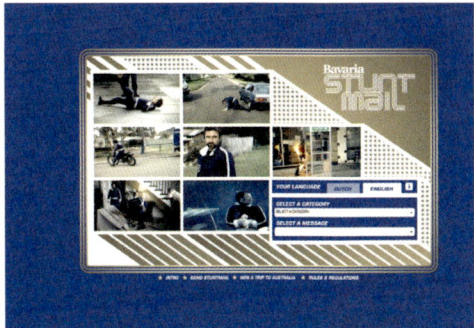

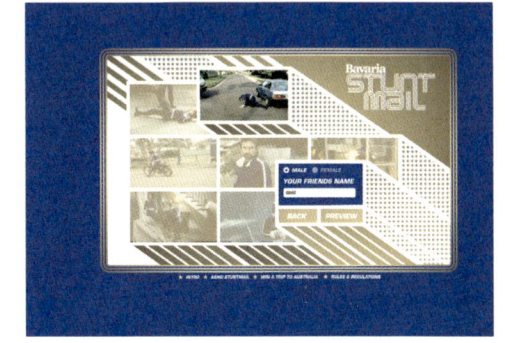

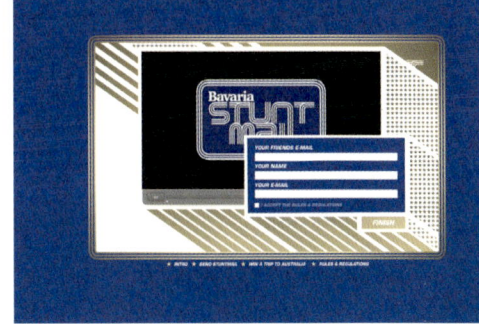

Bavaria, online films and website
Bavaria Stuntmail, the world's most manly way to communicate. Site visitors could select a message (choose between apologies, encouragements or congratulations) and this special service would generate a personal film stunt to your friend. Watch as the stunt actors break through glass, fall from great heights or get set on fire to help deliver your touching but tough memo.

Bavaria／インターネット・ビデオ、ウェブサイト：世界で最も男らしいコミュケーション方法、ババリア・スタントメール。同ウェブサイトの訪問者がメッセージを選択すると（あやまる、はげます、祝う、から選ぶ）、友人向けの個人的なスタント・ビデオができあがる。スタント・マンがガラスを突き破ったり、かなり高いところから落ちたり、火につつまれたりして、あなたの感動的だがタフなメモを届けるさまを見てみよう。

Uitburo, brand book and design toolkit
Uitburo is an independent, national Dutch organization providing reliable cultural calendar tips. This brandbox helped each city working within the Uitburo network develop a strong and single-minded identity, yet with their own local colour.
Uitburo／ブランド・ブック、デザイン・ツールキット：Uitburoは、信頼できる文化関連スケジュールを提供するオランダの独立型国立組織。この箱に入ったブランドキット一式は、当組織のネットワークに協力する都市が、地元の特色を活かしながら、強烈で一貫したアイデンティティを制作できるようにするためのもの。

2.81776 kilo

0

DE HUISSTIJL VAN HET UITBURO.
Vormen, typografie en kleuren.

TRUSSARDI
Necklaces and Gloves

Trussardi, print campaign
Trussardi is an Italian fashion company founded in 1911 as a glove-making business. The brand diversified into other luxury accessories, as well as ready-to-wear fashion for men and women. This campaign looked to communicate this wide assortment of goods in a quirky yet sophisticated way.
Trussardi／紙媒体キャンペーン：トラサルディは1911年に手袋メーカーとして設立されたイタリアのファッション企業。商品はその後、高級アクセサリーや女性・男性向けの既製服へと多様化。本キャンペーンはこの商品の幅広さを、ひねりがありつつも洗練された形で表現している。

2.82477 kilo

Trussardi, print campaign
More stylish combinations on behalf of the Italian fashion brand.
Trussardi／紙媒体キャンペーン：イタリアのファッション・ブランドを代表するスタイリッシュなコンビネーションのそのほかの例。

TRUSSARDI
Hats and Bags

TRUSSARDI
Gloves and Shoes

Shadow festival, poster campaign
This festival shadowed the IDFA, Amsterdam's international documentary showcase in an attempt to provide films that the more established event would or could not. A street campaign took the symbol of a shadowman to help direct audiences to the festival's venues.
Shadow festival／ポスター・キャンペーン：アムステルダムの国際的なドキュメンタリー映画祭IDFAの影の映画祭「シャドウ」は、有名映画祭がとりあげようとしなかった、また、とりあげることができなかった映画をとりあげる試み。街のキャンペーンではシャドウ・マンのシンボルを使って会場が案内された。

VANS
FOLLOW ME TO THE
SHADOW FESTIVAL
CREATIVE DOCUMENTARY FILMS
22-30 NOVEMBER 2005 AMSTERDAM
AMSTERDAM: MELKWEG, FILMMUSEUM VONDELPARK, DE UITKIJK
DEN HAAG: FILMHUIS DEN HAAG / EINDHOVEN: PLAZA FUTURA
WWW.SHADOWFESTIVAL.NL
shadow
festival

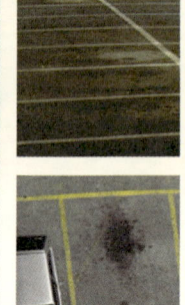

ER IS EEN KANS VAN 70% DAT DE AUTO VAN UW KLANT GEEN ALARMINSTALLATIE HEEFT.

DE AUTOVERZEKERING VAN
REAAL. REALIST IN VERZEKEREN.

Er zijn een hoop factoren die bepalen of een auto wordt gestolen of niet. Waar staat-ie geparkeerd bijvoorbeeld? Het zal geen verrassing voor u zijn om te horen dat de mensen in de grote steden eerder een lege parkeerplaats aantreffen dan de mensen in een dorp. De leeftijd van een auto is een andere factor. Er worden meer auto's gestolen die ouder zijn. Dat komt doordat nieuwe auto's vaak uitgerust zijn met een alarminstallatie. En daar houden dieven niet van. De leeftijd van de auto, en nog meer factoren, bepalen de premieberekening van onze autoverzekering. We hebben 'm nog meer verfijnd, zodat de premie zo goed mogelijk aansluit bij de realiteit van uw klant. Met behoud van de snelheid in verwerking. U kunt zelf voor uw klanten de premie berekenen via In Meetingpoint of Rolls.

REAAL Verzekeringen

REAAL Insurance, print campaign
Campaign for car insurance. Copy for the left-hand side reads: '70% chance that your client's car doesn't have an alarm system installed.' Copy for the right-hand side execution reads: 'There's a 61% chance that your clients would rather save than spend'.

REAAL Insurance／紙媒体キャンペーン：自動車保険のキャンペーン。左ページのキャッチ・フレーズは「あなたのクライアントの車に盗難警報装置が取り付けられていない可能性：70%」、右ページは「あなたのクライアントが、支出するより貯金したいと考える可能性：61%」

ER IS EEN KANS VAN 61% DAT UW KLANTEN LIEVER SPAREN DAN SPENDEREN.
REAAL COMBISPAREN: NU MET 4%* RENTE

Nederlanders, dat is u waarschijnlijk bekend, zijn gek op sparen. Ruim 61% geeft aan een uitgekeerd bedrag liever weg te zetten dan uit te geven. Een klein percentage hiervan verdwijnt overigens nog steeds onder het matras, maar dat is een ander verhaal. Nu het kabinet heeft besloten dat al het van 2001 tot en met 2004 gespaarde spaarloongeld zonder fiscale consequenties kan worden opgenomen, zal een groot deel van uw relaties binnenkort een beslissing moeten nemen omtrent de bestemming van het vrijgekomen bedrag. Een realistische optie, zeker voor de langere termijn, is REAAL CombiSparen. Dit is een combinatie van een spaar- en beleggingsrekening waartussen kosteloos geswitcht kan worden. Met een rentepercentage van 4%*, het hoogste in de markt, lijkt REAAL CombiSparen nu de meest voor de hand liggende keuze. Wilt u er meer over weten, neem dan contact op met uw REAAL-accountmanager.

* Rente per 8 augustus 2005. Rentewijzigingen voorbehouden.

REAAL Bancaire Diensten

ER IS EEN KANS VAN 100% DAT U DOODGAAT.

DE UITVAARTVERZEKERING VAN
REAAL. REALIST IN VERZEKEREN.

REAAL Verzekeringen
www.reaal.nl

ER IS EEN KANS VAN 25% DAT UW BEDRIJF BIJ BRAND FAILLIET GAAT AAN DE SCHADE.

HET BEDRIJVEN TOTAALPLAN VAN
REAAL. REALIST IN VERZEKEREN.

REAAL Verzekeringen
www.reaal.nl

REAAL Insurance, poster campaign
At the top, a poster for funeral insurance. Copy reads: '100% chance that you die.' At the bottom, a business insurance plan is advertised with the line: 'There's a 25% chance that your business falls victim to arson.'
REAAL Insurance／ポスター・キャンペーン：上図は葬儀保険用ポスターで、キャッチ・フレーズは「あなたが死ぬ可能性：100％」。下図は企業保険プランで、その広告は「あなたの会社が、放火の犠牲になる可能性：25％」

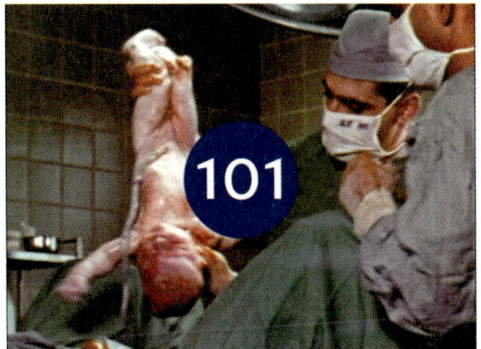

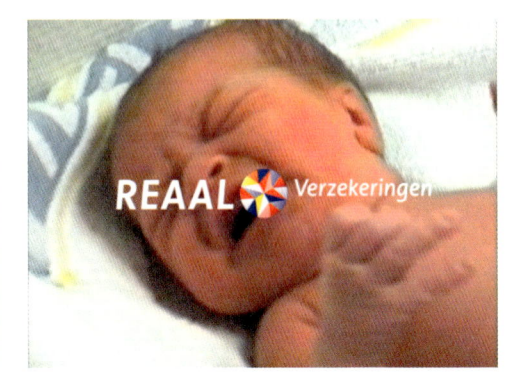

REAAL Insurance, TV campaign
A range of unlikely-but-true statistics are explored in this TV ad for REAAL.
REAAL Insurance／TVキャンペーン：ありそうもないが真実であるさまざまな統計が取りあげられた、REAAL のTVコマーシャル。

2.84346 kilo

KesselsKramer, stickers
Whenever KK sends a letter, staff have the opportunity to attach their email address with these stickers. The images are drawn from authentic 1970s high-school yearbooks and feature the staff member's apparent double. Some images are considerably more accurate than others.
KesselsKramer／ステッカー：ケッセルスクライマーから手紙を送るとき、スタッフはこのステッカーを貼って自分の電子メール・アドレスを知らせることができる。これらの画像は70年代の本物の高校卒業アルバムから選んだ、スタッフにそっくりな人物の写真。なかには驚くほど瓜二つなものもある。

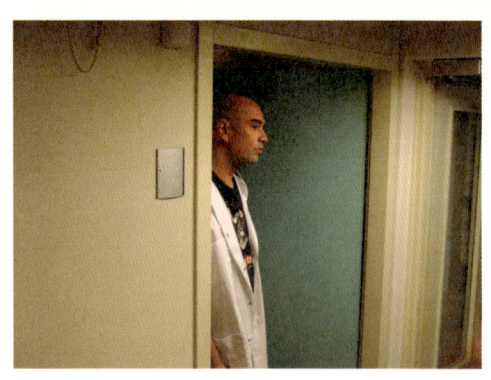

Opgezwolle, DVD
The introduction of a new genre, the album film for Dutch hip-hop band Opgezwolle.
The film 'My World' is based on the lyrics of the same CD from the band.
Opgezwolle／DVD：新ジャンルであるオランダ・ヒップホップ・バンド
Opgezwolleの音楽アルバム・ビデオ。ビデオ「マイ・ワールド」は同じCDに収録
されていた歌詞をベースにしたもの。

2.84813 kilo

Hans Brinker Budget Hotel, passport
This budget passport was handed out to backpackers on their arrival at the front desk of Amsterdam's favourite hostel to help them make the most of their travels.
Hans Brinker Budget Hotel／パスポート：アムステルダムの人気ホステルのフロント・デスクでは、バックパッカーが到着するとバジェット・パスポートが手渡される。バックパッカーたちはこれで旅行を最大限に楽しむことができる。

2.85280 kilo

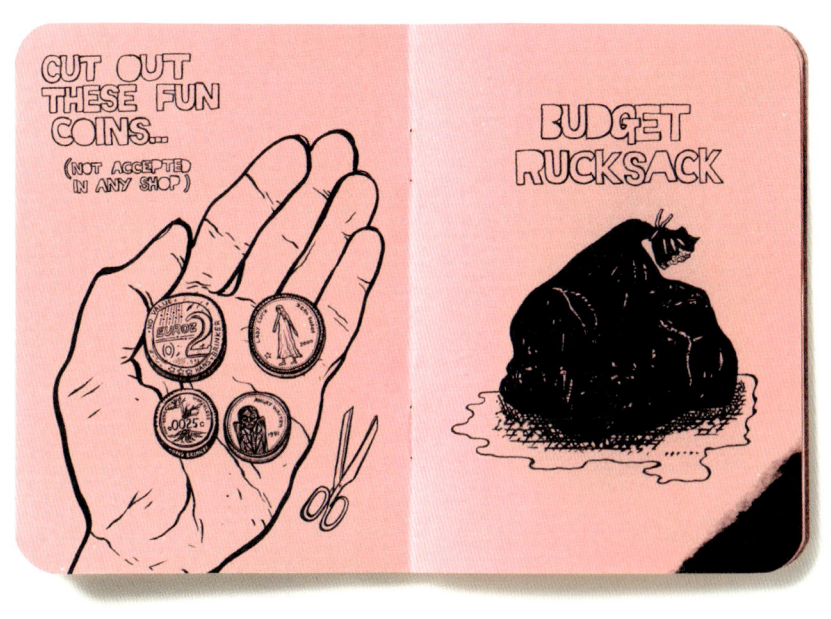

Footlocker, print and poster campaign
This high-street outlet for the world's best trainers and sneakers regularly communicated fresh collectables appearing only in their stores. This particular example highlights the Adidas Superstar Sign-Off, complete with Plasticine paparazzi.
Footlocker／紙媒体、ポスター・キャンペーン：世界でも最高品質のトレーナーやスニーカーを扱い、つねに大通りに店舗をかまえるフットロッカーは、同店限定の新しい特別商品を定期的に宣伝している。この例では、アディダス・スーパースター・サイン・オフに、粘土でできたパパラッチがはりついている。

adidas Superstar Sign-Off

Only At Foot Locker

in almost every picture, book collection
The first five books in the amateur photography series could now be offered as a complete set in a felt case.
in almost every picture／書籍セット：アマチュア写真コレクション・シリーズの1〜5巻がフェルト・ケース入りのセットとして登場。

2.85981 kilo

Gospel Festival, poster
In this poster for the third edition of the Gospel Festival, a performer is seen in action as her audience becomes absorbed in both her singing skills and her dress.
Gospel Festival／ポスター：第3回ゴスペル・フェスティバルのポスター。観客が出演者の歌唱力とドレスに引き込まれているようすが表現されている。

2.86215 kilo

zo kan het ook: in 2006

SNS Bank

SNS Bank, poster campaign
January 2006. A time of cultural restlessness in The Netherlands. This series by the Dutch bank SNS starts the year with a positive message on the subject by showing people from different cultures and backgrounds embracing each other to welcome in 2006. 'Zo kan het ook in 2006', the bank's motto, translates to: 'It could also be like this in 2006', a statement of hope.
SNS Bank／ポスター・キャンペーン：2006年1月。オランダは民族的ににぎやかな季節。オランダの銀行SNSのキャンペーン・シリーズは、異なる文化や背景をもつ人々が新年を祝って互いに抱き合う様子を、同銀行のモットー「Zo kan het ook in 2006＝2006年もこんな感じになるでしょう」という希望のメッセージとともに見せることで、テーマに対しポジティブなメッセージをはなち、一年をスタートした。

2.86449 kilo

zo kan het ook:
in 2006

SNS Bank

2.86682 kilo

SNS Bank

zo kan het ook:
klaar voor elke financiële tegenslag

SNS Standbykrediet
Er kan natuurlijk altijd iets met u of uw bedrijf gebeuren. Dus zorgt u ervoor dat u bij een tegenvaller niet meteen in financiële problemen komt. Met het SNS Standbykrediet heeft u altijd een extra potje met geld achter de hand. Zo heeft u altijd voldoende armslag om te kunnen blijven ondernemen.

U mag het SNS Standbykrediet gebruiken wanneer u het wil. En waarvoor u maar wil. Het staat altijd voor u klaar zonder dat het u geld kost. En daar hoeft u niet eens klant van SNS Bank voor te zijn. U profiteert hoe dan ook van de zeer lage rente van maar 4,65%. Bel voor meer informatie 0900-1890 (lokaal tarief) of kijk op snsbank.nl/zakelijk

SNS Bank, print campaign
A twin set of ads that appeared in entrepreneurial magazines. The visual metaphor of protective headgear communicated an easy-access loan that will shield you from financial setbacks.
SNS Bank／紙媒体キャンペーン：企業家向け雑誌に掲載された2種類で1セットの広告。保護用ヘルメットは、簡単に借りられて財政的な痛手からも守ってくれるローンの宣伝に、ビジュアル・メタファとして使われた。

2.86916 kilo

0

SNS Bank

5 2.87150 kilo

MONIQUE BESTEN ZIET VOOR JACQUELINE VAN HAPEREN

'Geur is voor mij belangrijk. Als ik in een kerk op een bankje zit, kan ik het verleden ruiken. De natuur heeft ook zulke prachtige geuren. Als de nacht overgaat in de dag,

maandag 27|2	dinsdag 28|2	woensdag 1|3	donderdag 2|3	vrijdag 3|3	zaterdag 4|3	zondag 5|3

SNS Bank, calendar
Calendar for SNS Bank in support of The Netherlands' Organisation for the Blind and Visually Impaired. A group of blind people took a photographer to a favourite or meaningful place. The photographer recorded the view and the images were over-printed in Braille, with a story to explain what each scene meant to them.
SNS Bank／カレンダー：オランダの視覚障害者支援団体を支援するためにSNS銀行が制作したカレンダー。目の不自由な人々が、自分のお気に入りの場所や大切な場所へカメラマンを連れて行き写真を撮影。視覚障害者たちが記録した風景は、各シーンが彼らにとってどんな意味があるかを説明した点字に重ね刷りされた。

2.87383 kilo

'Geur is voor mij belangrijk. Als ik in een kerk op een bankje zit, kan ik het verleden ruiken. De natuur heeft ook zulke prachtige geuren. Als de nacht overgaat in de dag,

| maandag 27\|2 | dinsdag 28\|2 | woensdag 1\|3 | donderdag 2\|3 | vrijdag 3\|3 | zaterdag 4\|3 | zondag 5\|3 |

HUNT!::EYEDOLLをさがせ

ヒントをたよりにEyeDollsをみつけて、日本最大級の音楽祭 Video Music Awards Japan のチケッをゲットしよう！ info PC>>>www.mtvjapan.com 携帯>>>v@mtvjapan.net

MTV Japan, posters, scavenger hunt, vinyl doll
A campaign created for the MTV Music Awards in Japan centred around the Eyedoll, a head-phone-wearing eyeball in sneakers. Japanese music fans were invited to search Tokyo for hidden Eyedolls – the lucky recipients would get free tickets to the event. Posters and commercials gave clues as to their whereabouts.

MTV Japan／ポスター、宝探し、プラスチック製人形：日本のMTVミュージック・アワード・キャンペーンの主人公は、ヘッドホンをかけてスニーカーをはいた目玉、アイドール。日本の音楽ファンは東京に潜伏したアイドールを探すよう求められ、運良く見つけられればミュージック・アワード・イベントへの無料チケットがもらえた。ポスターとコマーシャルがその居場所に関するヒントを提供。

HUNT!:EYEDOLLをさがせ

HUNT!:EYEDOLLをさがせ

HUNT!:EYEDOLLをさがせ

HUNT!:EYEDOLLをさがせ

2.88084 kilo

MTV Japan, TV idents
The search for the MTV Eyedoll continued on TV and on the music channel's website, with short films giving clues as to the vinyl collectable's whereabouts. Animated idents of the bouncing, ocular objects were then used during the live awards show.
MTV Japan／TV用イメージ・ビデオ：MTVアイドール探しはテレビやMTVのウェブサイトでも展開され、短編ビデオがプラスチック製ドールの居場所に関するヒントを提供。跳ね回る目玉のアニメーションはアワード・イベントでも使われた。

2.88551 kilo

55DSL, print campaign
The fall/winter collection of Diesel's younger brother brand, 55DSL, takes the theme of 'Feel at Home', in direct contrast to the outdoors mentality of most snow, surf and street wear brands. The models are seen being sucked, impaled or branded by seemingly harmless household appliances.

55DSL／紙媒体キャンペーン：ディーゼルの弟ブランド、55DSL の秋冬コレクションのテーマは、スノー・ウェア、サーフィン・ウェア、ストリート・ウェアを扱うブランドのアウトドア精神とは正反対の「家にいるようにくつろごう」。モデルたちは、一見害がなさそうな家庭用電化製品に、吸い込まれたり、突き刺されたり、焼印を押されたりする。

BEWARE
USING WRONG TYPE OF BATTERIES
CAN CAUSE SERIOUS INJURY
WWW.55DSL.COM
55DSL
FEEL AT HOME

55DSL, print campaign
Another execution in the 55DSL campaign that warns fashion fans about the incorrect use of everyday household objects.
55DSL／紙媒体キャンペーン：55DSL キャンペーンのそのほかの例。日用品の使い方を間違えないよう、ファッション・ファンたちに警告を発している。

BEWARE

IF USED INCORRECTLY, VACUUM CLEANER MAY BEHAVE IRREGULARLY

WWW.55DSL.COM

55DSL
FEEL AT HOME

55DSL, catalogue
The 'Feel at Home' theme is ironically pursued in this catalogue to accompany the 2005 fall and winter collection of 55DSL. It takes the form of a self-defence guide to give you hints and tips on how to protect yourself against the risk of attack by unruly household lamps, sofas or tables.
55DSL／カタログ:「家にいるようにくつろごう」のテーマは、55DSL の2005年秋冬コレクションのカタログでも皮肉な形で取りあげられた。カタログは、乱暴な家庭用ランプ、ソファ、テーブルの攻撃から自分を守るためのヒントを提供する自己防衛ガイド風の体裁。

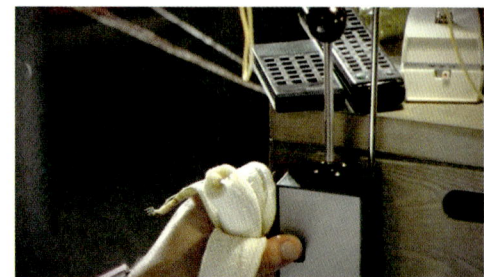

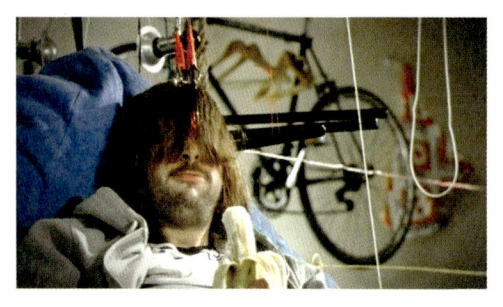

Bol.com, TV commercial
Laziness is celebrated in a campaign for online retailer Bol.com. This TV commercial shows a young man lying on a couch. Around him, an intricate system of pulleys and levers ensure that he gets what he wants without moving an inch – including a special delivery of electronic goods from Bol.com.
Bol.com／TVコマーシャル：インターネット・ショップ Bol.com のキャンペーンでは「怠けること」が讃えられた。このTVコマーシャルに登場するのは、ソファに寝そべる若い男性。その周囲には滑車やレバーでできた複雑な仕掛けが置かれ、男性はそれを使えば、少しも動かずに、Bol.com から特別配達された電気製品をはじめとした欲しいものが獲得できた。

KesselsKramer, van
KesselsKramer is the proud owner of over 30 bikes and just one fossil-fuelled vehicle. And since every outlet for communication is a viable one, the company car got its own branding, albeit with a series of messages that deliberately confused the public with what service KesselsKramer provided – does it offer pool cleaning or pizza delivery? KesselsKramer／ライトバン：ケッセルスクライマーは自転車を30台以上所有しているが、化石燃料で動く乗り物はたったの一台。広告においてはあらゆる販路が重要であることから、この社用車にも独自のブランディングをほどこした。とはいっても、そのメッセージは、ケッセルスクライマーの商売が、プールの掃除屋なのか、それとも、ピザの宅配なのか、見た人をわざと混乱させるようなものだった。

Zo Limburg, nu eerst zoeken naar een Bavaria Paaskrat.

Kijk achter bomen, til uw schoonmoeder op en wroet in aarde: Bavaria heeft maar liefst 10.000 Paaskratjes in Brabant en Limburg verstopt. En vindt u een Paaskrat, dan verdubbelt u uw Bavaria. Met een Bavaria Paaskrat krijgt u namelijk 2 kratjes Bavaria voor de prijs van 1. Of 8 voor de prijs van 4. Vrolijk Pasen.

Bavaria, print campaign

Bavaria beer was famous and widely available in the province of Brabant, but less so in the rest of The Netherlands. A distribution strategy was used in the communication – soon the whole country would enjoy their beer. During Easter, the traditional search for eggs was changed into a more desirable one for beer lovers everywhere – a hunt for blue crates of Bavaria, thousands of which were hidden throughout the country.

Bavaria／紙媒体キャンペーン：ババリア・ビールはブラバント州では有名で、あちこちで入手できるが、オランダのほかの地域ではそれほどでもなかった。そこで、ある流通上の戦略を宣伝に使った———このビールが全国で楽しまれるようになるのも時間の問題に違いない。イースターに卵を探すという伝統が、全国のビール愛好家にとって、より望ましいものに変わったからである。それは、国中に隠された数千個のババリアの青い木箱を探すことであった。

Bavaria, poster and TV commercial
The epic journey of man and goat is shown in this movie-trailer-style poster and accompanying TV commercial announcing the new Bavaria bock beer.
Bavaria／ポスター、TVコマーシャル：映画予告編スタイルのポスターとTVコマーシャルのテーマは男とヤギの大冒険。ババリアの新しいボック・ビールを宣伝した。

5

2.90888 kilo

Bavaria, print campaign
International campaign for the Dutch brewery took the theme of sharing around the world. A blue-spot device was used to literally pinpoint the moments where a Bavaria could be shared with friends.
Bavaria／紙媒体キャンペーン：世界中でシェアすることをテーマにした、オランダのビール会社の海外向けキャンペーン。友人どうしでバパリアをシェアできる瞬間を指し示すため、青い点のしかけが使われた。

José, Anna and friends, Buenos Aires
Bavaria Premium from Holland.
Where do you share?

Aaron & Emma, Brooklyn
Bavaria Premium from Holland.
Where do you share?

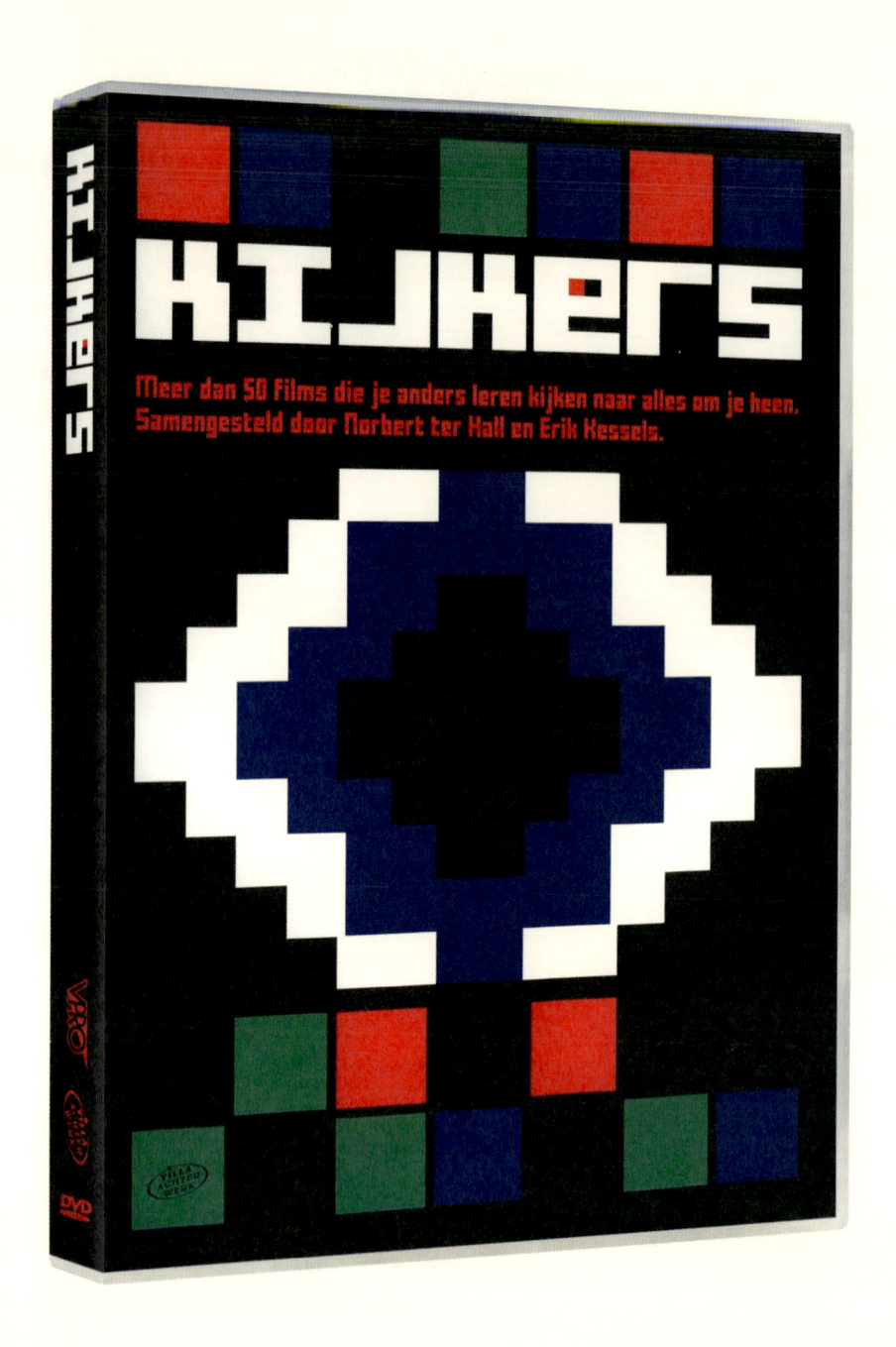

Kijkers, TV series and DVD
Kijkers ('Viewers' in Dutch) was the name given to this compilation of short films created by KesselsKramer in collaboration with Norbert ter Hall. They first appeared on children's television and soon after, in the form of a DVD. The films were diversely realized both in style and content and sought to fuel the imagination of young children without condescension.
Kijkers／TVシリーズ、DVD：Kijkers（＝視聴者）は、ケッセルスクライマーがノルバート・テル・ホールとのコラボレーションで制作した短編ビデオ集につけられた名。これらのビデオはテレビの子ども番組に登場した後、すぐにDVDになった。スタイルも内容も多様なビデオは、子どもの目線に立って幼児の想像力を高めることを目指したもの。

2.91822 kilo

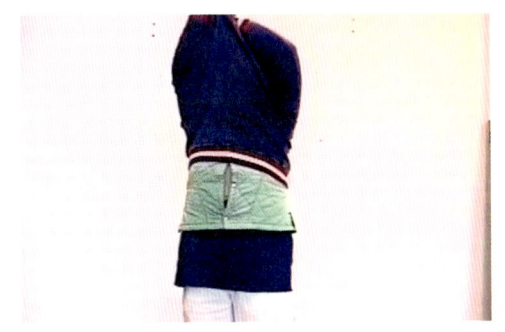

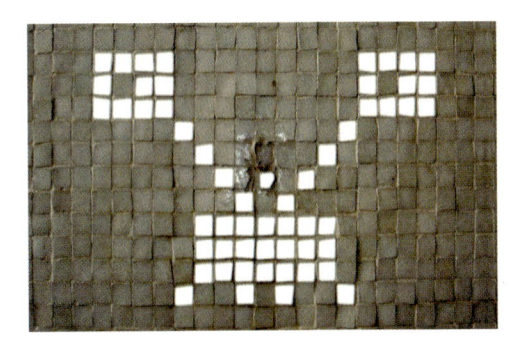

in almost every picture #4, book
The found photography collection continues with the story of two sisters in Barcelona during World War II. We witness the twins posing in identically arranged outfits until the war manages to invade the photographs and two sisters become one – the reader can only imagine what the cause of her absence could be.
in almost every picture #4／書籍：ファウンド・フォト・コレクションの第4巻がとりあげたのは、第二次世界大戦中にバルセロナで撮影された2人の姉妹の物語。写真にはまったく同じ服を着てポーズをとる双子たちの姿が写っているが、やがて戦争の影がしのびより、2人の姉妹は1人に。読者にできるのは、もう1人がいなくなってしまった理由を想像することだけ。

madrid october 17 1940

2.92523 kilo

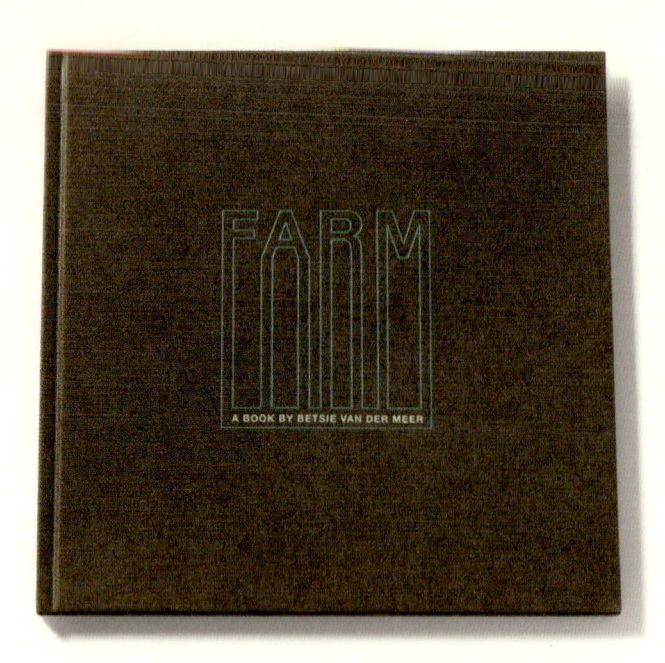

Farm, book
The photographer Betsy van der Meer wanted to bring attention to the disappearance of farms in The Netherlands – a subject close to home since she was born and raised on one. This book tells the story of a single farm, all the more emotive since it was the one she was brought up on. The photos were taken shortly before the farmhouse was demolished.
Farm／書籍：写真家のベッツィー・ファン・デル・メールが望んだのは、オランダの消え行く農地に関心を集めること。農村出身の彼女にとって身につまされるテーマだったからである。本書が伝えるのはある農園の物語。彼女が生まれ育った場所であるだけに、非常に情感がこもっている。写真は農家が取り壊される直前に撮影されたもの。

Gospel Festival, poster campaign
The world-renowned Gospel Festival compares the poses adopted by various people waking up in the morning to those of the passionate emotions displayed by the event's gospel singers. Gospel Festival／ポスター・キャンペーン：世界的に有名なゴスペル・フェスティバルのポスター。さまざまな人が朝目覚めたときにとったポーズと、イベントに出演するゴスペル歌手の熱い感情表現のそれとを比較している。

2.92757 kilo

Gospel Festival, TV commercial
Individuals wake up, stretch and yawn with movements that match the accompanying sounds of a gospel choir.
Gospel Festival／TVコマーシャル：人々が目覚め、伸びながらあくびをする動作が、ゴスペル聖歌のサウンドに合っている様子を見せるCM。

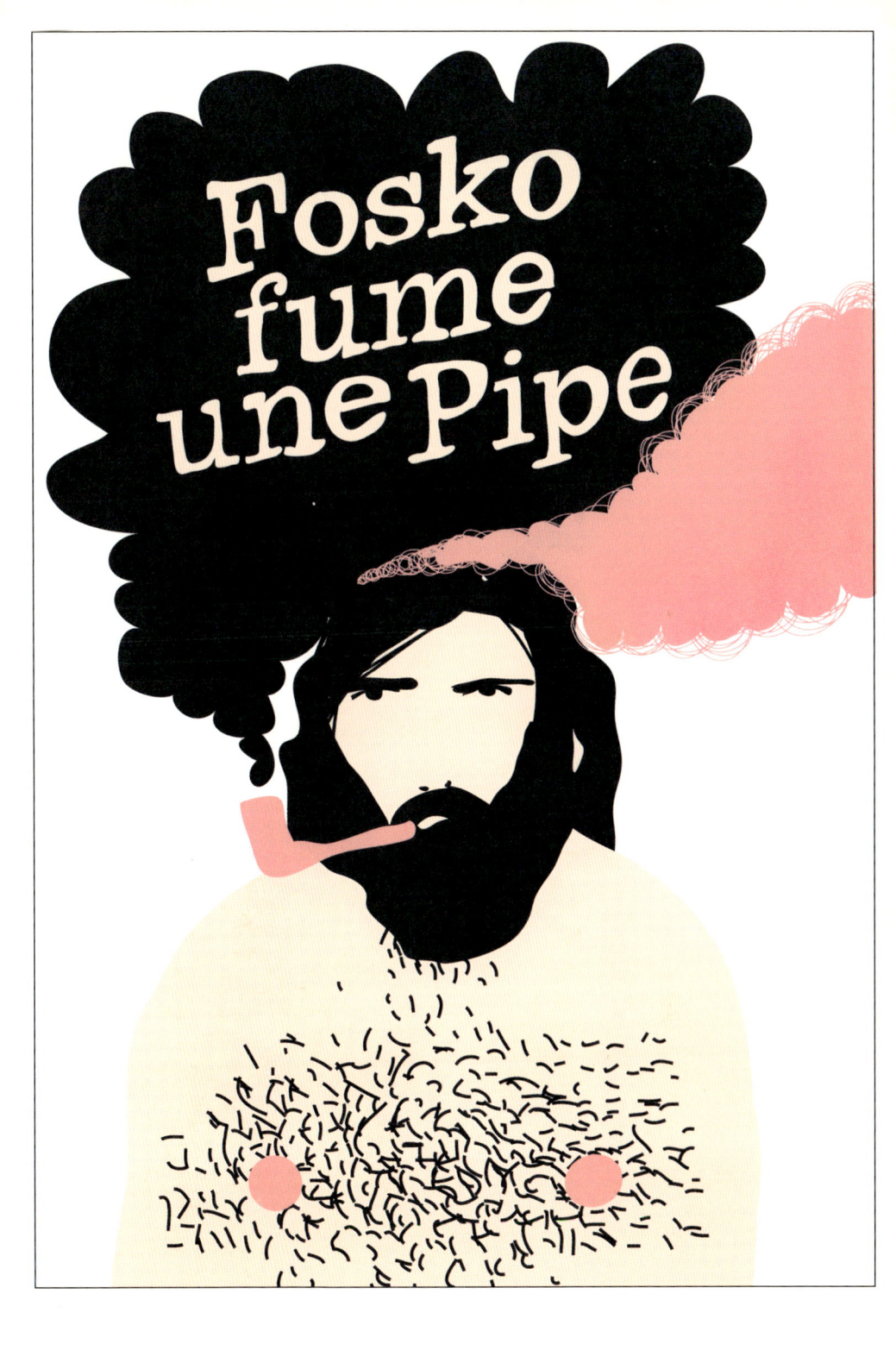

Bob Fosko, poster
A poster for the theatre-based tour of local singing legendary local actor and musician, Bob Fosko.
Bob Fosko／ポスター：地元の伝説的歌手であり、俳優であり、ミュージシャンであるボブ・フォスコの劇場ツアー用ポスター。

5   2.93224 kilo

Hans Brinker Budget Hotel, product and poster campaign
The hotel with no shame takes its first step into product development. Inspired by the tourists who leave the Van Gogh Museum with souvenir posters rolled in triangular containers, the Brinker offered its guests a chance to take home a memory of their stay – in the form of posters in triangular containers.

Hans Brinker Budget Hotel／商品、ポスター・キャンペーン：恥知らずなホテルが、商品開発にはじめの一歩を踏み出した。三角の箱に巻いて収められたお土産用ポスターを、ヴァン・ゴッホ美術館に忘れてきた旅行者がいたことから思いついたアイデア。ホテル・ステイの思い出をポスターにして三角の箱におさめ、ゲストが家に持ち帰られるようにしたのである。

HANS BRINKER
BUDGET HOTEL
AMSTERDAM
HANS-BRINKER.COM
WALLPAPER
BRING YOUR HANS BRINKER MEMORIES HOME

2.93692 kilo

Hans Brinker Budget Hotel, product and poster campaign
Guests could choose from the most infamous view from the Brinker – of a brick wall; a segment of the graffiti from the wall of the Brinker bar; or a life-sized cleaner with sponge at the ready. The wallpaper also came as posters within posters – acting as communication to tempt travellers to either buy the product or spend a night at the hotel.
Hans Brinker Budget Hotel／商品、ポスター・キャンペーン：ゲストは、ハンス・ブリンカー・バジェット・ホテルの特に評判が悪い眺め──レンガ壁、バーの壁のらくがき、スポンジをもって準備万端の等身大掃除婦──から好きなバージョンのポスターをチョイスすることができた。この壁紙は、旅行者に商品を買いたくさせる宣伝効果か、ホテルで過ごしたいと思わせる宣伝効果のいずれかを発揮した点で、ポスターとしての機能も抜群だったといえる。

HANS BRINKER
BUDGET HOTEL
AMSTERDAM
HANS-BRINKER.COM
WALLPAPER
BRING YOUR HANS BRINKER MEMORIES HOME

Bavaria, TV commercial
For this latest outing of Bavaria's quest to reach the whole of The Netherlands with their great-tasting beer, it enlisted the help of one of The Netherlands' most famous singers. Armed only with a van, hundreds of bottles of Bavaria and his voice, Albert West helped make the beer a hit.
Bavaria／TVコマーシャル：オランダ中においしいビールを行き届かせようとするババリアの取り組みにおける最新の活動として、オランダの有名歌手の助けを借りた。ライトバンと数百本のババリア・ビールと自分の声だけを武器に、歌手のアルバート・ウェストがビールをヒットさせようと協力。

Resilience, book
It's one year after the Indian Ocean tsunami had a devastating effect on Thailand and South East Asia. Photographer Pieter van der Houwen was commissioned to visit the provinces which were hardest hit to see how the funds of the Dutch development organization, Cordaid, helped rebuild their shattered communities. The result is a book whose title speaks volumes: Resilience.
Resilience／書籍：インド洋大津波がタイや東南アジアに壊滅的被害をもたらしてから1年がたったころ、写真家のピーター・バン・デル・ホーベンは被害が特に甚大だった地域を訪ねた。オランダの開発団体 Cordaid から、荒廃した地域の再建に、資金がどのくらい貢献したかを確認してくるよう依頼されたからである。その調査結果は一冊の本になり、貢献の度合いはタイトル『レジリエンス＝回復力』が物語った。

2.94626 kilo

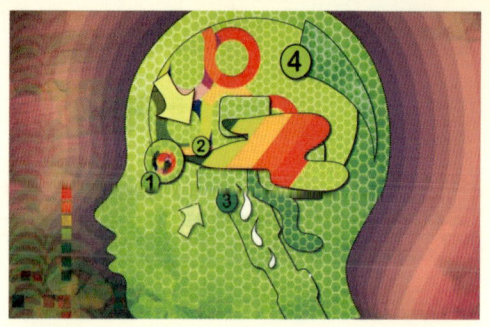

Lipton Ice Tea, TV and cinema commercial
A cinema commercial for the Green Tea version of Lipton's eponymous Ice Tea showed individuals creating their own soothingly, relaxing summers in increasingly inventive ways. The TV commercial, which clocked in at 24 minutes, won a Guinness World Record for its efforts.
Lipton Ice Tea Green／TV、映画用コマーシャル：夏をのんびりとリラックスして過ごせるよう自分なりの工夫をする人々をとりあげた、リプトン・アイス・ティー緑茶バージョンの映画用コマーシャル。紹介される工夫はどんどん独創的に。そのTV版は24分間を記録し、ギネス世界記録を更新した。

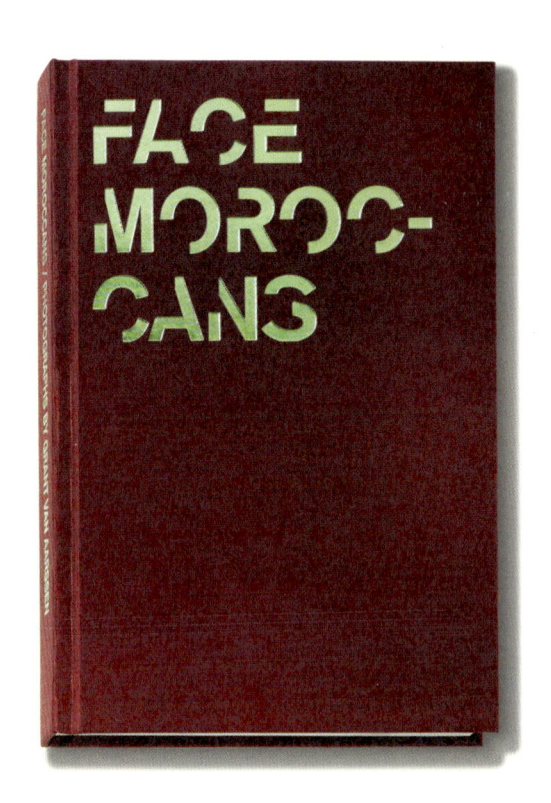

Face Moroccans, book
A book made by photographer Grant van Aarssen on his travels around Morocco in a van. This very personal journey avoids the landscape and instead captures Moroccan locals to help paint a portrait of Muslim men who live far away from their media image.
Face Moroccans／書籍：写真家グラント・バン・アーセンがライトバンでモロッコじゅうを旅したときの写真集。この非常に個人的な旅では、風景写真ではなく、地元モロッコの人たちの姿が撮影された。マスコミが報道するイメージとはかけはなれた、イスラム教の男たちの肖像を描くためである。

2.95093 kilo

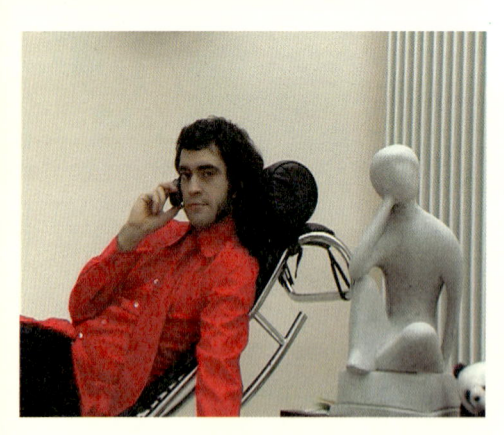

Jack Stafford, music video
Music video for British singer-songwriter Jack Stafford's hit 'Toy Boy' which shamelessly copies a hundred different sex-phone chat-line commercials, the likes of which are found lurking on TV channels after midnight. The band's singer cavorts suggestively in supremely kitsch settings as phone numbers and slogans flash incessantly on screen.

Jack Stafford／ミュージック・ビデオ：百種類のセックス電話チャットラインのコマーシャル───深夜によく放送されているような───を恥ずかしげもなくコピーした、イギリスのシンガーソングライター、ジャック・スタッフォードのヒット曲「トイ・ボーイ」のミュージック・ビデオ。画面上で電話番号とメッセージがひっきりなしに点滅するという極めて下品なムードのなかで、バンドのシンガーが意味ありげなポーズをとって遊んでいる。

Radio 1, brand book
A book offering the house-style and branding guidelines for the staff and reporters of the number one Dutch news and sports broadcaster.
Radio 1／ブランド・ブック：オランダNo.1のニュース＆スポーツ放送局のスタッフとレポーター用に制作されたブランド・ブック。スタイルガイドとブランドのガイドラインが掲載されている。

Useful Photography #005, magazine
Meet Lord Lily, a legend in his own field. This bull has sired over 150,000 descendants, a small selection of which appear in number five in the series of Useful Photography manuals. The images – fascinating in their repetitiveness – show the standard method used to photograph cows and bulls to allow farmers to examine the qualities of different breeds.
Useful Photography #005／雑誌：牧牛界の伝説、ミートロード・リリィは15万頭以上の子孫をうみだした種牛。『ユースフル・フォトグラフィ』シリーズ第5号は、その子孫のごく一部を掲載。魅了されるほど延々と繰り返し現れる写真は、雄牛と牝牛の標準的な撮影方法を示している。飼育業者はこの写真でさまざまな品種の品質を調べることができる。

2.95794 kilo

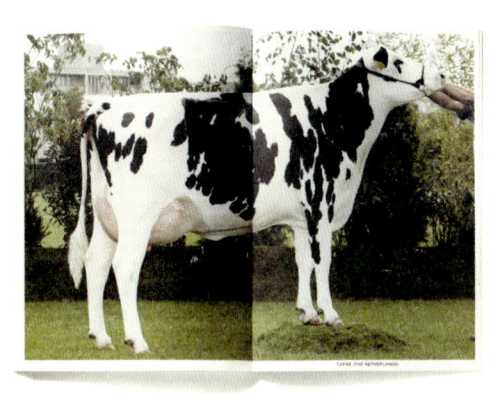

2.96028 kilo

Lipton Ice Tea, TV campaign
People drink ice tea in the summer, but avoid it in the winter. The tag line 'Create Your Own Summer' helped prove that Lipton can be enjoyed all year. These commercials showed individuals creating summer by using a gold-fish bowl to go snorkelling or constructing a homemade sun out of dozens of household lamps.
Lipton Ice Tea／TVキャンペーン：人は、夏にはアイス・ティーを楽しむが、冬はそうしようとはしない。キャッチ・フレーズの「自分の夏を作ろう」は、リプトンが一年中楽しめることを伝えようとするもの。これらのコマーシャルは、金魚鉢を使ってシュノーケリングしようとしたり、たくさんの家庭用ランプから自家製太陽を作ることによって夏を作り出そうとする人々を描いている。

Lipton Ice Tea, TV campaign
More 'Create Your Own Summer' commercials reveal a woman who slaps herself repeatedly – some say disturbingly – to rid herself of imaginary mosquitoes, and a couple who replace the summer waterslide with the construction chute on the side of a high-rise building.
Lipton Ice Tea／TVキャンペーン：「自分の夏を作ろう」キャンペーンのそのほかの例。想像上の蚊を退治しようと、少し気味悪いほどに、自分をくりかえし叩く女性と、夏のウォーター・スライドを、ビルの脇に取りつけられた建設廃棄物用のといと取り替えようとするカップルが登場。

5   2.96495 kilo

Magnum sees Piemonte, book and exhibition
A photographic look at this north-western region of Italy, host of the Winter Olympics in 2006. Eleven Magnum photographers documented the preparations of the games as well as the culture and colour of Piemonte, and the results were collected in this book, created in collaboration with Design Politie.
Magnum sees Piemonte／書籍、展覧会：2006年冬季オリンピックの開催地であるイタリア北西の地を、写真という視点でまとめたもの。11人のマグナム写真家がオリンピックの準備作業とピエモンテ州の文化と特色を詳細に報道した。その内容は、デザイン・ポリシーの協力のもと、一冊の本にまとめられた。

2.96963 kilo

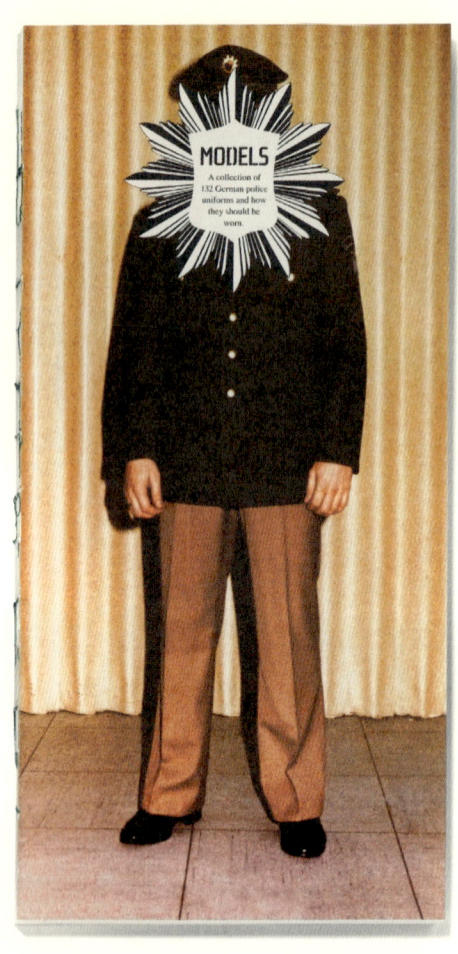

Models, book
German police-officer uniforms from the 1970s form an oddly fashionable parade in this limited-edition box collection. The figures also appeared as part of numerous exhibitions, in the form of life-sized boards.
Models／書籍：限定版のボックス・コレクションにくりひろげられた、70年代のドイツ警察の制服のオンパレードは、意外におしゃれ。登場人物たちは幾度となく開催された展覧会に、等身大ボードとして参加した。

Hamburg — Mittlerer Dienst/Hundeführer/Dienstanzug — Medium level/dog handler/service uniform

Medium level/service uniform with khaki jacket — Mittlerer Dienst/Dienstanzug mit Kakijacke — Hamburg

UITMARKT 2005
HET CULTURELE SEIZOEN
BREEKT LOS AMSTERDAM 26/27/28 AUGUSTUS

AMSTERDAMS UIT BURO

Uitmarkt, poster campaign
A series which expresses the opening of the Dutch cultural season by portraying different individuals abandoning their clothes and running freely through the great outdoors.
Uitmarkt／ポスター・キャンペーン：衣服を脱ぎ去り、気持ちのよい野外を自由に駆けまわるさまざまな人々を描くことにより、オランダ文化シーズンの始まりを表現したシリーズ。

2.97664 kilo

0

Uitmarkt, TV commercial
A woman encased in plaster cracks open her body-hugging mould to symbolize the breaking loose of the cultural season in The Netherlands.
Uitmarkt／TVコマーシャル：石膏に包まれた女性が、体にぴったりとはりついている型を砕き、オランダの文化シーズンの始まりを象徴。

5   2.97897 kilo

WOMEN INC.

300 vrouwen met lef – 24 en 25 september 2005
Beurs van Berlage Amsterdam – www.women-inc.nl
theater, debat, muziek, speeddating, documentaire, workshop, lezing, feest, film, fotografie

Women Inc., poster campaign
An annual festival of discussion, debate, exhibitions and workshops by and for 'women who stand for change.' The branding and posters depict a contrasting view of women by filling stereotypical silhouettes with more honest and modern representations continued within.
Women Inc.／ポスター・キャンペーン：「変化を支持する女性」による、「変化を支持する女性」のための毎年恒例のフェスティバル。議論、討論、展覧会、ワークショップが実施される。そのブランディングとポスターは、より率直かつ現代的な図像をステレオタイプな女性のシルエットで切り取ることによって、女性が抱える裏腹な気持ちを表現している。

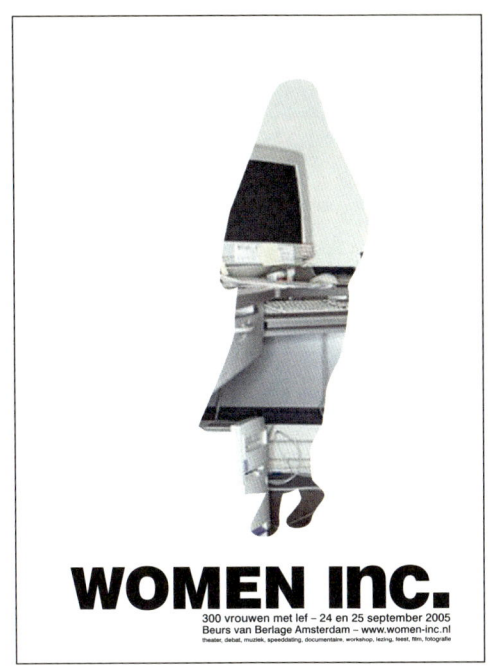

2.98598 kilo

2 kilo of KesselsKramer, van
Kesselskramer's resident van was transformed to advertise the arrival of its weighty book of collected work.
2 kilo of KesselsKramer／ライトバン：ケッセルスクライマー社用車のライトバンが、分厚くて重い作品集を宣伝するため改造された。

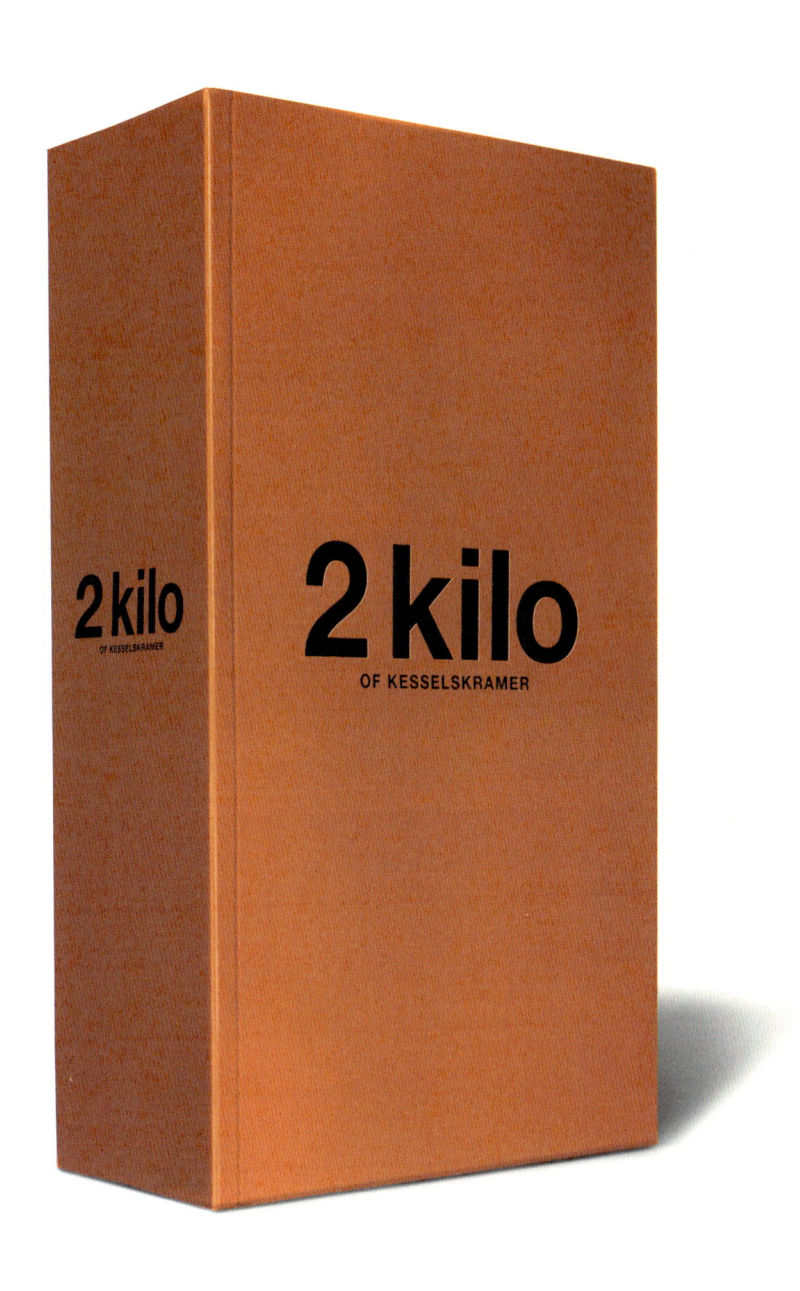

2 kilo of KesselsKramer, book
The book preceding 'a new kilo of KesselsKramer' looked like a brick and weighed precisely 2 kg. It contained 'the best and the not so best' of KesselsKramer's work from the years 1996 to 2005, including Diesel, Nike, Levi's and, of course, the Hans Brinker Budget Hotel.
2 kilo of KesselsKramer／書籍：『ケッセルスクライマーの新たな1キロ』の前に出版された作品集はまるでレンガみたいで、重さはちょうど2kgだった。同書は、ディーゼル、ナイキ、リーバイス、そしてもちろん、ハンス・ブリンカー・バジェット・ホテルなど、1996年から2005年にかけて制作されたケッセルスクライマーの「最高な作品と、まあまあな作品」を収録。

2.98832 kilo

1 kilo weight watcher
Guide yourself with this wobbly stack of colour-coded balls.
1キロ用重量チェッカー
クライアント別に色分けされたボールで構成されています。
多少でこぼこしていますが、索引としてご利用ください。

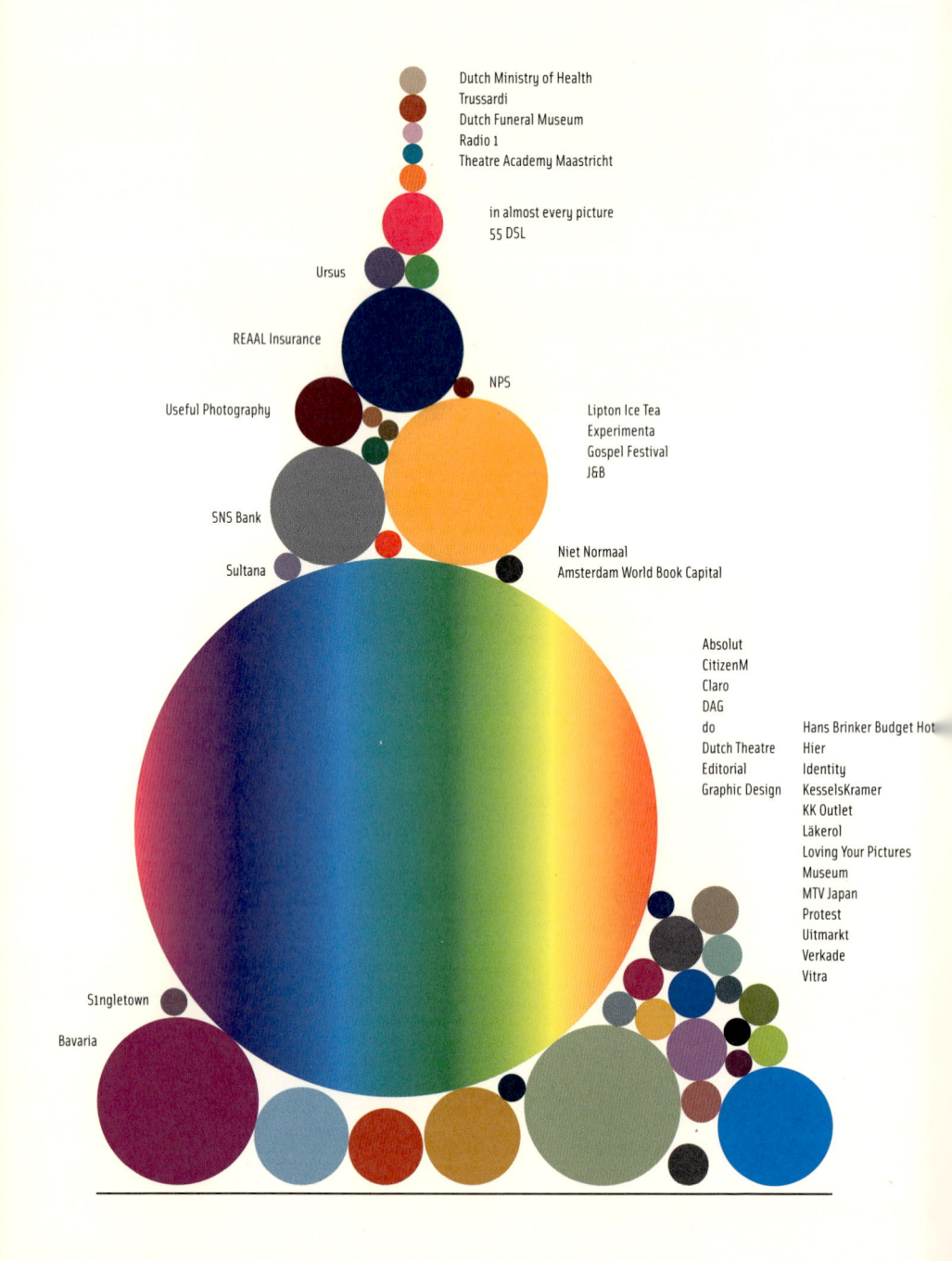

Dutch Ministry of Health
Trussardi
Dutch Funeral Museum
Radio 1
Theatre Academy Maastricht

in almost every picture
55 DSL

Ursus

REAAL Insurance

NPS

Useful Photography

Lipton Ice Tea
Experimenta
Gospel Festival
J&B

SNS Bank

Sultana

Niet Normaal
Amsterdam World Book Capital

Absolut
CitizenM
Claro
DAG
do
Dutch Theatre
Editorial
Graphic Design

Hans Brinker Budget Hotel
Hier
Identity
KesselsKramer
KK Outlet
Läkerol
Loving Your Pictures
Museum
MTV Japan
Protest
Uitmarkt
Verkade
Vitra

Singletown
Bavaria

2.99065 kilo

Category	Year	Weight
55 DSL		0.01170 kilo
55DSL, catalogue	2005	2.89720 kilo
55DSL, print campaign	2005	2.88785 kilo
55DSL, print campaign	2005	2.89019 kilo
55DSL, print campaign	2005	2.89252 kilo
55DSL, print campaign	2005	2.89486 kilo
Absolut		0.00936 kilo
Absolut, catalogue and underwear collection	2006	2.74533 kilo
Absolut, PR materials and underwear collection	2006	2.73832 kilo
Absolut, PR materials and underwear collection	2006	2.74065 kilo
Absolut, PR materials and underwear collection	2006	2.74299 kilo
Amsterdam World Book Capital		0.00936 kilo
Amsterdam World Book Capital, bags	2008	2.27336 kilo
Amsterdam World Book Capital, poster campaign	2008	2.27103 kilo
Amsterdam World Book Capital, poster campaign	2008	2.27570 kilo
Amsterdam World Book Capital, poster campaign	2008	2.27804 kilo
Bavaria		0.05616 kilo
Bavaria, books	2006	2.78972 kilo
Bavaria, books	2006	2.79206 kilo
Bavaria, online film	2006	2.80374 kilo
Bavaria, online film	2006	2.80607 kilo
Bavaria, online films and website	2006	2.81308 kilo
Bavaria, online films and website	2006	2.81542 kilo
Bavaria, packaging	2006	2.77804 kilo
Bavaria, poster	2006	2.77570 kilo
Bavaria, poster and TV commercial	2005	2.90654 kilo
Bavaria, poster and TV commercial	2005	2.90888 kilo
Bavaria, print campaign	2005	2.90421 kilo
Bavaria, print campaign	2005	2.91121 kilo
Bavaria, print campaign	2005	2.91355 kilo
Bavaria, print campaign	2007	2.52336 kilo
Bavaria, print campaign	2007	2.52570 kilo
Bavaria, product	2006	2.80841 kilo
Bavaria, product	2006	2.81075 kilo
Bavaria, T-shirts	2006	2.79907 kilo
Bavaria, T-shirts	2006	2.80140 kilo
Bavaria, TV and cinema commercial	2006	2.79439 kilo
Bavaria, TV and cinema commercial	2006	2.79673 kilo
Bavaria, TV commercial	2005	2.94393 kilo
Bavaria, TV commercial	2007	2.52804 kilo
Bavaria, TV commercial	2007	2.53037 kilo
Ben		0.03978 kilo
Ben, poster campaign	2008	2.19159 kilo
Ben, poster campaign	2008	2.19393 kilo
Ben, poster campaign	2008	2.19626 kilo
Ben, poster campaign	2008	2.19860 kilo
Ben, poster campaign	2009	2.08411 kilo
Ben, poster campaign	2009	2.08645 kilo
Ben, poster campaign	2009	2.08879 kilo
Ben, poster campaign	2009	2.09112 kilo
Ben, poster campaign	2009	2.09346 kilo
Ben, poster campaign	2009	2.09579 kilo
Ben, poster campaign	2009	2.09813 kilo
Ben, print campaign	2008	2.20561 kilo
Ben, print campaign	2009	2.14486 kilo
Ben, print campaign	2009	2.14720 kilo
Ben, TV commercial	2008	2.20093 kilo
Ben, TV commercial	2008	2.20327 kilo
Ben, website	2008	2.17991 kilo
citizenM		0.02574 kilo
citizenM, extra materials	2008	2.24299 kilo
citizenM, extra materials	2008	2.24533 kilo
citizenM, hotel	2008	2.23832 kilo
citizenM, hotel interior and online film	2008	2.24766 kilo
citizenM, hotel interior and online film	2008	2.25000 kilo
citizenM, packaging	2008	2.24065 kilo
citizenM, packaging	2009	2.12850 kilo
citizenM, poster campaign	2008	2.23364 kilo
citizenM, poster campaign	2008	2.23598 kilo
citizenM, website	2008	2.25234 kilo
citizenM, website	2008	2.25467 kilo
Claro		0.01404 kilo
Claro, billboard	2006	2.78505 kilo
Claro, billboard	2006	2.78738 kilo
Claro, brand identity and packaging	2006	2.78037 kilo
Claro, poster campaign	2006	2.78271 kilo
Claro, print campaign	2007	2.51869 kilo
Claro, print campaign	2007	2.52103 kilo
DAG		0.01404 kilo
DAG, brand manual	2007	2.55374 kilo
DAG, extra materials	2008	2.37850 kilo
DAG, extra materials	2008	2.38084 kilo
DAG, newspaper	2007	2.55140 kilo
DAG, newspaper	2008	2.38318 kilo
DAG, TV commercial	2008	2.38551 kilo
do		0.01638 kilo
do box, exhibition	2007	2.47897 kilo
do box, product	2007	2.47664 kilo
do camouflage, product	2008	2.28037 kilo
do change, editorial	2006	2.64019 kilo
do sin, product	2009	2.03505 kilo
do, editorial	2006	2.76168 kilo
do, editorial	2006	2.76402 kilo
Dutch Funeral Museum		0.00702 kilo
Dutch Funeral Museum, poster	2008	2.26636 kilo
Dutch Funeral Museum, poster	2009	2.16355 kilo
Dutch Funeral Museum, stunt	2008	2.26869 kilo
Dutch Ministry of Health		0.00936 kilo
Dutch Ministry of Health, extra materials	2009	2.11682 kilo
Dutch Ministry of Health, extra materials	2009	2.11916 kilo
Dutch Ministry of Health, poster, print and web	2009	2.11215 kilo
Dutch Ministry of Health, TV commercial	2009	2.11449 kilo
Dutch Theatre		0.00936 kilo
Dutch Theatre, poster, print and TV campaign	2007	2.57009 kilo
Dutch Theatre, poster, print and TV campaign	2007	2.57243 kilo
Dutch Theatre, poster, print and TV campaign	2007	2.57477 kilo
Dutch Theatre, poster, print and TV campaign	2007	2.57710 kilo
Editorial		0.01170 kilo
Antwerp Photo Museum, editorial	2006	2.72897 kilo
Antwerp Photo Museum, editorial	2006	2.73131 kilo
Libelle Anniversary Edition, editorial	2009	2.07710 kilo
Libelle Anniversary Edition, editorial	2009	2.07944 kilo
Libelle Anniversary Edition, editorial	2009	2.08178 kilo
Experimenta		0.00936 kilo
Experimenta, poster campaign	2008	2.25701 kilo
Experimenta, poster campaign	2008	2.25935 kilo
Experimenta, poster campaign	2008	2.26168 kilo
Experimenta, poster campaign	2008	2.26402 kilo
Gospel Festival		0.00702 kilo
Gospel Festival, poster	2006	2.86215 kilo
Gospel Festival, poster campaign	2005	2.92757 kilo
Gospel Festival, TV commercial	2005	2.92991 kilo
Graphic Design Museum		0.01404 kilo
Graphic Design Museum, campaign book	2008	2.36215 kilo
Graphic Design Museum, opening event	2008	2.36449 kilo
Graphic Design Museum, opening event	2008	2.36682 kilo
Graphic Design Museum, poster campaign	2008	2.35514 kilo
Graphic Design Museum, poster campaign	2008	2.35748 kilo
Graphic Design Museum, poster campaign	2008	2.35981 kilo
Hans Brinker Budget Hotel		0.05382 kilo
Hans Brinker Budget Hotel, book	2009	2.07009 kilo
Hans Brinker Budget Hotel, book	2009	2.07243 kilo
Hans Brinker Budget Hotel, clothing	2007	2.48598 kilo
Hans Brinker Budget Hotel, newspaper	2008	2.29907 kilo
Hans Brinker Budget Hotel, newspaper	2008	2.30140 kilo
Hans Brinker Budget Hotel, online film	2008	2.29439 kilo
Hans Brinker Budget Hotel, online films	2009	2.06776 kilo
Hans Brinker Budget Hotel, passport	2006	2.85047 kilo
Hans Brinker Budget Hotel, passport	2006	2.85280 kilo
Hans Brinker Budget Hotel, POS	2008	2.42523 kilo
Hans Brinker Budget Hotel, poster and films	2009	2.14019 kilo
Hans Brinker Budget Hotel, poster campaign	2007	2.48131 kilo
Hans Brinker Budget Hotel, poster campaign	2007	2.48364 kilo
Hans Brinker Budget Hotel, poster campaign	2008	2.28972 kilo
Hans Brinker Budget Hotel, poster campaign	2008	2.29206 kilo
Hans Brinker Budget Hotel, poster campaign	2009	2.07477 kilo
Hans Brinker Budget Hotel, product and poster campaign	2005	2.93458 kilo
Hans Brinker Budget Hotel, product and poster campaign	2005	2.93692 kilo
Hans Brinker Budget Hotel, product and poster campaign	2005	2.93925 kilo
Hans Brinker Budget Hotel, product and poster campaign	2005	2.94159 kilo
Hans Brinker Budget Hotel, stamp	2007	2.54673 kilo
Hans Brinker Budget Hotel, toilet roll	2008	2.29673 kilo
Hans Brinker Budget Hotel, website	2008	2.30374 kilo
Hier		0.01404 kilo
Hier, extra materials	2006	2.63551 kilo
Hier, extra materials	2006	2.63785 kilo
Hier, print campaign	2006	2.62617 kilo
Hier, print campaign	2006	2.62850 kilo
Hier, print campaign	2006	2.63084 kilo
Hier, print campaign	2006	2.63318 kilo

2.99299 kilo

Identity			0.01872 kilo
Caren Pardovitch Interior Design, house style		2008	2.32710 kilo
Concreet, branding		2007	2.56776 kilo
Het Klokhuis, brand identity and films		2009	2.16589 kilo
Prooff, brand identity		2008	2.41121 kilo
puC, brand identity and packaging		2008	2.33178 kilo
puC, print and poster campaign		2008	2.33411 kilo
TRUE, brand identity		2007	2.50870 kilo
TRUE, brand identity		2007	2.59112 kilo
in almost every picture			**0.02106 kilo**
in almost every picture #4, book		2005	2.92056 kilo
in almost every picture #4, book		2005	2.92290 kilo
in almost every picture #5, book		2006	2.65421 kilo
in almost every picture #5, book		2006	2.65654 kilo
in almost every picture #6, book		2007	2.59813 kilo
in almost every picture #7, book		2008	2.38785 kilo
in almost every picture #7, book		2008	2.39019 kilo
in almost every picture #8, book		2009	2.03972 kilo
in almost every picture, book collection		2006	2.85981 kilo
J&B			**0.05616 kilo**
J&B, billboards, online and event		2008	2.28505 kilo
J&B, billboards, online and event		2008	2.28738 kilo
J&B, DVD		2007	2.50467 kilo
J&B, DVD		2007	2.50701 kilo
J&B, extra materials		2008	2.35047 kilo
J&B, extra materials		2008	2.35280 kilo
J&B, films		2009	2.06542 kilo
J&B, online film		2009	2.05140 kilo
J&B, online films		2007	2.51168 kilo
J&B, online films		2007	2.58411 kilo
J&B, online films		2007	2.58645 kilo
J&B, poster and online		2009	2.04673 kilo
J&B, poster and online		2009	2.04907 kilo
J&B, poster, online and event		2009	2.05607 kilo
J&B, poster, online and event		2009	2.05841 kilo
J&B, print and poster campaign		2007	2.49766 kilo
J&B, print and poster campaign		2007	2.50000 kilo
J&B, print and poster campaign		2007	2.50234 kilo
J&B, print and poster campaign		2007	2.50935 kilo
J&B, print and poster campaign		2007	2.61682 kilo
J&B, print and poster campaign		2007	2.61916 kilo
J&B, product		2007	2.51402 kilo
J&B, product		2007	2.51636 kilo
J&B, TV and cinema campaign		2007	2.49533 kilo
KesselsKramer			**0.03276 kilo**
2 kilo of KesselsKramer, book		2005	2.98832 kilo
2 kilo of KesselsKramer, van		2005	2.98598 kilo
a new kilo of KesselsKramer, poster		2010	2.02103 kilo
KesselsKramer, stickers		2006	2.84579 kilo
KesselsKramer, van		2005	2.90187 kilo
KK Exports, exhibition		2009	2.10047 kilo
KK Outlet, exhibition		2006	2.70561 kilo
KK Outlet, exhibition		2006	2.70794 kilo
KK Outlet, exhibition		2006	2.71028 kilo
KK Outlet, exhibition		2006	2.71262 kilo
KK Outlet, poster		2006	2.70327 kilo
KK Publishing, website		2006	2.66589 kilo
On Hold at KesselsKramer, CD		2007	2.58178 kilo
Polar Bear Memorial Candle, product		2008	2.30841 kilo
KK Outlet			**0.00936 kilo**
KK Outlet, brand identity		2008	2.34112 kilo
KK Outlet, office		2008	2.34346 kilo
KK Outlet, posters and exhibition space		2009	2.14953 kilo
KK Outlet, posters and exhibition space		2009	2.15187 kilo
Läkerol			**0.01404 kilo**
Läkerol, brand book		2007	2.60280 kilo
Läkerol, poster campaign		2007	2.60514 kilo
Läkerol, poster campaign		2007	2.60748 kilo
Läkerol, poster campaign		2007	2.60981 kilo
Läkerol, TV campaign		2007	2.61215 kilo
Läkerol, TV campaign		2007	2.61449 kilo
Lipton Ice Tea			**0.00702 kilo**
Lipton Ice Tea, TV and cinema commercial		2005	2.94860 kilo
Lipton Ice Tea, TV campaign		2005	2.96262 kilo
Lipton Ice Tea, TV campaign		2005	2.96495 kilo
Loving Your Pictures			**0.01404 kilo**
Loving Your Pictures, exhibition		2006	2.67757 kilo
Loving Your Pictures, exhibition		2006	2.67991 kilo
Loving Your Pictures, exhibition		2006	2.68224 kilo
Loving Your Pictures, exhibition		2006	2.68458 kilo
Loving Your Pictures, postcard book		2006	2.67290 kilo
Loving Your Pictures, poster		2006	2.67523 kilo
MTV Japan			**0.01872 kilo**
MTV Japan, poster campaign		2006	2.76636 kilo
MTV Japan, poster campaign		2006	2.76869 kilo
MTV Japan, posters, scavenger hunt, vinyl doll		2005	2.87850 kilo
MTV Japan, posters, scavenger hunt, vinyl doll		2005	2.88084 kilo
MTV Japan, tape and brand book		2006	2.77336 kilo
MTV Japan, TV commercial and mobile film		2006	2.77103 kilo
MTV Japan, TV idents		2005	2.88318 kilo
MTV Japan, TV idents		2005	2.88551 kilo
Niet Normaal			**0.00936 kilo**
Niet Normaal, extra materials		2009	2.16121 kilo
Niet Normaal, online films		2009	2.15888 kilo
Niet Normaal, print, poster and online campaign		2009	2.15421 kilo
Niet Normaal, print, poster and online campaign		2009	2.15654 kilo
NPS			**0.00702 kilo**
NPS, brand identity		2008	2.41355 kilo
NPS, extra materials		2008	2.41589 kilo
NPS, extra materials		2008	2.41822 kilo
Protest			**0.03276 kilo**
Protest, brand manual		2008	2.22430 kilo
Protest, extra materials		2008	2.22664 kilo
Protest, extra materials		2008	2.22897 kilo
Protest, extra materials		2008	2.23131 kilo
Protest, hang-tag films		2009	2.10748 kilo
Protest, hang-tag films		2009	2.10981 kilo
Protest, poster, film and event		2010	2.03037 kilo
Protest, poster, print and online		2010	2.02804 kilo
Protest, print campaign		2009	2.10280 kilo
Protest, print campaign		2009	2.10514 kilo
Protest, print, poster and mobile campaign		2008	2.21495 kilo
Protest, print, poster and mobile campaign		2008	2.21729 kilo
Protest, print, poster and mobile campaign		2008	2.21963 kilo
Protest, print, poster and mobile campaign		2008	2.22196 kilo
Radio 1			**0.00702 kilo**
Radio 1, brand book		2005	2.95561 kilo
Radio 1, TV campaign		2006	2.73598 kilo
Radio 1, TV commercial		2006	2.73364 kilo
REAAL			**0.04212 kilo**
REAAL Insurance, booklet		2007	2.46495 kilo
REAAL Insurance, poster campaign		2006	2.84112 kilo
REAAL Insurance, poster campaign		2007	2.45794 kilo
REAAL Insurance, poster campaign		2007	2.46028 kilo
REAAL Insurance, poster campaign		2008	2.31075 kilo
REAAL Insurance, poster campaign		2008	2.31308 kilo
REAAL Insurance, poster campaign		2008	2.31542 kilo
REAAL Insurance, print		2007	2.47196 kilo
REAAL Insurance, print campaign		2006	2.83645 kilo
REAAL Insurance, print campaign		2006	2.83879 kilo
REAAL Insurance, print campaign		2008	2.32243 kilo
REAAL Insurance, print campaign		2008	2.32477 kilo
REAAL Insurance, stunt		2007	2.54907 kilo
REAAL Insurance, stunt		2008	2.31776 kilo
REAAL Insurance, stunt		2008	2.32009 kilo
REAAL Insurance, TV campaign		2006	2.84346 kilo
REAAL Insurance, TV commercial		2007	2.46262 kilo
REAAL Insurance, website		2009	2.17757 kilo
S1ngletown			**0.00936 kilo**
S1ngletown, exhibition		2008	2.43458 kilo
S1ngletown, exhibition		2008	2.43692 kilo
S1ngletown, exhibition materials		2008	2.42991 kilo
S1ngletown, exhibition materials		2008	2.43224 kilo
SNS Bank			**0.03978 kilo**
SNS Bank, booklet		2007	2.62150 kilo
SNS Bank, calendar		2005	2.87383 kilo
SNS Bank, calendar		2005	2.87617 kilo
SNS Bank, poster campaign		2005	2.86449 kilo
SNS Bank, poster campaign		2005	2.86682 kilo
SNS Bank, poster campaign		2008	2.42056 kilo
SNS Bank, poster campaign		2008	2.42290 kilo
SNS Bank, print campaign		2005	2.86916 kilo
SNS Bank, print campaign		2005	2.87150 kilo
SNS Bank, print campaign		2006	2.75701 kilo
SNS Bank, print campaign		2006	2.75935 kilo
SNS Bank, print, poster and event		2007	2.62383 kilo
SNS Bank, TV commercial		2006	2.64252 kilo
SNS REAAL, print campaign		2006	2.64486 kilo
SNS REAAL, print campaign		2006	2.64720 kilo
SNS REAAL, TV commercial		2006	2.64953 kilo

2.99533 kilo

SNS REAAL, TV commercial		2006	2.65187 kilo
Sultana			0.00702 kilo
Sultana, poster campaign		2006	2.72430 kilo
Sultana, poster campaign		2006	2.72664 kilo
Sultana, TV campaign		2006	2.71963 kilo
Sultana, TV campaign		2006	2.72196 kilo
Theatre Academy Maastricht			0.00936 kilo
Theatre Academy Maastricht, online films		2007	2.45093 kilo
Theatre Academy Maastricht, print campaign		2007	2.44393 kilo
Theatre Academy Maastricht, print campaign		2007	2.44626 kilo
Theatre Academy Maastricht, print campaign		2007	2.44860 kilo
Trussardi			0.00936 kilo
Trussardi, print campaign		2006	2.82243 kilo
Trussardi, print campaign		2006	2.82477 kilo
Trussardi, print campaign		2006	2.82710 kilo
Trussardi, print campaign		2006	2.82944 kilo
Uitburo			0.00936 kilo
Uitburo Rotterdam, poster campaign		2007	2.46729 kilo
Uitburo Rotterdam, poster campaign		2007	2.46963 kilo
Uitburo, brand book and design toolkit		2006	2.81776 kilo
Uitburo, brand book and design toolkit		2006	2.82009 kilo
UitMarkt			0.01404 kilo
UitMarkt, poster campaign		2005	2.97664 kilo
UitMarkt, poster campaign		2007	2.45327 kilo
UitMarkt, poster campaign		2007	2.45561 kilo
UitMarkt, poster campaign		2008	2.21028 kilo
UitMarkt, poster campaign		2008	2.21262 kilo
UitMarkt, TV commercial		2005	2.97897 kilo
Ursus			0.01404 kilo
Ursus, poster campaign		2008	2.18692 kilo
Ursus, poster campaign		2008	2.18925 kilo
Ursus, TV and poster campaign		2008	2.18224 kilo
Ursus, TV and poster campaign		2008	2.18458 kilo
Ursus, TV commercial		2007	2.54206 kilo
Ursus, TV commercial		2007	2.54439 kilo
Useful Photography			0.02340 kilo
Useful Photography #005, magazine		2005	2.95794 kilo
Useful Photography #005, magazine		2005	2.96028 kilo
Useful Photography #006, magazine		2006	2.71495 kilo
Useful Photography #006, magazine		2006	2.71729 kilo
Useful Photography #007, magazine		2007	2.47430 kilo
Useful Photography #008, magazine		2008	2.34579 kilo
Useful Photography #008, magazine		2008	2.34813 kilo
Useful Photography #009, magazine		2009	2.05374 kilo
Useful Photography, exhibitions		2006	2.70093 kilo
Useful Photography, magazine box set		2007	2.60047 kilo
Verkade			0.00936 kilo
Verkade, poster campaign		2006	2.74766 kilo
Verkade, poster campaign		2006	2.75000 kilo
Verkade, TV campaign		2006	2.75234 kilo
Verkade, TV campaign		2006	2.75467 kilo
Vitra			0.02106 kilo
Vitra, poster, print and in-store		2010	2.02336 kilo
Vitra, poster, print and in-store		2010	2.02570 kilo
Vitra, print and extra materials		2008	2.37383 kilo
Vitra, print and extra materials		2008	2.37617 kilo
Vitra, print and poster		2009	2.13084 kilo
Vitra, print and poster		2009	2.13318 kilo
Vitra, print and poster		2009	2.13551 kilo
Vitra, print and poster campaign		2008	2.36916 kilo
Vitra, print and poster campaign		2008	2.37150 kilo
Miscellaneous			0.18018 kilo
Amateurism, book		2008	2.39720 kilo
Amateurism, book		2008	2.39953 kilo
Anonymous, book		2008	2.32944 kilo
artoons, book		2008	2.39252 kilo
artoons, display		2008	2.39486 kilo
Bad Food Gone Worse, book		2006	2.69860 kilo
Bart Julius Peters, newspaper		2008	2.20794 kilo
Bangkok Beauties, book		2007	2.56075 kilo
Bangkok Beauties, book		2007	2.56308 kilo
Benthem Crouwel, poster campaign		2009	2.12150 kilo
Benthem Crouwel, poster campaign		2009	2.12383 kilo
BFI London Film Festival, poster camp., cinema commercial		2009	2.13785 kilo
Blender, website		2009	2.16822 kilo
Bob Fosko, poster		2005	2.93224 kilo
Bob Fosko, poster		2006	2.66355 kilo
Bol.com, TV commercial		2005	2.89953 kilo
Bombay Beauties, book		2009	2.03271 kilo
Brabant Cultural Capital, poster campaign		2009	2.12617 kilo

Bushmills, online films		2009	2.03738 kilo
Coffee Company, posters and cup designs		2007	2.53271 kilo
Coffee Company, posters and cup designs		2007	2.53505 kilo
Face Moroccans, book		2005	2.95093 kilo
Farm, book		2005	2.92523 kilo
Footlocker, print and poster campaign		2006	2.85514 kilo
Footlocker, print and poster campaign		2006	2.85748 kilo
Fruit Shoot, poster		2006	2.68692 kilo
Fruit Shoot, TV commercial		2006	2.68925 kilo
Held, poster campaign		2007	2.53738 kilo
Held, poster campaign		2007	2.53972 kilo
Het Goud Van Lopik, art installation		2009	2.06075 kilo
Het Goud Van Lopik, book		2009	2.06308 kilo
Het Wapen Van Geldrop, poster campaign		2008	2.33645 kilo
Het Wapen Van Geldrop, poster campaign		2008	2.33879 kilo
Jack Stafford, music video		2005	2.95327 kilo
Kijkers, TV series and DVD		2005	2.91589 kilo
Kijkers, TV series and DVD		2005	2.91822 kilo
Kind, poster campaign		2007	2.43925 kilo
Kind, poster campaign		2007	2.44159 kilo
LeLe, music video		2008	2.40654 kilo
LeLe, music video		2008	2.40888 kilo
Madre Perla, poster campaign		2008	2.42757 kilo
Magnum sees Piemonte, book and exhibition		2005	2.96729 kilo
Magnum sees Piemonte, book and exhibition		2005	2.96963 kilo
Mail & Female, print		2009	2.04439 kilo
Mavi, poster campaign		2009	2.04206 kilo
Models, book		2005	2.97196 kilo
Models, book		2005	2.97430 kilo
Morgan's Spiced, print and poster campaign		2009	2.17290 kilo
Morgan's Spiced, TV commercial		2009	2.17523 kilo
Mr Motley, poster campaign		2007	2.49065 kilo
Mr Motley, poster campaign		2007	2.49299 kilo
NEROC'VGM, book		2006	2.66822 kilo
NEROC'VGM, book		2006	2.67056 kilo
On Show, book		2008	2.30607 kilo
one hundred and one things to do, book		2006	2.69159 kilo
one hundred and one things to do, book		2006	2.69393 kilo
Opgezwolle, DVD		2006	2.84813 kilo
Platform 21, poster campaign		2008	2.40187 kilo
Platform 21, poster campaign		2008	2.40421 kilo
PTT post, poster and stamps		2007	2.59346 kilo
PTT post, poster and stamps		2007	2.59579 kilo
Queen, Bitch, Queer, poster		2007	2.56542 kilo
Resilience, book		2005	2.94626 kilo
Rude Chalet, posters, booklet, online, events		2009	2.17056 kilo
Shadow festival, poster campaign		2006	2.83178 kilo
Shadow festival, poster campaign		2006	2.83411 kilo
Shampoo Planet, poster		2007	2.57944 kilo
Strangers In My Photo Album, book		2007	2.48832 kilo
Tree Paintings, book		2009	2.14252 kilo
Vanishing trades, bus posters		2008	2.28271 kilo
Waater, product design and branding		2007	2.55607 kilo
Waater, product design and branding		2007	2.55841 kilo
Wakker Dier, poster campaign		2006	2.66121 kilo
Wakker Dier, TV commercial		2006	2.65888 kilo
Women Inc., poster campaign		2005	2.98131 kilo
Women Inc., poster campaign		2005	2.98364 kilo
Wonder, book		2006	2.69626 kilo

intro		2.00234 kilo
intro		2.00467 kilo
intro		2.00701 kilo
intro		2.00935 kilo
intro		2.01168 kilo
intro		2.01402 kilo
intro		2.01636 kilo
1 kilo weightwatcher		2.99065 kilo
index		2.99299 kilo
index		2.99533 kilo
index		2.99766 kilo
colophon		3.00000 kilo

2.99766 kilo

a new kilo of KesselsKramer Colophon

made by: KesselsKramer

1 kilo of thanks
Like everything else in the universe, the small communications agency of KesselsKramer depends on an intricate web of relationships rippling out into infinity. Without these relationships, KesselsKramer would cease to exist. It seems only fair then that we thank all those who helped make this book, as well as those who helped make the agency behind the book. These include the directors, runners, editors, sound studios and lighting technicians who created the films. The photographers who shot the images. The producers who made shoots run like a particularly efficient Swiss time-keeping device. The illustrators who turned scribbles into masterpieces. The designers who designed the designs, for fashion, websites and products. The web developers, printers, binders and typographers. The publishers who published the books. The office managers, receptionists and über-organized PAs. The handy man who ensures we don't work in the dark. The printer repair guy who fixes our printers an average of 8,456 times a year. And all our spouses, children, friends, relatives and domestic animals who make life just a little bit nicer. And finally, a very special thanks to our clients, who saw that risky work is also effective work.

published by: PIE BOOKS
2-32-4 Minami-Otsuka, Toshima-ku, Tokyo 170-0005 Japan
Tel: +81-3-5395-4811 Fax: +81-3-5395-4812
sales@piebooks.com1 editor@piebooks.com
www.piebooks.com

publisher: Shingo Miyoshi
translator: Yuko Wada
coordinator: Megumi Shimada

printed by: DAIICHI PUBLISHERS CO., LTD.

isbn 978-4-89444-860-5

First edition, first issue, August 4, 2010

© 2010 KesselsKramer

No part of this publication may be reproduced or utilized in any form or by any means, including photocopying or quotation, without prior written permission from PIE BOOKS. Books with missing or improperly collated page will be exchanged.

Printed in China

ケッセルスクライマーの新たな1キロ

2010年8月4日　初版第1刷　発行

制作：　ケッセルスクライマー

1キロの感謝
宇宙の万物と同様、小さな広告代理店、ケッセルスクライマーも無限に広がる網のように込み入った人々とのつながりに頼って生きている。この人々とのつながりがなくては、私たちは存在することができない。だから、本書の制作に協力してくれた人々や、本書を作れるよう私たちを導いてくれたすべての人々に感謝の意を述べたい。
その方々には、ビデオ制作に関わった監督、助手、編集者、録音スタジオ、照明技術者、写真を撮影した写真家、精巧なスイス製の時計のように撮影を管理してくれたプロデューサー、殴り書きを傑作に変えたイラストレーター、ファッション、ウェブサイト、商品をデザインしたデザイナー、ウェブ開発者、印刷会社、製本業者、タイポグラファ、本を出版した発行人、オフィス・マネージャー、受付係、非常にまめな製作アシスタント、私たちが暗いところで仕事をしなくてもよいようにしてくれた便利屋、私たちのプリンターを年に平均8,456回も修理してくれた修理担当者、そして、私たちの人生をちょっと楽しくしてくれている、配偶者、子ども、友人、親戚、ペットのすべてが含まれる。
最後に、危なっかしい仕事を、効果的だと思ってくれたクライアントに、特に深く感謝を申し上げたい。

発行元／ ピエ・ブックス
〒170-0005 東京都豊島区南大塚2-32-4
営業　TEL 03-5395-4811　FAX 03-5395-4812　sales@piebooks.com
編集　TEL 03-5395-4820　FAX 03-5395-4821　editor@piebooks.com
www.piebooks.com

発行人：　三芳伸吾
翻訳者：　和田侑子
制作進行：　島田 恵

印刷・製本　DAIICHI PUBLISHERS CO., LTD.

©2010 KesselsKramer

ISBN　978-4-89444-860-5　C 3070

本書の収録内容の無断転載・複写・引用等を禁じます。
ご注文、乱丁・落丁本の交換等に関するお問い合わせは、小社営業部までご連絡ください。

3.00000 kilo